THE RISE AND PROGRESS
OF NEGRO COLLEGES
IN GEORGIA
1865 - 1949

THE RISE AND PROGRESS OF NEGRO COLLEGES IN GEORGIA

1865-1949

by

Willard Range

DEPARTMENT OF POLITICAL SCIENCE
UNIVERSITY OF GEORGIA

THE UNIVERSITY OF GEORGIA PRESS
ATHENS

Paperback edition, 2009
© 1951 by the University of Georgia Press
Athens, Georgia 30602
www.ugapress.org
All rights reserved
Printed digitally in the United States of America

The Library of Congress has cataloged the hardcover edition of this book as follows:
Library of Congress Cataloging-in-Publication Data

Range, Willard.
The rise and progress of Negro colleges in Georgia, 1865–1949.
254 p.
Bibliography: p. 236–248.
1. African Americans—Education (Higher)—Georgia. 2. Universities and colleges—
Georgia. I. Title
University of Georgia Phelps–Stokes fellowship studies, no. 15
E185.5 .G35 no. 15
51-14571

Paperback ISBN-13: 978-0-8203-3452-3
ISBN-10: 0-8203-3452-9

Contents

		Page
	Foreword	vii
	Preface	ix

PART ONE: THE CRUSADE

I	Laying the Foundations	3
II	Founding the First Colleges	21
III	A Few Years of Failure and Success	34
IV	The Second Wave of the Crusade	49
V	The Hand, the Head, and the Heart	66
VI	Physical Expansion	92
VII	The Students and Their Teachers	116

PART TWO: TRANSITION TO THE MODERN COLLEGE

VIII	Decadence and the Upturn	157
IX	An Awakening State	176
X	Affiliation and Merger	193
XI	Characteristics of the Modern College	204
	Appendix	223
	Bibliography	236
	Index	249

Foreword

THIS STUDY OF THE RISE AND PROGRESS OF NEGRO Colleges in Georgia, 1865-1949, was made with the assistance of a Phelps-Stokes Fellowship granted to the author by the Phelps-Stokes Fellowship Committee of the University of Georgia. The terms of the grant, which must "be incorporated in every publication issued under the foundation," are as follows:

PHELPS-STOKES FELLOWSHIP

This fellowship has been endowed under the following resolutions of the Trustees of the Phelps-Stokes Fund:

"Whereas, Mrs. Caroline Phelps-Stokes in establishing the Phelps-Stokes Fund was especially solicitous to assist in improving the condition of the Negro, and

"Whereas, It is the conviction of the Trustees that one of the best methods of forwarding this purpose is to provide means to enable Southern youth of broad sympathies to make a scientific study of the Negro and his adjustment to American civilization:

"Resolved, That twelve thousand five hundred dollars ($12,500) be given to the University of Georgia for the permanent endowment of a research fellowship, on the following conditions:

"1. The University shall appoint annually a Fellow in Sociology, for the study of the Negro. He shall pursue advanced studies under the direction of the Departments of Sociology, Economics, Education, or History, as may be determined in each case by the President. The Fellowship shall yield $500, and shall, after four years, be restricted to graduate students.

"2. Each Fellow shall prepare a paper or thesis embodying the result of his investigation, which shall be published by the University with assistance from the income of the fund, any surplus remaining being applicable to other objects incident to the main purpose of the Fellowship. A copy of these resolutions shall be incorporated in every publication issued under this foundation.

"The right to make all necessary regulations, not inconsistent with the spirit and letter of these resolutions, shall be given to the President and Faculty, but no changes in the conditions of the foundation can be made without the mutual consent of both the Board of Trustees of the University and of the Phelps-Stokes Fund."

Preface

As the Foreword indicates, this study is one of the University of Georgia Phelps-Stokes Studies on Negro Life.

When I was appointed to make one of these studies, Dr. E. Merton Coulter suggested that the development of the Negro colleges in Georgia was a wide-open and worthy field for research. Negro history, it appeared, had already received considerable attention in a general way, and a few books were in print on various aspects of Negro education in the United States as a whole. But no detailed study had ever been made from which one could get a picture of the evolution of Georgia's Negro higher education from its beginnings in Reconstruction to the appearance of the full-fledged colleges of the twentieth century.

Dr. Coulter also pointed out that even though Negro higher education probably had developed somewhat more fully in Georgia than in most of the other Southern states the story of the rise and progress of the Negro colleges in one state would, very likely, be so similar to that in other states of the South that the study might also have some regional value.

The study has had, therefore, a two-fold aim: (1) that of creating a detailed picture of the development of Negro higher education in Georgia, and (2) that of drawing the picture in terms of "movements" that were experienced throughout most of the South.

Most of the material used in the study was gathered in or near the colleges themselves. Every Negro institution of higher learning in the state was visited and all available material was studied. In some colleges material was so abundant that several weeks had to be devoted to it. In some other institutions, however, fire or simply wanton neglect had made even catalogues scarce. When material was hard to find the narrative had to be accumulated from the memory of old-timers who had been close to the life of the college. No doubt this has given rise to inaccuracies, but every effort has been made to sift carefully the information collected and to use only that which seemed reliable. While working at the colleges, moreover, I acquired some facts and much insight by talking with presidents, teachers, students, graduates, and both Negro and white leaders who have been or were interested in the enterprises.

Needless to say, appreciation for much help on the study is due Dr. Coulter. In addition to suggesting the subject and supervising the research, he was also kind enough to edit the manuscript immediately prior to publication. A grateful hand must be extended also to other members of the faculty of the University of Georgia who read and criticized the manuscript: Drs. George H. Hutchinson, J. H. T. McPherson, S. Walter Martin, A. S. Edwards, and Albert B. Saye. Appreciation is also due the staffs of the various Negro colleges and all the important libraries in the state who were very helpful in making material available.

W. R.

Athens, Ga.

PART ONE

The Crusade

CHAPTER I

Laying the Foundations

ON A NIGHT LATE IN DECEMBER, 1864, ONLY A FEW weeks after the Union army had marched through Georgia to the sea, an unusual meeting was held in Charles Greene's fine old Savannah mansion, then the headquarters of the army. The meeting was unusual in that it was devoted to a subject hitherto generally considered heretical in the South—the establishment of schools to educate Negroes.

The importance of the meeting was heightened by the presence of Secretary of War Edwin M. Stanton. General William T. Sherman, the conqueror, was there also with his generals and aides, but the significant feature of the meeting was the presence of a colored committee of eight or ten ministers. Among these were Garrison Frazier, a colored man of some learning who acted as spokesman for the group; Alexander Harrison, the real leader of the movement; Charles Bradwell, John Cox, William J. Campbell, Arthur Vardell—in all, a group exhibiting an intellectual capacity that astonished even the Secretary of War.[1]

---

1. R. R. Wright, *A Brief Historical Sketch of Negro Education in Georgia* (Savannah, 1894), 16-17.

The existence of these few black ministers with a smattering of education was proof that book learning was not entirely new to the Negro of Georgia. Despite such laws as those of 1770 and 1829 making education the forbidden fruit of the Georgia Negro, certain ones with the will to learn and the initiative to see those larger vistas of the white man had filched the meaning of letters from books. As early as 1818-1819 a colored Frenchman out of Santo Domingo, Julian Froumontaine, operated a school in Savannah, and many of his pupils continued his work clandestinely until the Civil War.[2] For thirty years another Negro, a woman named Deveau, conducted a school in Savannah without being suspected. Also schools were established by liberal planters to fit slaves to live as "good free human beings" in days to come. One of these was uncovered by Sherman on his march to the sea.[3]

A few poor whites also eked out a paltry living by such teaching. Fearing the thirty-nine lashes of the law, free children went to the teacher's house ostensibly to "pick up chips" in case an officer appeared.[4] William Scarborough, later president of Wilberforce University, claimed he spent six to eight hours a day in school during his boyhood near Macon. Favored slaves of the wealthy were taught by their masters or members of the master's family, and some Negroes taught each other. A few employed as clerks were taught to read and write for the sake of business efficiency.[5] The universal fervor of the ministry to gather souls into the Kingdom was another boon to the black child of inquiring mind. Armed with the

---
2. *Ibid.*, 20; W. E. B. DuBois, *Black Reconstruction* (New York, 1935), 644.
3. H. F. Thomas, "Legislation as it Affected Public Education for Negroes in Georgia" (Unpublished Master's Thesis in Atlanta University, 1935), 3-5.
4. Wright, *Negro Education*, 19-20.
5. Thomas, "Legislation as it Affected Public Education for Negroes in Georgia," 5-6.

Bible, which few men could challenge without losing caste, some ministers often turned their Sunday schools into classrooms in the conviction that all men, white or black, should be able to learn the meaning of the Gospels. The Reverend Charles C. Jones, father of the Georgia historian, taught some Negroes in this fashion.[6]

Already in the North the Negro had experienced education in its higher forms. A few white colleges had been opened to them. The establishment of Avery College in Pittsburgh in 1852, and of Wilberforce in Ohio in 1854, entirely for colored students, had encouraged the black man of the deep South.[7] By 1860 only twenty-eight Negroes had graduated from American colleges,[8] but the movement was under way.

It was not alone a desire to uplift the black man that impelled the military commanders of the Union army to establish schools. It was a war measure based upon military expediency. Sherman and his fellow officers were men of war, driving on ruthlessly to bring the war to an end. They wanted victory swift and clear-cut so that they might return home and live like other men in the peace of a solid Union. But there was no shaking off the tens of thousands of dark, ragged vagabonds who clung to their military columns. Harried by these hordes of Freedmen who impeded the movements of the troops, commanders were forced to set them down and clothe and feed them as wards of the government. Accordingly the sea islands and coast of Georgia for thirty miles inland were turned over to General Rufus Saxton for the care of the refugees. Efforts were made to keep the Freedmen busy by organizing work in the cultivation of confiscated plantations. But many who had worked squandered their pay.

---

6. Wright, *Negro Education*, 19.
7. H. M. Bond, *The Education of the Negro in the American Social Order* (New York, 1934), 371.
8. C. S. Johnson, *The Negro College Graduate* (Chapel Hill, 1938), 7.

Crime was rampant and fighting, bickering, laziness, filth, disease, and death harassed the officers commanding the refugees. To alleviate these conditions schools were opened for the idling Freedmen in many of the camps.[9]

Then occurred that meeting in Savannah on a night late in December, 1864, out of which came the initial plan for the general education of the Negro race in Georgia. Little more was done than to decide to open schools for all colored people who should apply, and set a time for the examination of teachers.[10] But the campaign was set in motion.

Shortly after this meeting, the bars of the slave stalls were knocked out of the "Old Bryan Slave Mart" in Savannah and the first school was opened there.[11] Into these beginnings came the American Missionary Association. It was a strong and well-developed organization and to it more than to any other humanitarian body must go the credit for the establishment of a sound educational system for the black race of the South. It grew out of a group established for the defense of the Negroes who rebelled and captured the slave ship *Armistad*, which was brought into Connecticut in 1837.[12] W. T. Richardson was sent to Savannah, and he opened a school for the Association in Wesleyan Chapel.

"Like untrained animals, the children flocked in, without any ideas of order or application. Cleanliness was disregarded in many cases. Disorder prevailed. . . ."[13] As soon as other schools were organized, S. W. Magill, a native white Georgian working in Connecticut, was sent South

---
9. W. E. B. DuBois, *The Souls of Black Folk* (Chicago, 1922), 14-20.
10. Wright, *Negro Education*, 18.
11. *Ibid.*, 18.
12. DuBois, *Black Reconstruction*, 77.
13. *Annual Report of the American Missionary Association, 1865* (New York, 1865), 25.

with a corps of Northern teachers.[14] Thus began the trek of the New England school-ma'am that within a year was to swell into a small crusade of men and women bent on transplanting Northern civilization into the Southland and revealing to the black man the wonders of his new freedom. Within three months the schools of Savannah were turned over to these white teachers. More buildings were secured, and by the end of the year 500 and more pupils were enrolled.[15]

But more than this was needed to make the education of the Freedmen effective. The South was openly hostile to this new heresy which threatened to give the ex-slave more in intellectual tools than many of the whites themselves possessed. Moreover, poverty of the worst kind clutched these dark people who had fled from their former homes. In the suburbs of Atlanta women and children lived sheltered only by tattered canvas picked up in the wake of Sherman's army. Destitution and starvation sat heavily upon half-naked people everywhere, black and white alike.[16]

Appeals reached Congress from Union leaders in all parts of the South to alleviate these wretched conditions. Finally, in March, 1865, after nearly two years of parliamentary struggle, a bill was put through Congress setting up the Freedmen's Bureau, an organization designed to manage all affairs for the welfare of ex-slaves.

By a second bill passed a year later the Bureau was empowered to sell or lease any property which had belonged to the Confederate government and use the proceeds to lease or construct school buildings. Responsibility for pro-

---

14. *Ibid.*, 25; Wright, *Negro Education*, 21.
15. Wright, *Negro Education*, 21; DuBois, *Black Reconstruction*, 644-645.
16. E. T. Ware, "Sketch of the Life of Edmund Asa Ware" (MS. in Atlanta University Library).

tecting and aiding schools operated by benevolent associations was also placed upon the Bureau.

Backed by this arm of the government, the founding of schools went forward at a greater pace. Government buildings, no longer needed for military purposes, were fitted up for school houses. Transportation was provided for teachers by the Bureau. Books and school furniture were shipped at government expense, and superintendents for education were appointed in each state.[17]

In Georgia, agents of the Bureau traveled over the state aiding benevolent societies and establishing schools. The agents were of many sorts, ranging all the way from devout philanthropists to narrow-minded busybodies and rascals. One of the best agents concerned with education was William Jefferson White, a native Georgian, part Negro, who played a large part in the gradual rise of higher education for his race. Born of a white plantation owner and a Negro-Indian woman, he received his earliest education from his mother, who persuaded him to use his first money to buy a copy of Webster's famous "Blue-Back Speller." In 1853 he had organized clandestine schools in Augusta which operated two nights a week. As an agent for the Bureau, he traveled over the state establishing schools, sometimes being the first to announce to the Negroes their freedom.[18]

Meanwhile Frederick Ayer had arrived in Atlanta to begin the work of the American Missionary Association. He was a graduate of Yale and had worked among the Indians of the Great Lakes. He was a missionary of zeal, prompted by a large affection for mankind, and a religious fervor that made him known as a man of mercy. Tall,

---

17. Holmes, *Evolution of the Negro College*, 40; J. L. M. Curry, "Education of the Negroes Since 1860," *Occasional Papers No. 3 of the John F. Slater Fund* (Baltimore, 1894), I, 13.
18. *Spelman Messenger*, February 1938, p. 709; Letter from Mrs. C. W. Harreld to the author, January 31, 1939.

LAYING THE FOUNDATIONS

white haired, and simple, he was better working with his human wards than with his records and statistics.[19]

The work was no easy matter. Board for the white teachers was exorbitant. Constant appeals were rushed North for flour, vegetables, dried fruits, salt meat, lean meat, and the like to be sent in boxes marked "for teachers." They needed books, slates, pens, pencils, and paper. The demands on the North for supplies were never-ending. The government aided by transporting supplies and clothing from New York, Chicago, and Cincinnati. Often the supplies consisted of little more than cases of hymn books, easily parted with from musty basements of churches and private attics.[20] Yet with all this effort, the Freedmen's Bureau was able to report in October 1866 only 48 schools, 63 teachers, and an enrollment of 2,755 pupils.[21]

If the enrollment was small, however, it was largely because teachers were lacking. Over the months of 1866-1867 the slow trickle of teachers from the North swelled to a minor crusade. Wrote DuBois: "The annals of this Ninth Crusade are yet to be written. . . . Behind the mist of ruin and rapine waved the calico dresses of women who dared and after the hoarse mouthings of the field guns rang the rhythm of the alphabet. Rich and poor they were, serious and curious. Bereaved now of a father, now of a brother, now of more than these, they came seeking a life work in planting the New England schoolhouse among the white and black of the South. They did their work well. In that first year they taught one hundred thousand souls, and more."[22]

---

19. M. W. Adams, *A History of Atlanta University* (Atlanta, 1930), 55.
20. Leaflets in "Ayer Collection of Letters." Atlanta University Library.
21. J. W. Alvord, *Fourth Semi-Annual Report on Schools for Freedmen, July 1, 1867* (Bureau of Refugees, Freedmen and Abandoned Lands, Washington, 1867), 33.
22. DuBois, *Souls of Black Folk*, 25.

The missionaries were of all types ranging from pious pilgrims prepared to devote a lifetime to the work to inquisitive adventurers bent on a lark. Some came wise in maturity and fortified with a consuming determination to accomplish their task, willing to remain at it for the rest of their lives. The most famous missionary of this caste to come into Georgia was Edmund Asa Ware. Son of a middle-class New England family, a graduate of Yale in the class of 1863, he was sent to Atlanta in the latter part of 1866 to assist Frederick Ayer in the management of the schools. He was a slender, long-whiskered man with a full, rotund voice, and piercing eyes. Ware was a strict disciplinarian, applying the same Puritanical rules to himself and his teachers that he applied to the Negroes who came to him. Willing to sacrifice, he lived before his marriage to one of the teachers in a small basement room of the Teachers' Home on Houston Street, using boxes draped with calico for furniture, and sleeping on a single cot. To him more than to any other man must go the credit for the founding of higher education for the Negro in Georgia.

But little could have been done had it not been for the renaissance of the Negroes themselves. The election of Lincoln had brought politics home to the slave, and for the first time in his life he was awakened to the actual possibilities of the future and the power of the ballot box. Slowly, his dream of political power formed as a means to greater liberty.[23] "At a place of voting they look at the ballot-box," wrote an observer, "and then at the printed ticket in their hands wishing they could read it. The party politician is at their side with professions and assertions, and they feel their ignorance. Earnestly they desire, and silently they resolve, to become more intelli-

---

23. *Ibid.*, 7.

gent .... 'We must all now have learning' is the common remark."[24]

Also during the war the Negroes of the South traveled as never before. Fleeing to the Union lines they dogged the tracks of the armies north, south, east, and west, seeing wonders of the world that quickened the imagination of those with initiative and the will to rise so that by the end of the war great visions were theirs. After the war the new responsibilities of home, family, farm management, and earning a living brought home to the ex-slave his inadequacy to cope with his new freedom. So, too, with the large body of colored ministers who roamed the country in 1865. Many were skilled in handling audiences and some were able to read a little, but almost none were able to write. To these masses with centuries-long inheritance of heathenism, meagre vocabulary, and tattered, torn remnants of English words, the vision of education became the avenue to all the good things of the world.

Certainly for awhile at least the Georgia freedmen seemed "crazy to learn." Rice field hands around Savannah begged for schools. At Calhoun and Sandersville Negroes offered to support teachers. At Lexington, Columbus, Albany, Ellijay, Athens and other towns the freedmen eagerly awaited the arrival of teachers, with a "universal desire" for education. Said the Superintendent of Education in Georgia in 1867: "The desire of the colored people to learn appears to undergo no abatement; and every available means by which they can be aided in obtaining knowledge is most eagerly improved. Many of those who labor upon plantations are learning from each other, and are taught by members of the employers' families; while in the cities, children are teaching their parents; and in these ways, tens of thousands who cannot enjoy

---

24. Alvord, *Fourth Semi-Annual Report on Schools for Freedmen, July 1, 1867*, p. 79.

the benefits of regular schools are receiving at least sufficient instruction to enable them to read and write."[25]

It was the purpose of the aid societies, however, to establish schools only at central points as models for a more complete state public educational system. The American Missionary Association had established schools by February 1867 in only fifteen of Georgia's 131 counties.[26] But as the Federal government upset the natural order of the state with Reconstruction Acts, it was necessary to go further afield. By 1869 the Association had spent about $200,000 on education in Georgia. Old barracks, hospitals, churches, abandoned buildings, and shacks were used, while in some cases schoolhouses were built by the Freedmen's Bureau. In Atlanta two were built costing $10,000 and accommodating 500 pupils; in Macon, one costing $15,000 with similar capacity; in Athens, another costing $6,000 accommodating 250; and in Augusta, four small ones holding 400. Others were set up in Columbus, Americus, Griffin, Jonesboro, Milledgeville, Thomasville, Bainbridge, Dalton, Gordon, Stone Mountain, Canton, Perry, Cuthbert, and other places, in which students studied arithmetic, reading, geography and writing. Three hundred and fifty teachers were in the field.[27] Even within the gruesome palisades of Andersonville prison, 27 pupils gathered in spite of threats from the whites and their own mute fears, some of them walking three and four miles morning and evening to attend.[28] By 1869 the Freedmen's Aid Society of the Methodist Church was also supporting twenty schools.[29]

---

25. *Ibid.*, 34; Henry Lee Swint, *The Northern Teacher in the South, 1862-1870* (Nashville, 1941), 71.
26. *The American Freedman*, February 1867 (New York, 1867), 172.
27. *Atlanta University Bulletin*, December 1886; "Weekly Reports of the Freedmen's Bureau for 1870." Printed forms among papers in Atlanta University Library.
28. *Annual Report of the American Missionary Association, 1867*, p. 36.
29. Holmes, *Evolution of the Negro College*, 105.

LAYING THE FOUNDATIONS

Apparently there was no stopping the crusaders who were determined to impose on the Negro what the majority of Southerners looked upon as a mad experiment. Conditions of poverty, prejudice, and wretched surroundings meant nothing to many of them. "Whenever some Yankee lady was lucky enough to get the frame-work of a school house, she nailed up an old army blanket, or the like, to the windy side of the house and taught as if she were in one of our modern school houses." And the same witness describes the school he attended in Cuthbert, Georgia. It "scarcely had one of its sides covered or weather boarded. It was about 20 by 30. It had not more than 10 or 12 benches made of rough Puncheons and, of course, without backs. This house was packed as tightly with dusky children as a sardine box. The pupils were aged from 6 to 70. . . . Truly, almost any shelter, as old cribs or fodder houses, or no shelter except tree or brush arbors served as school houses for colored children in those days."[30]

One of the most famous schools in Atlanta was no more than an old railroad box-car purchased by the American Missionary Association in Chattanooga for $310. From the government and people of the North came lumber, paper, desks, pencils, inkstands, zinc, shovels, pokers, stove pipe, coal hods, rugs, copy books, tables, chairs, and a constant stream of boxes and barrels of food, clothing, and the inevitable hymn books.[31]

Also from the Negroes themselves came nickels and dimes and skill in carpentry. Obviously there was little wealth among the more than half million Freedmen who formed 46% of the population of Georgia at the end of the war. Yet out of their poverty and eagerness they built

---
30. Wright, *Negro Education*, 25-26.
31. "Monthly Reports to the Freedmen's Bureau, 1870." Printed forms in Atlanta University Library; letter from E. M. Cravath, July 9, 1866, in "Ayer Collection," Atlanta University Library.

schools and supported teachers, white and black. In Savannah 350 pupils were in schools supported by a colored association.[32] As early as 1865 the Negroes of Savannah contributed $1,000 for their first teachers.[33] The African Civilization Society also had its schools before financial embarrassment overtook it in 1869.[34] Of the 236 schools reported in 1867, 152 were entirely or partly supported by Freedmen who owned 39 of the buildings.[35] Reports for 1869 from General J. R. Lewis, Superintendent for Education of the Bureau in Georgia, claimed that in merely six months the Negroes of the state had contributed about $40,000 not counting contributions for erecting schoolhouses.[36]

So it was not solely a crusade of Northern humanitarianism and benevolence. Even a large percentage of the teachers were native white Georgians. This was accepted by some as an indication that the heresy of educating the black man was gradually becoming accepted by the South as another Northern blessing. Actually it was not that, and such teachers usually came from the lower class whites in the rural sections. Rather than starve they taught. Even salaries of $25 to $50 a month were better than nothing.[37] Thus wrote the Superintendent of Education for the Freedmen's Bureau in Georgia in 1867: "At the beginning of the current school year, scarcely any white persons could be found who were willing to 'disgrace' themselves by 'teaching niggers'; but as times grew hard,

32. C. M. Thompson, *Reconstruction in Georgia, Economic, Social, Political, 1865-1872* (New York, 1915), 125.
33. *Annual Report of the American Missionary Association*, 1868, p. 25.
34. T. J. Jones, *Negro Education* (Washington, 1916), I, 280.
35. Alvord, *Fourth Semi-Annual Report on Schools for Freedmen*, July 1, 1867, p. 35.
36. Alvord, *Eighth Semi-Annual Report on Schools for Freedmen*, July 1, 1869, p. 30.
37. Jones, *Negro Education*, I, 287-288.

and money and bread scarce, applications for employment became so numerous that I was obliged to prepare a printed letter with which to answer them. Lawyers, physicians, editors, ministers, and all classes of white people applied for employment; and while a few by their letters evinced only tolerable qualifications—none of them first class—a vast majority were unable to write grammatically, or spell the most simple and common words in our language correctly. Not a few appeared to think that 'anybody can teach niggers.' "[38] Several were hired, however, and the same report showed that of 147 white teachers, 83 were native Georgians.

It was all a heresy, of course, to the majority of Georgians. To that generation, bred by inheritance to a belief in the natural inferiority of the black man, living in mortal fear of rebellion (even if without cause), it was not strange that the new doctrine of knowledge for all men was opposed. Education of the black man meant dissatisfaction, revolution. Disregarding the obvious truth that through four years of war ninety per cent of the race had clung faithfully to the homes of their masters, white Southerners generally saw in the new experiment calling the black man to rise only danger that must be answered if necessary by insult, blood, and ashes.

Thus the Northern school-ma'ams often became special objects of ostracism. In some places they could find board only at exorbitant rates and often they had to lodge with Negroes whether they liked it or not.[39] The Reverend George Standing, coming from the North to teach in Newnan, found it hard to persuade storekeepers to sell him food to eat. In Greensboro, a man with whom a teacher boarded was taken from his house in the night and beaten.

---
38. Alvord, *Fourth Semi-Annual Report on Schools for Freedmen*, July 1, 1867, p. 34.
39. *Annual Report of the American Missionary Association*, 1865, pp. 11-12.

Other teachers were run off and schoolhouses were burned. At Hawkinsville a colored teacher was shot at and wounded. In Chattooga County a schoolhouse erected by a white farmer was torn down by a mob because it was considered too close to the school for white children. In Savannah, Edmund Asa Ware was refused permission to speak in a church for fear he would talk on politics.[40] Said the *Macon Messenger* of the Northern teachers in 1867: "They are all either fanatics or knaves . . . and their sole mission is to stir up strife and strew tares of hate and evil in the minds of their pupils. What propriety, then, is there in having them associated with *our* teachers."[41]

After touring the South in 1865, the General Superintendent of Education for the Freedmen's Bureau, J. W. Alvord, wrote: "Military force alone can save many of our schools from being broken up, or enable us to organize new schools."[42] While traveling through the state establishing schools, William J. White was "Ku Kluxed" once, shot at, and often threatened.[43]

Yet terrorism against the schools was not endorsed unanimously by all the people. Many whites believed the new freedom of the race demanded at least the simple rudiments of knowledge. Political leaders like Benjamin H. Hill, Herschel V. Johnson, Joseph E. Brown, John B. Gordon, and Alexander Stephens saw the futility of opposing the demands of the government, and believed that if citizenship must be given the race, the steps to knowledge should be provided. Many planters were willing to set up schools provided they could select the teachers

---

40. Thompson, *Reconstruction in Georgia*, 364; Holmes, *Evolution of the Negro College*, 42; Wright, *Negro Education*, 24; J. W. Alvord, *Letters From The South Relating to the Condition of Freedmen* (Washington, 1870), 22; W. H. Crogman, *Talks for the Times* (Atlanta, 1896), 101-102.
41. Ware, "Sketch of Edmund Asa Ware," 24.
42. Holmes, *Evolution of the Negro College*, 41.
43. Letter from C. W. White to the author, January 31, 1939.

and keep out Northern ideas.⁴⁴ In Atlanta there was much prejudice but little violence. There a man bought a book for his ex-slave, and his wife and daughter helped the boy with his lessons. So bold were two ladies of staunch secession principles that they visited a school out of curiosity and before leaving bestowed upon it a benediction of kindness. By 1870 it was noted in Savannah that although the old families excluded teachers from their social circles, they no longer denounced their "Christian work."⁴⁵ Said the Superintendent of Education in Georgia for the Freedmen's Bureau in 1867: "The opposition to the education of the Freedmen is disappearing, and the work has not been materially interfered with except in the burning of the school house at Jonesboro, Fayette County, by unknown incendiaries."⁴⁶

It was soon evident, however, that the crusade of the New England school-ma'am could not go on forever. Far from the land of their birth, working in a hostile country in which everything touched by Northerners was looked upon with suspicion, it took only a few months in the hard realities of Reconstruction humanitarianism to shatter many of their ideals. Those who could stand the gaff stayed and brought into being a system of higher education for the Negro. As the first outburst of enthusiasm for the campaign faded, it became evident that if any appreciable dent were to be made in the ignorance of the black masses, Negro teachers must be trained. For it must be noted that in all the work of the Freedmen's Bureau never more than 10 per cent of the colored children of school age got into school. Appeals for teachers rose from all parts of the South. Agents of the Bureau appealed to

---

44. Alvord, *Fourth Semi-Annual Report on Schools for Freedmen*, July 1, 1867, p. 78.
45. Alvord, *Letters from the South*, 14.
46. Alvord, *Fourth Semi-Annual Report on Schools for Freedmen*, July 1, 1867, p. 34.

their superintendents for trained teachers. "I want fifty," wrote one. Another wanted thirty, another twenty, and so on.[47]

The answer to these cries came quickly in Georgia in the establishment of normal schools in Savannah, Macon, Augusta, and Atlanta. Thus was made the second step toward the higher education of the Negro in Georgia. In 1865 the Ballard Normal School was set up in Macon, in 1867 the Beach Institute in Savannah, and the Storr's School in Atlanta.[48] In this same year the inspector of schools for the Bureau urged the improvement and enlargement of normal schools with endowments to secure their permanency.

Yet the missionaries and even the Negroes themselves knew that their groundwork must be no more than a prelude to larger systems. They could never hope to educate more than a small part of the great mass of blacks scattered throughout the fields and villages of the South. The largest enrollment for any one month in Georgia had been little more than 13,000 pupils, and this, out of a population of more than half a million illiterate Negroes, was no more than a dim light in a vast area of darkness. Certainly the state must be forced to do its part. Foundations for common school systems for whites, at least, already were being laid in all the Southern states.

It was no easy task, however, to convince most Southerners, or many Northerners for that matter, that schools should be supported by public taxation. The land-holding taxpayers, often able to send their own children to one of the many private schools, saw no reason why they should empty their pockets to educate other men's sons. In some places Jeffersonianism still lay over the land perpetuating

---
47. Holmes, *Evolution of the Negro College*, 46.
48. Thomas, "Legislation as it Affected Public Education for Negroes in Georgia," 33; *Annual Report of the American Missionary Association*, 1867, p. 17.

the belief that the fewer functions performed by a government, the better government it was. Moreover, the unrest of the Southern mind in Reconstruction, preoccupied with a political struggle for the survival of cherished institutions, was another hindrance to the adoption of novel ventures. The economic revolution caused by the freeing of the slaves at a loss to the South of two billion dollars in human property, the failure of the Freedmen to take quickly to the job of sustaining wealth in a country primarily agricultural, the cost of the war, destruction of property, repudiation of the Confederate debt, and the resultant tremendous burden of taxation imposed to pay the Union war debt and support the extravagance of Reconstruction—all this produced a poverty hitherto unknown in any spot in America. Georgia itself came out of the fiasco with banks ruined, capital destroyed, property worthless, and a state debt of eighteen million dollars. The taxable value of slaves in Georgia in 1860 was $302,694,855, far more than the value of all taxable land. With emancipation the structure collapsed.[49]

In the face of this poverty, however, the constitution written in Georgia in 1865 included provisions for public education. But it failed to include the Negro. To the majority of Georgians, despite the new ideals of democracy, the idea of educating the ex-slave was as ridiculous as attempting to educate a mule. Immediately a drive was begun by Negroes and their new guardians from the North to get the black race into the school system. By 1868, when another constitution was written, the Radicals had come into power both in Washington and in Georgia and the star of the black man rose with them. Of the 166 delegates in the new state convention, thirty-seven were Negroes, and about nine were white Carpet-baggers. The rest were native whites or Scalawags. Under the whip

---

49. Thompson, *Reconstruction in Georgia*, 40-42.

hands of ex-Governor Joe Brown, Rufus B. Bullock, and Ben Conley, a clause was written which guaranteed the Negro free public education for at least three months a year.[50] The Negro delegates themselves had exercised little influence. But with the desire of the Negro for education spreading through other states where the black man was in power, and the general preoccupation of the whites in other political affairs, the proposal was pushed through. And the victory won when the Negro succeeded in squeezing into the state program for public education was the greatest battle won by them in Reconstruction. Outlasting the ballot box and dreams of social equality, it remained and grew into the most powerful force shaping the new destiny of the race. When in 1871 the common school system finally opened in Georgia, 6,664 colored men, women, and children marched in. When the more permanent system of schools opened in 1873, the number of Negro pupils jumped to 19,755.[51] From there on, growth was steady and rapid.

Such were the foundations. Out of these beginnings, hasty and unstable though they were, accompanied by blood and ashes and the zeal of a small band of indomitable missionaries, the Negro college was to rise.

---

50. *Ibid.*, 189; J. L. Reddick, "The Negro and the Populist Movement in Georgia" (Unpublished Master's Thesis, Atlanta University, 1937), 8; Thomas, "Legislation as it Affected Public Education for Negroes in Georgia," 70.
51. *Report of the State School Commissioner of Georgia*, 1879-1880, p. 5.

CHAPTER II

Founding the First Colleges

ATLANTA UNIVERSITY

THE FIRST DEFINITE STEP IN GEORGIA TO MEET THE demand for education at a higher level than the normal school and designed to prepare leaders for the Negro race was taken in 1867 by the founding of Atlanta University. Under the aegis of the American Missionary Association, a board of trustees was organized consisting of eleven men, some white and some black. Important among the white men were Frederick Ayer, old and soon to pass from missionary fields into eternal green pastures, Erastus M. Cravath, founder of Fisk University, and Edmund Asa Ware, fresh from Yale, young, dynamic, and already dedicated to a life with the Negro race.

Obviously the title of "university" was more a hope than a reality. Preposterous at the beginning though the name was, it was the hope of the founders that this central institution should begin with normal and preparatory departments, grow into a college, and finally expand into a university. Ware was a man of high horizons. Out of his mind came the three-fold purpose of the institution: to develop individual Negro talent, provide inspiration and leadership for Negro communities, and train teachers. He believed that as little as the Negro knew of carpentry, agriculture, and industry, he knew still less of life, of civilization, of human contact, parentage and the home.[1]

After studying Atlanta, Augusta, and Americus for a site, Ware finally saw his vision on a barren hill, scarred by Confederate trenches and breastworks, overlooking Atlanta. With money from the Freedmen's Bureau and the American Missionary Association, the land was purchased and plans for a building were drawn up. Needing more money, Ware tried to tap the treasuries of the state and the city, but he failed. Immediately he went North, but passing the hat there among influential people was almost equally unsuccessful.[2] After returning to Atlanta, he found Negroes willing to dig the foundation of the first building for $80 for which white contractors had asked $300. Then the work began. By 1869 the first building, North Hall, was completed at a cost of $35,000 and two years later the second building, South Hall, was finished at a cost of $41,000.[3]

The first class of the Normal Department was assembled in April 1869, even before the first building was completed. It was a conglomerate of 89 students including the more promising from Storr's School and other advanced pupils from Albany, Andersonville, Athens, Augusta, Cuthbert, Dalton, Milledgeville, Savannah, Macon and other towns.[4]

Denominational Rivalry Produces Clark and Morehouse

At the same moment that brick and mortar were going into the creation of this first Negro college in Georgia, a profound change was taking place in the character of the

---
1. *From Servitude to Service* (Boston, 1905), 156.
2. Adams, *Atlanta University*, 11; Ware, "Sketch of Edmund Asa Ware," 31.
3. Adams, *Atlanta University*, 9.
4. E. H. Webster, "The Georgia Negro's Fight on Ignorance," (MS. in possession of Prof. Webster, Fairhope, Ala.), 9.

church societies that had been at work since the war. Sectarian competition began to divide the missionaries into separate camps. The majority of the first crusaders were sincere missionaries endowed with an incorruptible determination to bring light to the souls of Negroes. And during the first years of effort the agencies and denominations cooperated with commendable honesty free from the spirit of gaining renown for themselves or their churches. But as the first flush of humanitarianism subsided, this spirit gave way to sectarian competition. Denominations began drives for Negro members. They strove for control of the churches that were to be. They developed schools which they hoped would become the favorite resorts of ministers and scholars, and the rallying points of religious culture.[5]

Into this struggle among the churches, two more Georgia colleges were born, Clark University in Atlanta and Augusta Institute in Augusta, which later moved to Atlanta and finally became Morehouse College.

The birth of Clark University was inauspicious. Early in 1869 a primary school was opened in Clark Chapel in Atlanta by the Rev. J. W. Lee and his wife. It became successful and was soon adopted by the Freedmen's Aid Society of the Northern Methodist Church. After a short stay in the old Summer Hill schoolhouse classes were moved in 1870 to a building at Whitehall and McDaniel streets. Because of interest shown by Bishop D. W. Clark of the Northern Methodist Church, who visited Atlanta shortly after the war, and the philanthropy of his daughter, the school was christened Clark University. It immediately assumed higher education as an ultimate objective.[6] In its earliest years it did considerable staggering, however. Dur-

---
5. Jones, Negro Education, I, 252; E. B. Reuter, *The American Race Problem* (New York, 1927, 1938), 265-267.
6. *Catalogue of Clark University, June, 1879,* p. 29; 1924-1925, p. 13.

ing the first five years no less than seven principals or presidents were in charge. Gradually, it became more stable and before long 450 acres were secured for it by Bishop Gilbert Haven, the inveterate New England reformer. The land lay on a hill two miles south of the city. With no pavements or lines of transportation running to it, the purchase was looked upon by many as the work of a mad cap. Provisions had to be brought up by mule-cart. In wet weather the red clay roads were almost impassable. There was no adequate water supply, and during rains the drinking water took on a rusty color so that foods cooked in it came out with a startling tint of redness.[7] But the students felled trees and made roads. By 1880 a building was completed at a cost of $30,000 and dedicated as Chrisman Hall in honor of a Northern woman who had supplied $10,000.[8]

Of the three institutions founded during this period of the crusade and destined to become colleges, only the Augusta Institute was without ambition to offer higher education. It was designed for the training of teachers and preachers, professions which then demanded only the rudiments of formal education. If the Negro masses were to have churches of their own, it was decided, ministers must be trained. Thus there was more to it than sectarian jealousy. Few colored ministers were able to write, much less able to impart the blessings of an intelligent Providence to their flock.

The seed for the Augusta Institute (later Morehouse College) was sown by an ex-slave named Richard C. Coulter. He had been taken from Augusta to Virginia by his master, with the Confederate army. He escaped and walked to Washington. By day he worked, attended

---

7. J. S. Stowell, *Methodist Adventures in Negro Education* (New York, 1922), 67-68.
8. *Catalogue of Clark University, 1879-1881*, p. 20.

FOUNDING THE FIRST COLLEGES 25

school at night, and finally studied in the National Theological Seminary. He returned to Augusta in the fall of 1866 with a letter from the seminary authorizing him to establish a branch school. With the help of William J. White, enrollment began and in February 1867 the school was opened with 38 pupils in the Springfield Baptist Church. The first teachers were three women missionaries. Classes were held at night. About this same time the school came under the wing of the American Baptist Home Mission Society which had absorbed the National Theological Seminary, and the Rev. J. W. Parker was placed in charge. The school, small as it was, dwindled to nothing, and two years later the society sent W. D. Siegfried to revive it. He rented a room in down-town Augusta and opened a school for teachers and preachers. In 1870 the society purchased for $5,700 a lot containing some ramshackle buildings on Telfair Street in the heart of the city. But the times were politically unsatisfactory for success. Early records of these attempts to found Augusta Institute tell of warnings from the Ku Klux Klan which necessitated police protection from the city. In the end, Siegfried was run out of town because of an offensive letter he had written to a Northern paper describing mistreatment of Negroes in Augusta. The school languished again. Finally, in 1871 another attempt was made that proved successful and permanent. This time the Rev. Joseph Thomas Robert arrived. He was a Southern man of some culture, better adapted to the task than his Northern predecessors. He was a graduate of Brown University and had studied medicine at Yale and the South Carolina Medical College, but had finally abandoned medicine for the ministry. Augusta was not encouraging. The white people were hostile, buildings were dilapidated, and a "few nails in the walls and a few books on a bench constituted the entire equipment."⁹ Gifted with an uncanny amount of spiritual fortitude, Robert conducted the school four years without even an assistant, raising money for support, hearing recitations five hours a day, and delivering two lectures a week on Biblical and scientific subjects. In the fifth year two advanced students aided him, and by another year he had an official assistant sent by the society.¹⁰

A more central location in the state was desired, however, and in 1879, with the influence of a prominent Negro Baptist, the famous "Father" Frank Quarles, Robert moved his school to Atlanta and renamed it the Atlanta Baptist Seminary. Classes were held in the basement of the Friendship Baptist Church during the first few weeks. Finally, four acres were purchased from Richard Peters at Elliott and West Hunter streets and a building was set up at a cost of $7,500. But the location was bad. Surrounded by railroad shifting yards and a lumber mill, the smoke and noise were unbearable. Boarding facilities were so bad that many students were forced to prepare their own meals. Far from an intellectual atmosphere, the licentious temptations of the booming city proved too seductive to those of primitive piety. But it was not until several years later that a final and permanent location was secured southwest of the city near the well established walls of Atlanta University.¹¹

Thus within a decade, the three institutions destined to become the first sanctuaries of Negro higher education in Georgia had crowded into Atlanta, one non-sectarian, one Methodist, and one Baptist. Not until near the turn of the century were other parts of the state to be similarly benefited.

---

9. Benjamin Brawley, *History of Morehouse College* (Atlanta, 1917), 12-24.
10. *Catalogue of Atlanta Baptist Seminary, 1888-1889*, pp. 20-21.
11. Brawley, *Morehouse College*, 31-36.

Early Curricula

The curriculum set up in these schools by the Northern missionaries was lifted body and soul from the small New England college. It was the only road to knowledge they knew. A false belief has been accepted widely that the crusaders imposed their classical course of Greek, Latin, and mathematics upon the ignorant Negro with little concern for the actual conditions of Negro life and with the firm conviction that the classics contained all the worthy secrets of the universe. But a study of the period shows plainly that from the beginning many practical subjects were taught and there were constant gropings, innumerable experiments, a myriad of changes, all in hope that a curriculum might be devised of practical everyday value to the Freedmen.

There is no space here to record these endless changes and only the general structure may be described. In the beginning the primary purpose was to prepare preachers and teachers. But so few Freedmen knew even the alphabet that before this could be done the three R's had to be taught. Said President Robert in 1875, the "ministers, indeed, with but few exceptions, were entirely untaught, and unable to read the scriptures."[12] The colleges began by setting up primary departments (excepting Atlanta University which began with normal and later added the primary) teaching reading, writing, geography, and a smattering of history. As soon as a few students were sufficiently advanced, normal and theological departments were inaugurated, plus an academic course designed to prepare a few in the classics for college study.

By 1872 the preparatory departments of Atlanta University had developed a graduating class, and a college department was opened with some of these graduates forming a freshmen class of twelve students. The college was

---
12. *Catalogue of the Augusta Institute, 1875-1876,* p. 3.

opened one year at a time as this first class advanced. In 1876 six of this first class graduated and received the first bachelor's degrees given to Negroes in Georgia. It was not until 1879 that Clark University opened a college department with four freshmen, to be followed two years later by the Atlanta Baptist Seminary, with a class of only one student. The first college graduate of Clark, Walter H. Nelson, finished in 1883.[13]

Admission to the college class of Atlanta University in the 'seventies demanded that students pass examinations in common English branches, algebra, geometry, history, geography, composition, and the inevitable several books of Latin and Greek. Or they could be accepted by passing through the preparatory departments of the University itself. Admittance to the college departments of the other schools varied only slightly from these requirements, sometimes being less strict in their demands because of the general lack of preparation which unavoidably interfered with the maintenance of high standards.

The catalogues of those years were masterly records of human expectation and optimism. Although it was not until the twentieth century that the college enrollment was more than a small fraction of the student body, the college departments and their elaborate curricula held the place of all honor and glory in the catalogue. Yet honest efforts were often made to carry out the program. The catalogue of Clark for 1879 listed a four year college course covering the English classics, eleven Latin and Greek authors, algebra, geometry, trigonometry, surveying, mechanics, English composition, rhetoric, modern literature, Greek geography and history, natural philosophy, geology, botany, mental philosophy, and logic—all for the first three years of college. In the final year subjects listed were chemistry, astronomy, physiology, political economy, history

---

13. *Catalogue of Clark University, 1883-1884*, p. 4.

FOUNDING THE FIRST COLLEGES 29

of civilization, civil government, evidences of Christianity, moral science, Greek Testament, and original orations.

Certainly such a curriculum was a far-fetched hope for four students and five instructors with practically no equipment, no matter how honest the intentions. Indeed, it is safe to say that the colleges, despite the catalogues, applied only an insignificant amount of effort to teach the classical curriculum; it was the matter of practical, everyday fundamentals that consumed their energy. Surely the tradition charged against them has little basis.

In Atlanta University there was a larger staff and fair equipment. The records of the few college students of those days reveal that about three-fourths of the above list was really attempted. In addition, Atlanta University in the 'seventies taught courses in the social sciences, such as international law, Constitution of the United States, Lieber's civil liberty, history of the Reformation, and occasional courses in German and pedagogy.[14] But since here also only a fraction of the students were in the upper classes, the records are misleading.

As early as 1873 Atlanta University offered a scientific course, mostly classical, however, and an agricultural course, both leading to bachelor of science degrees.[15] A farm was a natural appanage of the Negro college. But despite a boast that the agricultural department of Atlanta University offered practical instruction in farming and ground beautifying under an "eminent" landscape gardener, there are no records of any appreciable number of students either in it or the scientific course.[16] Scientific agricultural instruction, expensive and demanding costly equipment, is a comparatively new development in Negro

---

14. Adams, *Atlanta University*, 18.
15. *Catalogue of Atlanta University, 1873-1874*, pp. 18-19.
16. *Ibid., 1869-1870*, p. 10.

colleges and was hardly to be thought of in the days of the crusade.

All other departments were below the level of what is generally accepted as higher education. Even certain of the college courses would not have passed muster in the average college of the day. But it is impossible to tell where the overlapping began and ended. Faced with a class of ignorant black men, women, and children nourished in the background of the log cabin and the hoe, with scientific equipment in the schools consisting only of copybooks and a blackboard, and with untutored minds searching in fanciful colors for a short cut to the wonders of the white world, it was inevitable that those be colleges more in name than in fact.

In the beginning all three of the institutions taught theology. By 1876 Atlanta University had graduated three in this subject, but being in a non-denominational institution, the course soon "gave up the ghost."[17] At the Atlanta Baptist Seminary theology went through a precarious career, vanishing for a while in the 'eighties despite the efforts of the school to develop ministers, and then returning to continue as an important means of building the Baptist ministry.[18] At Clark the course had 14 students in 1879 and they were listed in the college department. But the work was not of college level.

The lack of a sufficient elementary school system for Negroes in the state forced each institution to enroll its largest numbers in the primary departments. But the incessant plea for teachers quickly made the normal department, if not the largest, the most important branch of the schools. The normal courses ranged from two to six years in length, undergoing constant changes and overlappings with the academic (high school) and preparatory depart-

---

17. Adams, *Atlanta University*, 16-18.
18. Brawley, *Morehouse College*, 41-44.

ments, sometimes extending even into college subjects. By 1883 Atlanta Baptist Seminary alone had 111 normal students. The courses were the usual school subjects of the day. As early as 1869 Atlanta University was offering also pedagogy, including methods of teaching in science and the common branches. In addition to all this, the faculty of Atlanta University voted in 1879 that women in the Higher Normal course be taught plain sewing, cooking, nursing, and housekeeping.[19]

Whatever were the dreams of these missionaries to bring into being centers of higher learning modeled on Oxford, Cambridge, Harvard, and Yale, even their smallest hopes were not destined to be realized until many years after the founders had passed from the stage. Enrollment in the college departments remained infinitesimal. Until 1879 when Clark began college work, the only students of that rank were in Atlanta University, and there they never numbered more than thirty. At Clark and Atlanta Baptist Seminary, there were never more than ten until the end of the century. In 1885, out of a total enrollment of more than 700 in the three institutions, there were only 28 in the college departments. About one-third were normal students and the rest were largely in the elementary branches. By that time Atlanta University had granted 41 bachelor's degrees and 101 normal certificates. This university was the largest of the three schools, having a total enrollment in 1880-81 of 341 students who were by then coming from ten states.

The smallness of the college departments was due in part to the belief at first of many Negroes that reading and writing were sufficient for any education they would need in life. President Robert of Augusta Institute wrote in 1878 that the first students came only for a few weeks or months and went away with their "vast" acquirements of

---
19. Minutes of the Faculty of Atlanta University, May 6, 1879, p. 155.

culture, convinced that they were prepared to face the vicissitudes of their new freedom. But Robert noted that students soon perceived the larger purposes of education and stayed for longer and more faithful study.[20]

The poverty of the black man was the greatest bar to college growth. Although the 725,000 Negroes in Georgia made up 47% of the population in 1880, the value of their real and personal property with fifteen years of freedom was only $5,700,000 compared to $238,000,000 for the whites. While this accumulation of wealth was a notable beginning for an illiterate race turned loose with no tradition of responsibility, scarcely able to count the coins of their wages, it was not enough to keep children in school over a long period of years. Farm laborers worked for an average of 40c and 50c a day plus board and room.[21] In 1880 tuition was $1 a month at the Atlanta Baptist Seminary and $2 a month in Atlanta University. It was small enough for students living in the city. Board and room cost only $8 to $10 a month and could be secured for as low as $5 in the neighborhood. But even these small sums put a terrific burden on the family working on little more than a slave basis.

The annals of students and families alike are grim with toil and sacrifice. All three of the institutions made desperate appeals for student aid funds. As early as 1869, students in Atlanta University were being helped by the Peabody Fund. At Clark, small loans were available, and the records of Augusta Institute for 1877 tell of 18 students receiving $5 a month toward their subsistence.[22] Attempts were made at Clark for students to support themselves through work on the farm.[23] Other work was provided on grounds and

---

20. Brawley, *Morehouse College*, 30.
21. W. H. Crogman, *Talks for the Times* (Atlanta, 1896), 112.
22. Brawley, *Morehouse College*, 28.
23. Stowell, *Methodist Adventures*, 68.

buildings. But facilities were limited, endowments were slow in coming, and after a few months of school, many students were forced to renounce their books and return home with only a smattering of knowledge.

CHAPTER III

A Few Years of Failure and Success

IF THE BEGINNING OF NEGRO EDUCATION IN THE SOUTH had not been the result of religious and humanitarian impulses, it is doubtful if the pockets of the nation would have opened for its support. The schools and colleges of the crusade were conceived in poverty. Some, like Atlanta University, quickly attained financial support of considerable amount for that day, but none achieved any degree of wealth until the educational renaissance following the First World War. In the aggregate, however, large sums of money were poured into the crusade by the North. More came from the Southern states also with the beginnings of public school systems. And the nickels and dimes of the Negroes themselves must not be forgotten. But for a population of nearly five million Negroes, 95 per cent illiterate, these sums were like a light shower falling on a parched land.

At the beginning of the crusade, the North opened its coffers in the belief that it had fought a war of unselfish humanitarianism not to be ended until all men of the South, black and white, were free and equal. In many churches sermons were preached and collections were taken for the education of the ignorant Freedmen. Sunday schools sent food, clothing, and supplies.[1] Sorrowful tales went North from the missionaries and agents of the Freedmen's Bureau of Negro suffering and poverty, stories of the results of their year's labor being stolen by the whites, of prejudice and injustice and violence of a kind to open hearts and pocket-books.[2] Each summer, teachers returned North with reports, glowing and enthusiastic, that the Freedmen were as capable or perhaps more so than the whites, that they might even become the superior race of the South. Intoxicated with their fervor, some teachers' mental and spiritual mirages magnified everything. The reports were listened to by audiences and congregations who, already elated by the conquests of their armies and the fruits of emancipation and Reconstruction, poured forth money and treated the missionaries like heroes engaged in the greatest campaign of modern times.[3]

The Federal government also entered into the work. Of the $89,000 spent by Atlanta University in the first two years of its life, 1869-1871, $52,400 came from the Freedmen's Bureau. The Morrill Act of 1862 was also a boon to Atlanta University. By the provisions of that Act 30,000 acres of public land for each Congressman were donated to the various states, the proceeds of which were to be used for colleges of agriculture and the mechanical arts. With the influence of the Negroes in the legislature, backed by the Republican regime of Governor Rufus Bullock, $8,000 a year was given to Atlanta University. A state Board of Commissioners was appointed to approve

---

1. Letters to Edmund Asa Ware, 1869 (in Atlanta University Library).
2. *Annual Report of the American Missionary Association,* 1869, pp. 28-32.
3. A. D. Mayo, *Southern Women in the Recent Educational Movement in the South* (Washington, 1892), 89-90.

the expenditure of the money, and Examiners were appointed to visit the institution annually to examine the buildings and teaching and see to it that subversive ideas were not promoted among the students.

Other money came from the North through the channels of philanthropic and church missionary societies. Of the $89,000 spent by Atlanta University in its first two years, $19,000 had come from the American Missionary Association. In the case of Clark University, entire support, such as it was, came from the Freedmen's Aid Society of the Northern Methodist Church. There was no endowment and growth was slow, but the limited income of the little school was secure and free from the constant demands of begging. The help of the American Baptist Home Mission Society which sponsored the Atlanta Baptist Seminary was hardly enough, however, for even a decent beginning. President Robert struggled continuously for a bare existence. Some classrooms were entirely unfurnished. Many pledges for the Atlanta building were never collected. Its usual expenditures in the 'seventies shifted between $2,000 and $4,000 a year.[4] When the first college student was graduated in 1883, its expenditures reached the sum of only $7,000 while Atlanta University had $32,000 to spend.

Despite constant appeals for endowments for the colleges there was little response during the period. Before 1882 Atlanta University could boast only of the Plainfield Scholarship of $300.[5] Student aid was provided in part by the Peabody Fund which gave from $500 to $800 a year to the University. Students and teachers were urged to join in campaigns for funds among themselves and their friends.[6] Catalogues were sent North carrying appeals.

---

4. Brawley, *Morehouse College*, 36.
5. Adams, *Atlanta University*, 25.
6. Minutes of the Faculty of Atlanta University, December 3, 1878, p. 145.

Their use as an advertising medium explains in part their display of an elaborate college curriculum. The catalogue of Atlanta University for 1869-1870 also appealed for books for a library, a bell, a clock, maps, charts, and scientific apparatus. The best medium of advertising soon came to be the bulletin or college paper, printed on the school's own printing presses. Atlanta University established its *Bulletin* in 1882 and similar papers soon followed and were sent throughout the North and South by all the institutions to raise money and create interest in the cause.

Some institutions kept agents traveling in the field, speaking in churches, clubs, mass meetings, chautauquas, and soliciting individuals for private gifts. As president of Atlanta University, Edmund Ware himself spent several months of every year in the field. In the long lists of donors to the University in the 'eighties are found such prominent names as "Rev. Phillips Brooks, $100"; "Cornelius Vanderbilt, $100." Agents, presidents, teachers on summer leave— all went over the land with a fine tooth comb collecting from every rank and class.

At best, it was a difficult matter to keep the institutions floating. With the failure of the South to provide public education on higher levels and the insistence of church denominations to establish their own schools, private institutions sprang up throughout the South like mushrooms. Competition for their support was keen. As early enthusiasm for the cause dwindled pockets were harder to open. Conflicting statements soon began to filter into the North concerning the condition of the South and the capacity of the Negro. Travelers in the South who heard a few students spout Latin and Greek reported the race unsurpassed in scholarship. Others who saw bunches of indolent black men loafing disorderly about railroad stations wrote only of their demoralization. Non-plussed by these conflicting statements the North often was unable to know whether to give or not. On the completion of a third building, Stone Hall, in 1882, President Ware of Atlanta University was at his wit's end to find furnishings to put in it.[7]

Beset with such poverty it was impossible for the colleges to secure sufficient equipment to teach college subjects efficiently. Scientific apparatus was not to be thought of. The catalogue of Clark University for 1879, however, made the proud boast of a cabinet of minerals. But little was added to it, and the collection was of doubtful use.

The development of libraries was more successful. In the second year of its life, 1870, Atlanta University recorded a gift for books from the "Rev. Giles Pease, Boston, Mass., $300." Three years later R. R. Graves of Brooklyn, New York, provided an endowment of $5,000 for the library. The number of volumes had increased to over 2,000. A room 11 by 15 feet was set aside for the "Graves Library" as it was named, and by 1883 more than 6,000 volumes were on its shelves. It was a better library, said Atticus Haygood of Emory College, than most Southern white colleges possessed.[8] The Augusta Institute also had a small collection of 503 volumes by 1877, which increased within four years after moving to Atlanta to more than 1,200. There was little popular literature among them. The collections were composed chiefly of books on religious, classical, and scientific subjects in keeping with the educational mood of the period.

THE EARLY MISSIONARY SPIRIT

However small these advances seem in the light of swiftly moving educational developments of the twentieth century, the men and women of the crusade built solid foundations. Considering the thanklessness of the task

---

7. Crogman, *Talks for the Times*, 153-156.
8. Adams, *Atlanta University*, 86-87; A. G. Haygood, *Our Brother in Black, His Freedom and His Future* (2nd ed., Nashville, 1887), 171.

and the hostility of the South wherein they were forced to renounce most human association to which they were accustomed, it is a wonder that any of them remained at all. Said one missionary of his treatment in a rural section of Georgia: "We are shut out from white society, until it is really a treat to have a white child speak to us. My wife has spoken to but two white women since we came here, and that on business . . . .

"Bands of armed and masked men are prowling around nights whipping some, and murdering others. Politicians, at a public meeting, have threatened our schools, and being isolated from every human protection, we are in great fear and peril. I have devoted the nights to watching, for the protection of life, and to guard our buildings against fire. To be for weeks in constant expectation of being murdered or burned out, and without losing faith in God, is something of a strain on the nerves.

"Mr.---, who assisted me last year, and two other white teachers who are teaching a short distance west of us, were allowed twenty-four hours to leave."[9]

Such violence was usually confined to the rural sections. Yet after a speech in Macon in 1868 Edmund Asa Ware was favored by a Ku Klux Klan warning that if he persisted in his course, "The sun will shine on a new made grave."[10] But on the whole, the native spirit in Atlanta and other cities was expressed only in distant opposition and silent contempt. Much of the hostility was due to the tactlessness and uncontrollable fervor of the missionaries themselves. They understood little of Southern culture and the traditions of generations that had made it what it was. In many cases the missionaries came already convinced of their social ostracism and made no attempt to change it.

---
9. C. H. Walker, "The Attitude of Georgia Toward the Education of Negroes" (Unpublished Master's Thesis, Atlanta University, 1935), 21.
10. Ware, "Edmund Asa Ware," 27.

Working hard for long hours in districts remote from good white neighborhoods, they had little chance for proper contacts and remained on, believing they were persecuted apostles.

But they were opposed, of course, because they were bent on lifting the Negro out of his place in the Southern scheme of life. They were popularly known as "N. T.'s" or "Nigger Teachers" and were as severely let alone as were the Negroes themselves.[11] During Reconstruction the doors of the Republicans were open to them in Atlanta and they were often seen in the homes of Governor Rufus Bullock, State School Commissioner J. R. Lewis, and A. E. Buck.[12] But with the end of that regime, the homes were no more and the teachers were forced to create their own social life among themselves and their students. The hostility of the whites forced many teachers in the earliest years to board in the homes of Negroes. But as quickly as possible, cottages were built on the campuses or bought near-by, and they then had homes of their own.[13]

Only men and women of stalwart faith were able to remain in the face of all the obstacles. Those who took part in the beginnings of higher education were, for the most part, the highest type of the missionaries. Whatever their beliefs in the capacity of the black race, in social equality, and the injustice of the South, they were crusaders of unquenchable spirit, with lusty courage, and a powerful driving will. They believed sincerely in the righteousness of their cause and many devoted their lives to it.

Hardly less notable than Edmund Asa Ware, at Atlanta University, were three other people who made up the famous quartet of the period. Thomas N. Chase was

---

11. *Atlanta University Bulletin, June, 1890.*
12. Notes on early Negro education prepared for the author by Prof. E. H. Webster, of Fairhope, Ala., 1939.
13. Ware, "Edmund Asa Ware," 21.

YEARS OF FAILURE AND SUCCESS 41

the first to come. A graduate of Dartmouth College, he arrived at the University in 1869. Not only a good business man but also an efficient teacher, he remained for thirty-eight years, acting as president three short periods, and instructing in Greek, Latin, and mathematics.[14] Another, Cyrus W. Francis, came to Atlanta in 1867 as pastor of Storr's Church. He was a classmate of Ware at Yale and joined with him as a charter member of the Board of Trustees which founded Atlanta University. In 1873 he joined the faculty and remained for twenty-seven years.[15] The fourth member of the quartet was Horace Bumstead. He was a member of two old New England families, the Bumsteads and the Willises, a gentleman of the old school, courteous, patient, and dignified. Like Francis, he was a member of Ware's class at Yale and joined the faculty in 1875. Eventually he followed Ware to the president's chair, proved himself a good money raiser, attracted friends, and guided the university through the most perilous years of its existence for two decades.[16]

For many years none of the teachers taught solely college subjects and their work was usually more in the preparatory grades. The teachers of the lower branches were, of course, of less fame, the majority of those in the grammar departments being women with no more than a normal school education. The fact that the faculties were all small often resulted in large classes. In 1878 Clark University had only five instructors for 179 pupils. Salaries were commensurate with the poverty of the schools. In 1874 Edmund Asa Ware received only $1,500 as president of Atlanta University, while Francis received only $450. The average salary was rarely more than $700 or $900 a year.

---
14. Adams, *Atlanta University*, 57.
15. *Ibid.*, 57.
16. *Ibid.*, 58.

Under such conditions of poverty, all the faculty were forced to be hard workers. In 1880-1881 President Robert of the Atlanta Baptist Seminary taught five and six classes a day, each class enrolling from 26 to 109 pupils. In 1884-1885 William Holmes taught eight classes daily, each having between 107 and 152 pupils.[17]

But it was not all a dreary life of hard work and hostility. The eagerness of the students and the friendly recognition of a few important white men like Atticus Haygood and ex-Governor Joe Brown were bright spots in their lives. Their pupils were extremely docile. It also pleased the teachers to have the state Board of Visitors in 1871 notice that many students were especially bright. Said the Board: "At every step of the examination we were impressed with the fallacy of the popular idea (which, in common with thousands of others, a majority of the undersigned have heretofore entertained) that the members of the African race are not capable of a high degree of intellectual culture. . . .

"Many of the pupils exhibited a degree of mental culture which, considering the length of time their minds have been in training, would do credit to members of any race."[18]

It was noted also, to the delight of the teachers, that in the buildings "no ink spots, knife marks, or other blemishes" were visible.[19] New England fastidiousness was reflected in the report in 1877 which said that the visitors "found neatness and order in the school rooms, far in advance of what is usually found in the academies and colleges of the whites."[20]

The teachers refused to respect the color line and founded their work on a basis of social equality, often

---
17. Brawley, *Morehouse College*, 37.
18. *Catalogue of Atlanta University, 1875-1876*, p. 26.
19. *Ibid., 1875-1876*, p. 27.
20. *Ibid., 1877-1878*, p. 27.

eating with their students and joining in the social life of the Negro community. It brought upon them the curse of the land. Yet the reports of the state Board of Examiners for Atlanta University were replete with praise for the thoroughness, patience, ability, and moral examples of the teachers. Leaders like Ware enjoined their teachers to use tact with the Southern whites. While insisting himself that so far as the races were concerned, he was afflicted with color blindness, he wished to antagonize no one. In 1879 his faculty voted to use the terms "young men" and "young women" rather than "young gentlemen" and "young ladies." And they prescribed that it was not desirable to say "mister" in addressing the boys.[21]

Although corporal punishment was forbidden for all but extreme cases of discipline, the colleges were characterized by a reign of law. The administration made and enforced its own law. It was severe and Puritanical, often insisting on narrow and intense piety. But it was characteristic of the day in many white institutions also. As men and women of stern religious principles, the crusaders knew no other way. They may have erred in their enthusiasm and righteousness. They may have placed too much emphasis on the printed page of the classics and too little on everyday knowledge applicable to common life. But they represented the golden age of the missionary spirit in America.[22]

It was natural that the state should look with fear at the hills around Atlanta where these institutions and their teachers were encouraging the submissive black man to rise. So great was the opposition to Atlanta University during Reconstruction that an attempt was made to abolish it by a city ordinance designed to cut up the campus and

---
21. Minutes of the Faculty of Atlanta University, April 1, 1879, p. 154.
22. Jones, *Negro Education*, I, 11.

run Mitchell Street through the boys' building. Ware won the contest, however, and disregarded the fiery and bitter speeches that resounded against him.

Constant vigil was maintained by the state to keep doctrines of heresy and disloyalty out of the masses. The power of the schools threatened the whole structure of the social order. For three months every summer advanced students went out to teach in the public schools of the state. Others who had finished or graduated were teaching regularly. In the summer of 1874 alone 115 students went out from Atlanta University to teach. It was estimated that during the 'seventies and 'eighties students and former students gave instruction to no less than 10,000 Negroes every year.[23] Much was done in these campaigns to arouse interest in education and develop the common school system. But what would be the result, asked the legislature, if ideas of social equality and political freedom were carried into the highways and byways of the state? The report of the Examiners for 1875-1876 reflected this dread. The Board felt that Atlanta University could not fail to achieve much good for the African race "so long as no improper or sinister attempt is made to foster jealousies and hatred against the whites among the pupils of the school, and to encourage future antagonisms, or social equality maxims. . . ."[24]

The report of 1877 was even more fearful and significant. Speaking of Atlanta University, the Examiners "would call attention of the General Assembly to the fact that it can, to a great extent, shape the public opinions of the colored race, and make them true and loyal citizens of Georgia . . . or it can turn all their prejudices and feelings against their native state, as the former scene of their

---

23. *Catalogue of Atlanta University, 1875-1876*, p. 28; *1885-1886*, p. 30.
24. *Ibid., 1875-1876*, p. 28.

YEARS OF FAILURE AND SUCCESS 45

slavery and the present home, as charged by our enemies, of their oppressors and natural enemies."[25]

It was emphasized that the educated Negroes would control nearly one-half the voters of the Empire State of the South. It was suggested that courses be taught in United States government, but that all textbooks be examined for political opinions. The report said, concerning the students: "They seem much attached to the school, and for the present they will take instruction from Northern teachers more readily and confidently than they would from us.

"The Board suggests, however, that our authorities insist that these Northern teachers do not try to alienate them from old masters and home, and from their native state; or even use such instruction or place around them such influences (by sectional books, etc.) as will have that tendency.

"Probably the present teachers are not so careful in this respect as the interests of this people and of our state demand."[26]

The fear of the Examiners was partially aroused by the discovery of a few sectional books in the library, and they were horrified to learn that the most worn volumes on the shelves were of an incendiary nature against the South. They included Allen O. Abbott's *Prison Life in the South*, Augustus C. Hamlin's *Martyria; or Andersonville Prison*, and Charles C. Coffin's *Four Years of Fighting*. It was urged from some quarters that the state withdraw its $8,000 annual appropriation and use the money on a white normal school. But with his usual tact, Ware pleaded that he had no knowledge of the presence of the books, and he promptly removed them from the library. The report the following year stated that such books were no

---
25. *Ibid., 1877-1878*, p. 26.
26. *Ibid., 1877-1878*, pp. 26-27.

longer to be found and that the teachers were being careful not to alienate the race.

End of the First Wave of the Crusade

The forward rush of the first generation of missionaries culminated in the early 'eighties and the first half of the crusade came to an end. New viewpoints in American life, different ideals, and a different spirit of endeavor had already seeped into the field of education and were destined to change its course from the Atlantic to the Pacific.

Any evaluation of what the first part of the crusade actually accomplished must emphasize not so much its failures as its successes. If Negro education in Georgia produced what to the modern mind seems insignificant, it must be remembered that education among whites was also a rather sterile affair. America before the Civil War was not conscious of the value of mass education. As late as 1850 there were only eight graduate students in American colleges and no great advance in education was begun until the 'seventies.[27]

With almost no foundation to build on then, the achievements of the crusade are little short of amazing. In Georgia the task was made somewhat easier by the existence of a more democratic people. Here, in 1880, fifteen years after the end of slavery, the state was able to report nearly 90,000 colored men, women, and children in schools, public and private. The majority of these were taught by colored teachers and only a few whites were left in the field, mostly in private schools.[28] Three embryo Negro colleges had been born, wielding an influence over the ignorant black masses of the state far beyond proportions of size.

By 1882 these three colleges had acquired land and build-

---
27. F. L. Paxson, *Recent History of the United States, 1865-1929* (New York, 1929), 55.
28. *Proceedings and Reports of the John F. Slater Fund, 1883* (New York, 1883), 12.

ings valued at nearly $250,000. It was a far cry from basements and rented rooms. With a plant worth $132,000 Atlanta University was surpassed in Georgia only by the University of Georgia, Mercer, and Wesleyan, the latter two of which were each valued at only $150,000. Emory, Shorter, and others had much less.[29]

By the end of the first half of the crusade, moreover, many friends had been won to the cause. At the opening of the Atlanta Baptist Seminary in Atlanta in 1879, Governor A. H. Colquitt and G. J. Orr, the State Commissioner of Education, made speeches of great praise.[30] A year later at Clark, ex-Governor Joe Brown, with the supporting presence of three ex-governors of the state and bishops of Southern churches, publicly thanked the Northern missionaries for doing what the South had been too poor to do.[31] Such eulogies were often no more than political stunts to catch votes, but there was some sincerity. By 1883 the pages of the *Atlanta Constitution* were condemning the tardiness of the white South in the education of the Negro, saying that if the Negro hated his Southern masters, it was because the white man had turned his back on the Negro and such hatred was deserved.[32] In 1881, Atticus G. Haygood, president of Emory College, published *Our Brother in Black*. He pleaded for justice and aid, socially and educationally, for the Negro. As editor of the *Wesleyan Christian Advocate* he campaigned for better race relations.[33]

The end of the crusade was not yet. It is impossible to measure it by time. But by the 'eighties the early spirit

---

29. *Report of the State School Commissioner of Georgia, 1880-1881*, p. 13.
30. Brawley, *Morehouse College*, 34.
31. Holmes, *Evolution of the Negro College*, 110-111.
32. *Atlanta Constitution*, May 19, 1883.
33. C. W. Dabney, *Universal Education in the South* (Chapel Hill, 1936), II, 434.

which had flared into a bright flame had dimmed noticeably, and the second generation that moved in to rekindle it was of a different clay. On a day in the fall of 1885, Edmund Asa Ware fell while walking up a hill near Atlanta University. He was carried into a house and frantic efforts were made to revive him. But it was no use. His life dimmed, flickered, and went out. While his death did not mark the end of the missionary spirit there was no doubt that its brightest star over Georgia had fallen. The new era of industrialism was already on its way. From then on, the rise of the Negro college in Georgia would continue to be beset by difficulties. But the effort was to be cast in a different mould, based more on materialism and the actual conditions of everyday life.

CHAPTER IV

The Second Wave of the Crusade

THE SECOND WAVE OF THE CRUSADE IN GEORGIA WAS marked by the practical application of four desires that had been growing in America and the South during the decade of the eighteen-seventies. First, the movement for the emancipation and education of women expressed itself in the founding of Spelman College in Atlanta. Second, the willingness of the South itself to take part in the higher education of the Negro resulted in the establishment of Paine College in Augusta. Third, the urge of the Negroes themselves, after a generation of white tutelage, to have schools of their own matured in the setting up of Morris Brown College in Atlanta. And fourth, the desire for a Negro ministry equipped with more than the simple lessons of the "Blue-Back Speller" was fulfilled in the erection of the Gammon Theological Seminary, also in Atlanta.

SPELMAN

Now free to desert the hoe and the wash-tub of slavery, many Negro women of the South became determined to assert themselves. In Georgia, Clark and Atlanta universities had been coeducational from the beginning. At Atlanta Baptist Seminary, where only men were enrolled, an attempt had been made to build a dormitory to include women. But the money could not be raised and the plan fell through.[1]

Then in 1880 Sophia B. Packard had come out of New England to see the South. As an officer of the Women's Baptist Home Mission Society it was her business to gain a better knowledge of the black race which her society was attempting to help. She was an excellent example of that type of stern, self-willed maiden woman that New England civilization took pride in producing. A product of the usual round of female seminaries, she had taught school, and later in her middle years, had experienced the advantage of European travel. At fifty-six, when she came South, she was a mature and dominating woman, progressive and aggressive, impelling and compelling as a March wind, but the rigors of Southern travel in days when railroads were not famous for comfort, proved too much for her, and in New Orleans she fell sick. There an old friend, Harriet E. Giles, came to her rescue, and after Miss Packard recuperated the two ladies continued their journey. Nothing so impressed them as the need of education among colored women. In every state the Baptists had established schools for men. Yet, even in Georgia, with the largest Negro population in the South, but little provision had been made for the elevation of women.

Immediately Miss Packard and Miss Giles made plans for a school and returned North to raise money. To their dismay, the treasury of their young women's missionary society was empty, and many people looked upon the scheme as a wild venture that could never succeed. Finally, with $50 in cash from the congregation of the West Medford Baptist Church, and $50 in pledges, the two crusaders returned to Atlanta and began their work.

---

1. *Historical Sketch and General Catalogue of Spelman Seminary, 1881-1921* (Atlanta, n. d.), 8.

Backed by the kind-heartedness of the famous Negro preacher, "Father" Quarles, the basement of the Friendship Baptist Church was turned into a school room. By canvassing the neighborhood from house to house, they persuaded eleven women to become students.[2] And with equipment consisting of two Bibles, two note-books, and two pencils, the first class of the Atlanta Baptist Female Seminary assembled on April 11, 1881.[3]

Within three months eighty students were enrolled, and by the end of the first year no fewer than 175 girls and women had crowded into the dark basement. They were mostly women out of slavery, one third of them being between thirty and fifty-five years of age.[4] Although often ridiculed they hid their books beneath their shawls and went to school determined to learn. "What will become of our homes if our women take to book learning?" said the husbands. And a movement was organized by colored ministers to stop the school.[5]

But this prejudice or suspicion was not the least of the trouble. On cloudy days the basement was damp and the dim light that filtered through the tiny windows made reading almost impossible. Three teachers had classes in the same room. In 1882 a Miss Champney came to help, and then Miss C. M. Grover. With no desks and only rude benches the classes gathered into the corners of the room, overflowing even into the coal bin.

By touring the North in the summer of 1882, Miss Packard and Miss Giles attempted to raise money for a building. Their efforts failed, however, and they returned sorrowfully to their cheerless basement. But a year later the American Baptist Home Mission Society purchased

---
2. *Spelman Messenger*, October 1930, p. 32.
3. *Catalogue of Spelman Seminary, 1887-1888*, p. 33; *Catalogue of Spelman College, 1924-1925*, p. 35.
4. *Historical Sketch of Spelman*, 6-7.
5. *Spelman Messenger*, June, 1927, p. 31.

for $17,500 the "Old Barracks" and drill field used by the Federal army after the war. It was a nine acre tract containing five frame buildings, located within sight of Atlanta University. On the condition that Miss Packard raise $15,000 to pay the balance of the cost, the new site was turned over to her. A boarding department was opened and the enrollment immediately increased to over 500. Teachers volunteered their services and missionary societies and individuals sent clothing, furnishings, and supplies.

But their troubles were not over. Money came slowly and the note of $15,000 hung menacingly close to their heads. A second campaign in the summer of 1883 again failed to bring the needed amount. Negro Baptists in Georgia gave $3,000 and other friends provided $1,300, but it was not enough. The note was extended twice, each time in the hope of a miraculous harvest. For whatever Miss Packard and Miss Giles lacked in business acumen, they had the same love and simple, boundless faith that had set Ware's dreams successfully upon the breastworks of Diamond Hill.

At last a savior appeared. John D. Rockefeller had sat in the congregation of the Wilson Avenue Baptist Church in Cleveland in the summer of 1882 when Miss Packard made her appeal to Northern churches. Impressed, he emptied his pockets into the collection plate. Once assured of the permanence of the school he sent in a large donation. In the spring of 1884, while in the South, Rockefeller came to see the new venture. Surrounded by the hundreds of Negro girls and women who swarmed the acres of the old barracks, he was enthusiastic in praise. Not only did he pay off the final balance of the ominous $15,000, but he supplied a greater sum of many thousands, and the first brick building, Rockefeller Hall, was built. The school was immediately renamed for the Spelman family of Mrs. Rockefeller, and future prosperity was assured.[6] Work was opened very shortly in education, industrial arts, home economy, and nurse training. With this broad appeal churches and agencies came with helping hands. Within two years the second brick building, Packard Hall, had been completed, and by 1888, twenty-five teachers and four student-assistants were instructing more than 600 students.[7] At first study was confined to the lower branches, but by 1890 an ambition to offer higher education asserted itself and a collegiate department was opened teaching Latin and German.[8] It was not until 1897, however, that a full-fledged college department was installed and two students, Jane Anna Granderson from far-off Mississippi, and Claudia T. White, the daughter of William J. White, entered as the first freshmen.

PAINE

While these efforts of Northern missionaries and philanthropists were answering the desire of Negro women for education, quite another movement, entirely divorced from the missionary impulse, was taking shape in Augusta to answer the demands of colored Methodist ministers. The Southern Methodist Church had long been active among the Negroes of the South. As early as 1829 Bishop William Capers had begun plantation mission work. The effort was more evangelical than educational, and by 1860 more than 200,000 Negroes had been gathered into the church. The upheaval of war and Northern objections to the Southern church, however, weaned many away, and by 1866 only 78,000 members were left. At the request of this remnant, the white church organized them into their own body under the name of the Colored Methodist

---

6. *Catalogue of Spelman Baptist Seminary, 1883-1884*, p. 3; *Catalogue of Spelman College, 1927-1928*, pp. 8-9.
7. *Catalogue of Spelman Seminary, 1892-1893*, pp. 9-10, 55.
8. *Ibid., 1890-1891*, p. 5.

Episcopal Church South, and let them go their own way under a mild paternal guardianship.[9]

Some progress was made by the new body, but no facilities were available for training preachers or teachers. Here the same desire for church members that had stirred the Northern churches to found schools developed into a strong force. At the General Conference of the white church in 1882 the need for a school was emphasized. It was declared that those of the colored ministry who were educated at all were taught by men and women of other denominations and of other sympathies. Obviously, it was the duty of the white church to see that something be done.[10]

Augusta was selected as the proper site for a college. It lay in the heart of the black population belt that swung in a gentle curve from Maryland to the western borders of Alabama. The Rev. Morgan Callaway was appointed president. He was a native Georgian born of aristocratic slave-holders, had served as a Confederate officer during the war, and at this time was Haygood's right hand man as vice-president of Emory College. Temporarily, at least, the kind hand of Providence hovered over the coming school.

But the raising of funds was a different matter. Apparently the white South had not yet gone beyond the conversational stage of racial cooperation. The first two donations were $7.15 from the Virginia Conference and $8.85 from the South Georgia Conference.[11] It was hardly enough to establish a college. Yet in November of 1883, Warren A. Candler, chairman of the finance committee, reported a balance of $27 in the treasury, and a motion

---
9. *Catalogue of Paine College, 1911-1912*, p. 13.
10. *Catalogue of Paine Institute, 1894-1895*, p. 16.
11. Minutes of the Trustees of Paine Institute, December 12, 1882, p. 37.

was moved and carried that the school be started.[12] Two months later rooms were rented for $25 a month on Broad Street in Augusta, and classes began. The school was named Paine Institute in honor of the senior bishop of the white church. Within a year about 150 students were enrolled.

The pitiful struggle for existence was too much for President Callaway, however, and he gave way to a white teacher in the school, the Reverend George Williams Walker. In Walker the missionary spirit was dominant. Born in Augusta, the son of a clergyman, he had enlisted in the Confederate army at the age of fifteen, graduated from Wofford College, taught school, and finally entered the Methodist ministry. Then for twenty-seven years he labored to develop the new college until death stopped his hand.

Two years after these beginnings the Douglas Place in Augusta was purchased at a cost of $8,000. It was a site of ten acres, containing an old dwelling house and two stables. The house was used for living quarters for teachers and girl students and the stables were turned into classrooms and a boys' dormitory. In 1888 college work was begun with a four-year curriculum and a freshman class of three students, George C. Taylor, R. A. Carter, and John Hope, later president of Morehouse College and Atlanta University. Despite the earnest appeals of Walker and his constant efforts to rally the churches to the cause, growth was slow, and it was not until the end of another decade that the stables were abandoned for a larger structure of brick and mortar.

Morris Brown

During these same years of the early 'eighties another Negro church, the African Methodist Episcopal, was moving forward in Atlanta to attain its birthright of a college

---
12. *Ibid.*, November 21, 1883, p. 39.

for itself—but this time without white patronage or control. In 1881 the North Georgia Annual Conference, being assembled in Bethel Church in Atlanta, expressed a desire for a college. With church schools rising all about them on the hills of the city, what would become of their own church if these schools of other faiths weaned their children away? Two weeks later the question was put to the Georgia Annual Conference meeting in Savannah. Together, the conferences began their work and promptly purchased a plot of land for $3,500 at the corner of Boulevard and Houston streets in Atlanta. The ideal of the ministers was to prepare young men and women for Christian leadership in the church, and also to give industrial training, then coming into fashion, to boys and girls.[13] It was a noble and yet practical aspiration. But to draw money for education from the ragged pockets of their poor congregations in only the state of Georgia was a goal hardly short of a fantasy.

With great faith and hope, but with little money, plans were drawn and the school-to-be was christened Morris Brown College in honor of an early bishop of the African Methodist Church. By 1885 a modest building was set up at a cost of about $9,000 and named for the Reverend W. A. Gaines, who had supplied not only the supervision, but the inspiration as well. At its dedication, 107 students flocked in.[14] Survival was a harrowing affair, however, and by the time courses on a college level were added in 1894, no less than five men and women had been at the helm. But the Conferences struggled on, establishing a huge board of trustees so that by assessing each member, a permanent income could be assured. After six years the second building was begun and by the end of the century the school was one of the largest in the entire state enrolling

---
13. *Catalogue of Morris Brown College, 1907-1908*, p. 20.
14. *The Wagon Wheel*, Morris Brown College (March, 1939), p. 3.

500 students or more in all branches. At last a portion of the Negro race in Georgia had acquired a sense of independence and responsibility for the enlightenment of its own people, and had struck out for itself toward the ultimate goal of a civilization unsheltered by the white world.

Gammon Theological Seminary

A fourth path was being cut at the same time in these early years by the second wave of the crusade, which resulted in the separate establishment of Gammon Theological Seminary. Here it was a purely missionary venture sponsored by the Northern Methodist Church that had set up Clark University. The Freedmen's Aid Society of the Church had hoped that Clark would prove a means of training preachers. But the several institutions of the Society were too much a burden for this specialized kind of work to be carried on. The study of theology had gone through a varied and meagre history in that church's many schools, and by 1880 there were still no efficient facilities for systematic training of the 1,500 or more ministers needed in the twenty-odd Negro conferences scattered throughout the South.[15]

By 1883 Bishop Henry W. Warren of the white church had managed to persuade Elijah H. Gammon to give $20,000 for a permanent chair of theology at Clark. A building named Gammon Hall had also been put up at a cost of $25,000. Gammon himself had been a Methodist minister. He had been born in Maine in 1819 and had grown up as a typical Yankee farmer boy, chopping wood, clearing fields, farming, and building stone walls on the sturdy New England plan. After teaching school a few years he had entered the Methodist ministry, turning abolitionist meanwhile, but the calamity of ill health had cut this work short. By the time of the war he had wandered into Illi-

---

15. *Catalogue of Gammon Theological Seminary, 1888*, p. 3.

nois and had begun amassing a considerable fortune in the manufacture of harvesting machinery. With the heart of a clergyman and abolitionist still in him, he was easily persuaded by Bishop Warren to invest in the humanitarian cause of the crusade.[16]

With this handsome endowment, a young white preacher, W. P. Thirkield, was called from Cincinnati, and a separate department of theology opened at Clark. At first in 1883, there were only two students, and by the end of the year only 19 had come.[17] A three-year course was installed but it was not of college grade.[18] Even at this date, few ministers had passed beyond the rudiments of reading and writing. But bringing into his work the hot blood of youth, Thirkield soon raised the enrollment to twenty-nine, to forty-eight, and in four years, to sixty-one. And the young preacher remained for seventeen years, organizing and building the most efficient Negro seminary in the South.

This development was made possible, however, only by Elijah Gammon's faith and riches. Once he was satisfied with the beginnings he determined to create a school for Negro ministers unsurpassed by whites or blacks. To do this, in 1886 he gave $200,000 for an endowment on the condition that the school become separate and independent.[19] Naturally, his demands were fulfilled. Then before the decade was out he had increased his gift to over $400,000. Although ninety per cent of the students were Methodist, no denomination was excluded and Baptist, Holiness, Congregational, Christian and all sects came in a small trickle to the new seminary. In 1888 eleven states, one

---

16. Stowell, *Methodist Adventures*, 35-38.
17. *Catalogue of Gammon Theological Seminary, 1888*, p. 5.
18. *Catalogue of Clark University, 1882-1883*, p. 15.
19. *Ibid.*, 1886-1887, p. 16.

foreign country, and twenty-two preparatory schools and colleges were represented.[20]

Thus within the space of six years four more institutions of higher learning had been planted among the black people of Georgia. Each different in the scope of its work, sometimes prompted by jealousy, three of them pressing into the already crowded field of Atlanta, yet each filling a definite need, they remained and grew into centers of education that played a definite role in the new social world the Negro was beginning to build. Within less than twenty-five years after the end of slavery, Georgia had become the nation's center of Negro higher education and the home of seven potential colleges—Atlanta University, Clark University, Morehouse College, Spelman College, Paine College, Morris Brown College, and Gammon Theological Seminary.

THE FIRST STATE COLLEGE

No less significant in this period than the founding of these four colleges was the entrance of the state into the field of Negro higher education with the founding of Georgia State Industrial College at Savannah.

The fires of opposition to Atlanta University, which Edmund Asa Ware had taken such pains to smother during the 'seventies, had left a few sparks that were easy to rekindle. Having failed in its attempt to snuff out the young institution, the state could do no more than assume a pose of watchful waiting. Georgia was quite willing, after all, to satisfy the demands of the Negroes for education by the haphazard gesture of public schools feeding slow dribbles of the three R's to students three to five months a year. By 1887, 133,429 Negroes were in these schools. But very few got beyond the second or third grade of this supposedly harmful pursuit and there was

---

20. *Catalogue of Gammon Theological Seminary, 1888*, p. 5.

little trouble. Yet the steady increase and growth of private embryo colleges within sight of the state capitol was a different matter. There were the beds of discontent, and of all, none was so vigorous in the drive for racial equality as Atlanta University, to which $8,000 of Federal aid was going each year through the state's treasury.

Finally the watchers saw their cue. In 1887, ten years after the uncovering of incendiary books in the library, the Board of Visitors discovered a few white children attending the school. It was strange that the discovery had never been made before, since the sons and daughters of teachers and missionaries had enrolled from the beginning. They were few, never more than six among the advanced students, and none ever graduated.[21] Probably it was hard to distinguish them from the cream colored mulattoes in the lot. Yet every catalogue had carried the declaration that the institution was open "to all of either sex without regard to sect, race, color, or nationality."[22] On this creed the institution had been founded and money had been given.

Nevertheless, the legislature immediately branded this newly discovered practice a misuse of public funds. On July 11th the famous Glenn Bill was introduced into the House. By it, all trustees and teachers of any institution in the state instructing both races would be liable to a fine and imprisonment. The bill passed the House 124 to 2, the two negatives coming from the only colored members of the body.

Although the Senate refused to pass the bill, a controversy was stirred up that rang from Maine to Texas. Indignation sprang from the Northern press condemning the "barbarism" of Georgia. Again, as in Reconstruction, hate and venom rose in a popular wail and the "bloody

---
21. Adams, *Atlanta University*, 29.
22. *Ibid.*, 24.

shirt" flung out its colors. Churches held mass meetings. And in Boston the Old South Church was turned into a forum where Phillips Brooks, and even George W. Cable of the New South, rendered stern protests.[23]

The state Senate next attempted a compromise bill barring those educated in mixed schools from teaching in Georgia. But it too failed. In the end, both Houses had to be satisfied with the Calvin Resolutions restraining the Governor from signing any more money over to Atlanta University until the wishes of the state were complied with.

But Horace Bumstead, who had followed Ware to the president's chair, had no intention of complying. Strong, self-willed, unwilling to accept the Southern experience that mixture of the races was impractical, he refused to relinquish the ideals upon which the university had been founded. The institution had never encouraged white students, he declared, but it could never refuse them.[24] And what of those with less than one-eighth African blood who, in spite of state laws, society would not allow to "pass over"? Teachers' children had enrolled for convenience, it was said, and it was unlikely anyway that they would have been fairly accepted in the white schools. And more than that, such a reversal of policy would be no less than a breach of faith with friends and those of the Freedmen's Bureau and the American Missionary Association who had contributed money on the condition that Atlanta University exclude no one on account of race.

But Bumstead was helpless and the money was withheld. Working swiftly to capitalize on the fame the feud had brought to Atlanta University, Bumstead launched a campaign throughout the press and churches of the North for $16,000. It came quickly, that and more.[25] But

---
23. *Boston Journal*, March 5, 1888.
24. Adams, *Atlanta University*, 24-27.
25. *Atlanta University Bulletin, February, 1889*.

this spirit of generosity failed to live long, and the college, for all the vigor and financial wizardry of its president, fell into debt.

It was three years after this unpleasant wrangle that the Federal government loosed the power of its patronage to force the state into re-accepting the Negro. The first Morrill Act of 1862, whence the disputed $8,000 had come, had not insisted that proceeds from the land-grant be divided according to color. Now in 1890 a second Morrill Act granting an additional $50,000 to each state for education, demanded that the Negro race receive its share. It was a bitter pill for the state to swallow, especially now that the Populists had risen and were ringing the death knell to Negro political activity. The prospect of taxing Negro colleges out of existence was even gaining ground. And on the commencement platform of the University of Georgia, R. W. Patterson of the legislature won favor by his appeal to give the black man only the education for which he paid taxes. Thereby each white child would receive thirty-five times the schooling of a black one, as was considered proper, and the extravagance of these wasteful Negro schools would be curtailed.[26] But the state was forced to divide the money or receive none of it.[27] There was no doubt among most state leaders that Atlanta University was not a proper medium to receive such bounty. Faced with these affairs, Governor John B. Gordon recommended to the legislature in November that a state normal school be established for colored teachers.[28] And by the end of the month a bill was approved setting up the school as a branch of the University of Georgia.

---

26. *Ibid., June, 1890.*
27. A. J. Klein, *Survey of Land-Grant Colleges and Universities* (Washington, 1930), 839.
28. *Journal of the House of Representatives of the State of Georgia,* 1890, pp. 52-56; Walker, "Attitude of Georgia Toward the Education of Negroes," 33.

THE SECOND CRUSADE 63

Whatever the intentions of the state, however, she moved grudgingly. Only after further prodding from Washington, which declared no subsidy would be sent until the Negro college was in operation, did the state bestir herself to action.[29] With a board appointed, headed by P. W. Meldrim of Savannah, towns were invited to make their bids. The college would go to the one offering the best property. In Augusta, Americus, Macon, Columbus, and Savannah, Negro leaders began a scramble.[30] In April Savannah won. The Board of Commissioners accepted the old Warren Place near Thunderbolt, six miles from the city. It was a beautiful site of several acres shaded by a grove of magnificent water oaks festooned with moss. G. W. Parsons, the wealthy owner of Wassaw Island, had been persuaded to give this from his mainland holdings by Meldrim, who willingly bought a strip of ground which he also gave. It was bounded on one side by the old Taylor Road over which Sherman's troops had rumbled to victory.

Meanwhile the state needed money. To satisfy Washington, therefore, a temporary school was set up for three months in the Baxter Street School in Athens. Richard R. Wright, the principal of the Ware High School in Augusta, was called to be its head. This was a good omen, for the Negroes had hoped for a colored president. Wright had come out of a boyhood of slavery into the first class in Atlanta University, and he was a man of some parts who knew the ways of his race. At last Wright moved his school to Savannah and on October 7, 1891, a crowd of about 1,200 people, black and white, gathered under the oaks of the new campus to hear Governor W. J. Northen proclaim the opening of the college. The Morrill Act had provided specifically that emphasis must be placed

---
29. *Savannah Tribune*, January 31, 1891.
30. *Ibid.*, February 14, 1891.

on industries, on the teaching of agriculture, the mechanic arts, the physical, natural, and economic sciences, mathematics, and English—all with reference to their practical application to everyday life.[31] But this was a fond hope, hardly to be well realized until the coming of a new order in the next century. It was more than the state was willing to pay for, a fact which suited the Negro, for he preferred Greek and Latin. For generations the plow and hammer had held him subdued and he was happy to leave them now for "higher culture."

Naturally, Georgia State Industrial College had to prepare its own college students for there were still only one or two public Negro high schools in the state. Of the forty-odd boys who entered when the institution opened, none was ready for college. In 1892, however, it was noted that four "bright young men" were received as members of the first freshman college class.[32] Not until 1898 did Richard R. Wright, Jr., the son of the president, go out as the first college graduate. Meanwhile the school grew. Within a year after opening, three buildings were scattered over 86 acres of land of which fifty-four acres were in cultivation. Co-education was then introduced, and within a decade thirty-four college students were numbered in an enrollment that had soared to over 500.

To some Negroes, here was the greatest victory won since emancipation.[33] The state had moved reluctantly in all these doings, leaving entire support to the Federal government and the benevolence of a few friends. But it had permitted the Negro to get up as he could, which in itself was a privilege in days when the "nigger howl"

---

31. *Federal Laws, Regulations, and Rulings Affecting the Land-Grant Colleges of Agriculture and Mechanic Arts* (Washington, 1911), 6. Hereafter cited as *Federal Laws*.
32. *Savannah Tribune*, January 16, 1892.
33. *Ibid.*, June 4, 1892.

rang from the pine barrens to the mountains. Now eight Negro schools stood out in Georgia offering at least a semblance of higher learning to the sons and daughters of former slaves.

Chapter V

The Hand, the Head, and the Heart

The Doctrine of Industrial Education Becomes Popular

The second wave of the crusade that appeared in Georgia in that lively decade of the 'eighties brought with it ideals symbolic of a new era in American life. Ideals of materialism, hard and tangible as brick and steel, worked at the old foundations of democratic and national idealism. Naturally there was conflict with the old order. Ideals cherished for generations do not give way without some struggle. In all ages there are those of gifted insight who keep their heads in the floating clouds of philosophic contemplation, seeing the universe over distant horizons, and saying boldly to themselves there is no sense in all this earthly materialistic scramble for brick and steel and gold that fade into a cheap glitter under the bright light of time. But these dreamers were too few in the America of that time. The result was that education, that which had been man's guide to the end and aim of life, now became his means to a living. Man had little time in the new order for high vistas. So back to primeval he went, urged to turn the schoolhouse of his fathers into a machine shop that he might learn to tear wealth from the bowels of the earth.

Yet this descent of education from head to hand did not go so hard with the Negro. With the majority of his vast tribe still lingering in the primeval, the means to a living was his greatest necessity. He needed to be taught how to do, to saw, hammer, sew, lay bricks, so that he might keep body and soul together even if on a basis little above slavery. Thus when the new theories of industrial education crept into the new framework of American life, black men and white alike took to them in hope that here was the answer to the Negro's eagerness to learn. The fanciful curriculum of classical studies that had been imposed on colored schools by the first crusaders had been brought in because it was the only kind known. And the Negro took it because he wanted to be a "gentleman." There was no way for him to know that this tradition was already on the decline when it was offered him.[1] The learning of something about tools and toil had no appeal for many. For generations they had known only the hard labor of slavery in field and mill. That had been enough for them. They wanted to study the great life of the white man.

But by 1880 this classical education for the Negro had fallen into very definite disrepute. The Negro had no background or preparation to study its great lessons. Confronted with the necessity of making a living, he had got what he could in snatches a few weeks or months at a time and had gone forth to display his ignorance. Serene in the belief that they had acquired the blessings of a university education, some students had aroused the ridicule of the whites.[2] Criticism arose in both the North and the South.

---
1. Reuter, *American Race Problem*, 267.
2. A. G. Haygood, *The Case of the Negro as to Education in the Southern States* (Atlanta, 1885), 17-18; T. J. Jones, *Educational Adaptations, Report of Ten Years' Work of the Phelps-Stokes Fund*, 1910-1920 (New York, 1920), 28.

It was a shock to see these dusky, ragged people hardly able to put together the words of their own language, work out classical tongues. "Mandy, is yo' did yo' Greek yit?" was a witticism that promoted high mirth.[3]

A general re-evaluation of Negro education resulted. The intellectual capacity of the race was still an unsolved question. Whatever the capacity, many people were convinced that the New England method had been a costly mistake. Even Henry Grady pointed to the increase of Negro crime and traced its seat to the colleges (overlooking, however, that white crime had increased even more rapidly).[4]

It was charged also that this abstract and lifeless education of an old dying world had demoralized the Negro as a worker. In the ten years from 1860 to 1870 farm lands in Georgia had decreased by three million acres.[5] The Negro had dropped the plow for the city and books. And there was a need of workmen, a pressing need. A host of blacksmiths, carpenters, painters, and wheelrights bred on the plantations of earlier days were dying, and who was to take their place? No wonder the white man protested. What good to him was a Negro with a smattering of "*hic, haec, hoc*"?

Gradually the Negro too began to see himself more clearly. He began to see where he could not rise, and he took to the task of adjusting his education to the facts of his life. Without the ballot and with poverty that made him see himself as a member of a race distressed, he lowered his ideals and began a zealous chase for the new craze.[6] Above and beyond social equality, he began desiring economic equality.

---
3. Bond, *Education of the Negro*, 362.
4. *Ibid.*, 418.
5. Thompson, *Reconstruction in Georgia*, 280.
6. DuBois, *Souls of Black Folk*, 10.

Of course, industrial education was not a new venture in the world. But it was Samuel Chapman Armstrong who finally emerged in America with the first successful and permanent example of the new doctrine. Armstrong was born in Hawaii in 1839, the son of New England Scotch-Irish missionary parents. There on the quiet islands of the Pacific his father had schools for the natives, both in books and tools. As a youth Armstrong was impressed with the failure of literary education to affect the lives of the primitive natives no matter how proficient they became in books. He noted that in the Hilo Labor School where hand and eye and head were brought together in a practical study of handicrafts, the effort was far more effective.

The beginnings of his new work sprang from the tragedy of war. As an officer in the Union army it fell to Armstrong's lot to herd the contraband hordes of black folk who dogged the flanks of the troops. From his work in a Virginia camp came Hampton Institute. It was not a school designed to teach the Negro to make a living. He taught thrift, cooperation, the moral effect of honest labor, the folly of education without discipline, self-reliance, and the principles of work for service.[7] Although he intended to train teachers, he was without the New England tradition. But little was heard of the school, and it was not until the 'eighties emphasized the new needs of American industry that the idea began to flourish. By that decade the doctrine had crept into Alabama and Armstrong was asked to send a teacher to begin a similar school. A likely lad among the students at Hampton was Booker T. Washington. Young and ambitious, with pride in his race, a temperamental dislike of conflict, and a desire to work as Armstrong worked, Washington went South and built Tuskegee.

It was in 1881, the same year Spelman was founded,

---

7. Dabney, *Universal Education*, I, 458.

that Washington began his campaign for industrial education. In the same year, Dr. J. L. M. Curry of the Peabody Fund had praised the work at Hampton in glowing terms.[8] Immediately the doctrine became popular. From the program of Armstrong and Washington, designed to build character, citizenship, respect for Negro labor, and a general knowledge of mechanical skills, the white race evolved a less idealistic theory of education for their black brethren designed to make carpenters, bricklayers, and blacksmiths.[9] It was an ignoble descent of aims. But at last the white man thought he had discovered the proper way to educate the Negro. Here was salvation for an inferior race destined to play always the God-given parts of servant and worker. In the South, Curry and Haygood were behind the new doctrine. The rest of the white South approved it because the theory was in harmony with the Negro as a laborer. And the North backed it because it seemed practical and in keeping with the advance of physical science and materialism.

Georgia's College Experiment

From the very beginning the Negro colleges in Georgia had initiated students into the manual labor required on the grounds, buildings, farm, dining hall, and kitchen.[10] And as early as 1879 the faculty of Atlanta University had voted that girls in the higher normal department be taught the household sciences of plain sewing, "cookery," and nursing.[11] Very soon printing presses were secured by the schools and the printing trade was taught. In Atlanta University the first issue of the *Bulletin* was printed on the school press in 1883. A year later Paine was printing its own catalogue and *The Paine Institute Herald*, a monthly

---
8. Jones, *Negro Education*, I, 256-257.
9. *Ibid.*, I, 10.
10. Adams, *Atlanta University*, 96.
11. Minutes of the Faculty of Atlanta University, May 6, 1879, p. 155.

student journal. Clark and even Spelman were teaching the trade. And by 1892 Atlanta Baptist Seminary had printed its first issue of the *Advance*.

In the early 'eighties training was also begun with metal and wood. At Clark especially, the new doctrine took hold quickly and by 1884 Haygood was able to report instruction in agriculture, carpentry, iron-work, printing, housekeeping, telegraphy, and phonography. There the carpentry department had built eight frame houses besides bookcases, chairs, and tables.[12] By working at their trades during the summer many students were able to make more than the paltry wages of teaching school. With the usual practice of embellishing the catalogue, carpentry and building construction were called "architecture."[13] At Clark too, students were busy making harness, carriages, hearses, and express wagons. In 1885-1886 the shops turned out five heavy six-horse wagons, and several buggies and hacks. The following year four mechanics and twenty-two students were kept busy from morning till night filling similar orders which included "two fine undertaker's wagons."[14] Even bricks for a new building were being fashioned in the school's own plant.[15]

In Atlanta University Ware attempted silk culture, an experiment that had failed miserably in the Georgia colony the century before. But it was Ware's fond hope that every family in the South could learn to produce between $50 and $200 worth of silk a year.[16] Here also a large brick building, Knowles Hall, was set up in 1884 at a cost of $8,000 for practical training in industrial and manual arts. In 1886 the State Board of Visitors was grati-

---
12. *Proceedings and Reports of the John F. Slater Fund*, 1889, pp. 12-13.
13. *Catalogue of Clark University, 1879-1881*, p. 18.
14. *Proceedings of the Slater Fund, 1887*, p. 16.
15. *Catalogue of Clark University, 1885-1886*, p. 33.
16. *Atlanta University Bulletin*, June, 1883.

fied to report that the best feature of the university's work was its mechanical course. If practical work like this was added to all the schools of the state, said the Visitors, "within a few years, Georgia would not find it necessary to draw upon other sections for the practical development of her resources."[17] At all schools practical farming was attempted, usually under a foreman rather than a scientific instructor. And at Paine, a cobbler shop was installed where the shoes of the students were repaired in the act of learning the trade.[18]

Although Georgia State Industrial College in Savannah lingered lovingly for its first year over the hope for a classical curriculum, the second year saw the introduction of industrial work. Both the first and second Morrill Acts of Congress had insisted that land-grant colleges specialize in the fields of agriculture, the mechanic arts, and home economics. Accordingly Georgia State Industrial College saw fit to open its second session in 1892 with an advertisement reading "Industrial Education, a Specialty."[19] Manual training was introduced. A year later, blacksmithing and wheelwrighting were added and in 1894-1895, carpentry and masonry.[20]

Nor were women forgotten. In all colleges household duties were taught, partly through the usual necessities of school dining halls, kitchens, laundries, and buildings, and partly in classes. As early as 1886 Spelman established a training school for nurses, to be followed six years later by a similar department at Clark. In addition to this, the catalogue at Spelman for 1889-1890 listed an industrial department teaching cooking, washing, ironing, chamber work, sewing, garment making, needle-work, printing, and telegraphy.

---
17. *Catalogue of Atlanta University, 1885-1886*, p. 32.
18. *Catalogue of Paine Institute, 1892-1893*, p. 9.
19. *Savannah Tribune*, October 1, 1892.
20. *Catalogue of Georgia State Industrial College, 1905-1906*, p. 36.

In the midst of the 'nineties a great impetus was given to the movement in Atlanta. There, in 1895, the directors of the Cotton States Exposition saw fit to recognize the Negro and provide a building for the exhibition of his progress. For the first time, thousands of eyes were opened to the industrial possibilities of the black man. Standing in the Negro building before an audience of whites and blacks, Booker T. Washington preached and pleaded with the oratory that was his gift. He pleaded with his race to give up for a time the complete fulfillment of their three most insistent desires that alienated them from the white South: political power, civil rights, and the higher education of Negro youth. To him, the idea of Negroes poring over French in the midst of poverty and squalor was ridiculous. He was a peace-loving man. He saw in conflict only a continued oppression for his race. While remaining socially apart, the two races could come together in friendship and progress as the fingers come together in the hand. In no other way could the hostility of the white South be disarmed. The speech echoed North and South. Washington arose to national prominence. Cast down your buckets where you are, cried the orator to his race, learn the dignity of labor, the thrift of honest toil, and the rest of man's blessings shall follow.[21]

With this push, industrial education in Georgia Negro colleges reached its fullest flower. From then on the catalogue of Georgia State Industrial College proclaimed the ideal of manual labor, showing the advantage of laying bricks at $3 a day above selling goods over the counter at $5 a week.[22] In addition to former trades, courses were listed in architectural drawing, mechanical drawing, plastering, painting, decorating, sign writing, glazing, shoe-

---
21. E. D. Washington, ed., *Selected Speeches of Booker T. Washington* (New York, 1932), 31-36.
22. *Catalogue of Georgia State Industrial College, 1896-1897*, pp. 22-24.

making, tailoring, dressmaking, cooking, and laundering. By 1901 the industrial course covered a period of three years, demanding that each student devote four hours a day to his trade.[23] Paine added basketry and millinery. Morris Brown began nurse training. And by 1907 Spelman listed 153 girls studying agriculture, 85 in basketry, 172 in cooking, 37 in dressmaking, 47 in millinery, 26 in printing, 424 in sewing, and 17 in nursing.[24]

The spread of industrial education did not go forward, however, without opposition from the old guard of the New England tradition. Missionaries from the North upheld the liberal arts tradition of their homeland. And the question was argued from the rostrums of Negro schools and the pulpits of churches up and down the land.[25] Yet there was really no conflict. Both theories had their place in the broad scheme of Negro life. But money was given chiefly to the schools where trades were taught, and the champions of the liberal arts began to stifle. Not a few schools, seeing the flow of Northern money into trades, set up make-shift industrial departments without equipment, teachers, experience, or a desire for efficient work.

Machinery and tools for shop instruction were costly and for all their approval and philanthropy neither the whites of North or South were willing to increase their bounty sufficiently for this most expensive of all forms of education.[26] By the 'nineties, President George Sale, of the Atlanta Baptist Seminary was forced to forego his hopes for carpentry, gardening, and shoemaking and be satisfied with his printing shop.[27] And in the late part of the decade

---

23. *Ibid.*, 1901-1902, p. 23.
24. *Catalogue of Spelman Seminary, 1907-1908*, p. 28.
25. T. E. McKinney, ed., *Higher Education Among Negroes* (Charlotte, 1932), 18.
26. Walker, "Attitude of Georgia toward the Education of the Negro," 64.
27. Brawley, *Morehouse College*, 78-79.

even printing was made an adjunct to the English department. For one year, 1894-1895, even the comparatively stable Atlanta University was forced to suspend industrial work for the lack of funds.[28] Despite the early flourish of the work at Clark, where at one time as many as ten different trade diplomas were offered, by 1896 the school was begging for aid. The making of wagons and carriages by which the school had hoped to support that department, came to a sad end with the discovery that factories could make them cheaper and faster. Eventually aid from the Slater Fund, which since 1882 had been aiding industrial education, was withdrawn and by 1903 the once blossoming trade departments of Clark taught only shoemaking. Even farming proved too costly for Atlanta University and in 1897 the trustees voted to close the department and sell the stock and tools.[29]

In the face of the controversy the North knew not if it should give. Excepting Spelman, no college in Georgia was properly equipped for efficient industrial education. Working without the means, there was no help but to turn out students only half-trained. Without seeing this handicap, many people again began to doubt the Negroes' capacity to learn. What few Negroes got into mills and factories failed for lack of training. Neither good journeymen nor scholars were being turned out of the colleges and this fact created a bad taste in white mouths.

Many of the Negro students themselves opposed industrial education. They knew hard labor and cared little for the dignity of it. While students in the lower branches were forced to study trades in most of the institutions, very few in the college departments could be enticed. By

---
28. Letter from H. Bumstead to Wallace Buttrick, September, 1902 (in Atlanta University Library).
29. Minutes of the Trustees of Atlanta University, October 21, 1897, p. 23.

the late 'nineties Clark gave up attempting to attract students into a mechanical course in the college department and ceased announcing it in the catalogue. At Georgia State Industrial College attempts to foist the demands of the Morrill Act on the college were frustrated by faculty and students alike. The desire of the Negro for classical wonders overwhelmed the lure of the shop. In 1894 the Commissioners of Georgia State Industrial College ordered that the classics be removed to make room for industries, but the faculty juggled the curriculum to include both.[30] In the same year President Wright, who had a tender yearning for the classics, wrote that trade work in all Negro schools was poor and the number of students who learned a trade well enough to follow it was hardly worth mentioning.[31] Other opposition, moreover, came from organized white labor which feared Negro competition.

Far more effective was opposition that came from the ranks of leading educators. To many, the submissive doctrines of Booker T. Washington meant the eternal subjection of the race. It meant perpetual disfranchisement. It meant a lowering of standards and the giving up of ideals of leadership and aspirations for a Negro civilization based on the fruits of human intelligence. Some, however, merely disapproved the over-emphasis of the fad, seeing value in both industrial and liberal arts study, yet applying their vision to the end that leaders, teachers, preachers, doctors, dentists and idealists were needed to lead the race to good citizenship and a righteous life. As early as 1885, Atticus Haygood opposed the Slater Fund plan of concentrating benefits in a few trade schools. As agent for the Fund he approved industrial education and supported it vigorously; but he wanted more than that for the Negro. "It is un-

---
30. Minutes of the Faculty of Georgia State Industrial College, November 14, 1894, pp. 72-73.
31. Wright, *Negro Education*, 54-55.

thinkable," he wrote to former President Rutherford B. Hayes, "that I make the superintending of three or four machine shops my life work . . . ."[32] Atlanta University, while not discounting the value of industrial study, worked to the end of training teachers in mechanical arts rather than laborers. To President Bumstead, the salvation of the race depended on its exceptional men. When faced with the charge that the masses of Negroes could not absorb classical studies, Bumstead retorted that the masses of whites were scarcely better. He contended that the greatest work of the world is done with brains, and leaders must be prepared for it.[33]

The same sentiment was expressed by William T. Harris, United States Commissioner of Education, in a speech before the students of Atlanta University in 1896. He urged the pupils to preserve their Latin and Greek despite opposition, so that they might carry their civilization beyond the drawing of water and the cutting of wood.[34] In the same year Charles W. Eliot of Harvard spoke from the pulpit of Trinity Church in Boston for Atlanta University and its liberal doctrine.[35] In 1897 W. E. B. DuBois came to the faculty of the university. Immediately he became the champion of cultural education. He fought with the high passion of youth to convince his race that the true college must ever have one goal—not to earn meat but to know the end and aim of life which meat nourishes. Through *The Souls of Black Folk*, which he published in 1903, and a series of social

---

32. C. W. Garrison, ed., "Slater Fund Beginnings; Letters from General Agent Atticus G. Haygood to Rutherford B. Hayes," in *The Journal of Southern History*, V, 2 (May, 1939), p. 235.
33. H. Bumstead, "The Practical Value of the Higher Education of the Negro" in *Proceedings of the Third Capon Springs Conference for Education in the South* (N. p., 1900), 57, 62.
34. *Catalogue of Atlanta University, 1900-1901*, Cover page.
35. *Ibid.*, p. 49.

studies on the Negro, he struck the most eloquent blows yet given the commercialism of the new fad which threatened to make "money changers" out of men. He too believed that the race must depend on its exceptional men. Some were fitted to dig, and some to know. Some were fitted to be blacksmiths, and some to be university men.[36] At Paine also President Walker plodded in poverty and opposition, determined to keep the training of leaders above the temptation of numbers.

Even without the opposition of these leaders the grand scheme of industrial education would have broken down by the sheer weight of its costliness, and that is what happened. Although Booker T. Washington continued to range in the land ringing the door bells of the rich and drawing many dollars to Tuskegee by his oratory, it is safe to say that after 1900 most schools had abandoned their dreams. They reverted to their first love of a liberal arts curriculum and satisfied the advocates of the trade system with a few industrial courses carried on in tumble-down shops.

During this controversy that lasted for more than two decades, each college had done its best to preserve and develop the liberal arts tradition. The inadequacy of public schools compelled each institution to continue elementary branches, but the normal department remained, by far, the most important. The failure in 1878 of several students from Atlanta University to pass examinations for teaching in the city, promptly turned the faculty into improving the common and normal branches.[37] During the 'eighties the Atlanta Baptist Seminary elevated its normal branch by adding algebra, rhetoric, civil government, English literature, and similar studies beyond elementary levels.

---
36. DuBois, *Souls of Black Folk*, 82-83.
37. Minutes of the Faculty of Atlanta University, November 6, 1878, p. 144.

And in the next decade additions were made of psychology, principles of teaching, history of education, and practice teaching. Spelman had emphasized its normal department from its very first year, 1881. A year's work was added at a time so that by 1884 a four-year course had been established.[38] By the early 'nineties only graduates of the academic course were admitted to the normal training department. Further improvement was made by a greater interchange of students and teachers from the Atlanta Baptist Seminary. By that time, Paine required examinations for admission to normal training. About 1896 examinations for teacher's certificates became more rigid in Georgia and the schools were forced to further elevate normal work. In 1894 Massachusetts had taken the lead in making graduation from high school necessary for admission to normal schools.[39] Immediately after the turn of the century, Atlanta University followed suit and made admission to the normal branch the same as to its college department. At Georgia State Industrial College normal study overlapped the college department one year. No students under fourteen were received in any of the departments, and they had to be comparatively well versed in English branches and mathematics.[40] In all the schools pedagogics had advanced to include several courses beyond those begun in the early days of Atlanta University. At Paine, normal class students also studied bookkeeping, while at Georgia State Industrial College studies were listed in educational psychology, the psychology of childhood, school economy, plus a unique course called "Good Morals and Gentle

---

38. *Catalogue of Spelman Baptist Seminary, 1883-1884*, p. 21.
39. A. Caliver, *Education of Negro Teachers* (Washington, 1933), Intro., v.
40. *Savannah Tribune*, October 10, 1891; *Catalogue of Georgia State Industrial College*, 1896-1897, p. 15.

Manners."⁴¹ Practically all maintained model elementary schools for practice teaching.

Meanwhile the college departments also had been reaching upward. As early as 1887 Spelman announced that graduates of the scientific and higher normal courses would be given Bachelor of Science degrees. Ten years of schooling or the equivalent was demanded for admission to the course. After receiving the Bachelor of Science degree students were offered a Master of Science degree for three years additional work "provided they have meanwhile been engaged in literary or scientific pursuits, and present a written thesis approved by the Faculty."⁴² It was realized quickly, however, that the school had stretched itself too far and that such work was really not above a secondary level. Accordingly the degrees were abolished. In the early 'nineties a collegiate department was initiated again, but this too was soon changed to be called the Collegiate Preparatory Department. In the meantime two teachers began instruction in Latin and German for graduates of secondary branches in the hope that a genuine college department might be evolved. But it was not until 1897 that a regular four year course leading to a bachelor's degree was put into operation. Then the work was carried on with the Atlanta Baptist Seminary. In 1899 Benjamin Brawley studied literature and themes at Spelman. In 1900-1901 twelve boys from the Seminary were studying history, Latin, geometry, astronomy, and evidences of Christianity in the girls' school, while some of the girls studied in the boys' school across the road.⁴³ Thirty-three college courses were available in the two seminaries. In the same year that Spelman began regular college work, 1897, the Atlanta

---
41. *Catalogue of Paine Institute, 1901-1902*, pp. 5-7; *Catalogue of Georgia State Industrial College, 1901-1902*, pp. 30-33; *1896-1897*, p. 18.
42. *Catalogue of Spelman Seminary, 1887-1888*, pp. 32-35.
43. Students' Record of Spelman Seminary, 1899-1901.

Baptist Seminary revised its charter and became incorporated as a college. Bachelor's degrees had been offered since the early 'eighties, but as at Spelman, the work had not been of a calibre to warrant them until the 'nineties, at least.

French and German had come into greater prominence in all the colleges. While Latin continued to hold sway as the leading subject of the classics, Greek suffered a descent. The first two graduates of the Spelman college course studied Greek not at all in their four years.[44] It was added later, but substitutes were available there as elsewhere.

The most notable advance of the second wave was in the physical and natural sciences. By 1905 Atlanta University had built fully one-half its college curriculum in these fields. In mathematics, calculus was introduced. Spelman added chemistry. Mineralogy and geodetic survey courses were attempted at Georgia State Industrial College. By 1898 Atlanta Baptist Seminary was able to follow the example of Atlanta University and set up equipped science laboratories where mineralogy, geology, chemistry, and physics were offered on a reputable basis. True, most of the colleges were forced to stumble along in the sciences under a handicap of meagre equipment unequal to college demands. And although they failed to keep up with the physical development of the country they raced after it diligently with what they had.

The decade of the 'nineties also saw the rise of psychology, sociology, and economics in practically every college. Sociology especially reached an important position at the turn of the century. Here for the first time the Negro began to see his race objectively. Race consciousness, a pride of heritage, and a realization of social conditions developed. At Spelman, sociology was designed par-

---

44. *Ibid.*, 1897-1901.

ticularly as a study of Negro conditions in town and country.⁴⁵ The pace had been set by a series of social studies begun by Atlanta University in 1896. Other colleges quickly took up the theme and included the infant science in their curricula. From them on, the Negro began to see that he too had a background and a civilization out of which the conditions of his racial culture grew.

In addition to these conventional curricula several of the colleges tried to branch out into specialized fields. For a time Morris Brown entertained a dream of a law school. In 1899-1900 three students were enrolled. But the scheme was premature and soon folded up. There too a commercial department was established to train stenographers. In the last year of the century the course had twelve students, but it, too, was soon dropped. In the 'eighties Clark listed an elaborate business college, teaching bookkeeping, actual business, commercial law, phonography, and banking. But little came of the attempt.

The Teaching of Theology Languishes

While the crusaders of the second wave were concerned with these many schemes of education, theology received little attention. Although the training of preachers continued to be a publicly avowed aim of many colleges, it was sadly neglected, and advances were miserably small. After graduating three theological students by 1876, Atlanta University refused to bother further with the matter. In the years that followed, the Negro ministry fell into very definite disrepute all over the South. The great number of preachers and the poverty of their parishes failed to attract men of either high morality or ability. Bishop Daniel A. Payne, himself a Negro preacher, condemned his brethren for this laxity. "I say emphatically, that no more than one-third of the ministers, Baptist and Methodist, in

---

45. *Catalogue of Spelman Seminary, 1898-1899*, p. 36.

the South are morally and intellectually qualified."[46] Booker T. Washington condemned them in even greater numbers: "Three-fourths of the Baptist ministers and two-thirds of the Methodist are unfit, either mentally or morally, or both, to preach the gospel or to attempt to lead anyone."[47]

The average student seeking a preaching post, satisfied himself with fleeting snatches from speller and primer and then went merrily on his way in a frock coat with high faith in his capacity to drive the hosts up to Zion.

But it was not all a day of darkness for theology. Among educational leaders there were some who were determined to maintain this one aim for which the colleges had been founded. Theology flourished somewhat at the Atlanta Baptist Seminary during the 'eighties. For a few years in the 'nineties all advanced theological study was transferred to the Richmond Theological Seminary in Virginia by order of the American Baptist Home Mission Society. But in 1897, when the Atlanta school became a college, theology returned. The department took on new life and missionaries were sent into the state to hold ministers' institutes. In 1904 a divinity school was organized with its own full time instructors and the two degrees of Bachelor of Divinity and Bachelor of Theology were introduced.

After trying for nine years to found a theological school, Morris Brown finally succeeded in 1894. At Paine also, a three year course held sway almost from the beginning.

Naturally, Gammon Theological Seminary was most able of all to train preachers efficiently. Constant efforts were made to admit only college graduates to the Seminary. The Bachelor of Divinity degree was given only to holders of a previous bachelor's degree. But the inability of the colleges to turn out graduates in numbers and the

---
46. *Proceedings of the Slater Fund*, 1891, p. 14.
47. *Ibid.*, 1891, p. 14.

failure of the ministry to attract them forced the seminary to accept what students it could get. Usually, no more than two or three at a time were college graduates. In 1890, there was one, and in 1897, three. The privilege of completing college work at Clark was allowed, but few were able to spend the time or the money to do so. Admission for the majority could be set no higher than proficiency in the grammar grades. The least advanced students were admitted only to an elementary theological course lasting one year. Others worked in a three-year course studying the usual historical, exegetical, systematic, and practical theological studies. At the end of the century Hebrew was made an elective and other electives followed to broaden the curriculum. But in the main the course changed but little over the years until theological study met the impact of the renaissance and social welfare tide following the First World War.

Under the circumstances almost none of the efforts to train preachers reached beyond a high school level. In his estimate of Negro education in 1900 DuBois refused to recognize any of it as college grade.[48] The degrees in most cases were hollow things. And as the era of materialism swept over the land the halls of theology remained quiet, half-deserted retreats for a handful of scholars.

Yet the religious and missionary spirit of the crusade continued to reproduce itself in some of the colleges. In 1891 Spelman opened a missionary training department. Taught there were the Bible, family organization, church work, household duties, nursing, and missionary work.[49] Four years later at Gammon, the Stewart Missionary Foundation for Africa was founded. It developed from

---

48. See W. E. B. DuBois, *The College-Bred Negro* (Atlanta University Publications, No. 5, Atlanta, 1902).
49. *Catalogue of Spelman Seminary, 1892-1893*, p. 13.

the philanthropy of the Reverend William F. Stewart, a Northern Methodist minister who had amassed a fortune from real estate. Its object was to arouse an interest in the American Negro for missionary work and support in Africa. Prizes were given for missionary hymns, orations, and essays. Libraries were established. And from this effort at Gammon and the work at Spelman a few ardent students were impelled to the broader field of dark Africa where some labored many years to service and a glimmer of fame.

It was in this period of the second wave that the Negro colleges of Georgia first began to project themselves into the communities of the state to improve the social conditions of the race. Not long after going to Tuskeegee, Booker Washington had inaugurated farmers' conferences. In 1893 Georgia State Industrial College took up the idea. Each year people were gathered to the campus "to consider the agricultural, mechanical, and intellectual development of the colored people in Georgia." In the first conference such subjects were discussed as: "How may farming be improved?", "To what extent have colored men become contractors and builders?", "How may the grade of teachers for county schools be raised?"[50] Fertilizers and implements were exhibited. Here again, however, the poverty of the school and of the colored people made the conferences small affairs touching but a few people of the state. Yet a new consciousness of Negro conditions was being aroused. At Atlanta Baptist Seminary conferences were held for moral and religious training.

By far the most effective effort of the colleges to improve the community, however, resulted from the Negro Life Conferences begun by Bumstead at Atlanta University in 1896. While the gatherings themselves were insig-

---

50. Minutes of the Faculty of Georgia State Industrial College, April 18, 1893, p. 52.

nificant, the social inquiries published each year won fame far beyond America. Studies were published with such titles as *Morality Among Negroes, The Negro in Business, The Negro Church, Notes on Negro Crime, The College Bred Negro, The Negro American Family*, and others numbering twenty over a period of years. In 1897 DuBois came to the faculty and took over the work. He used scientific methods of sociological inquiry in gathering data and his studies, issued as *Atlanta University Publications*, resulted in practically the first sizable body of examination into the actual conditions of life among free Negroes in America. They were taken into the libraries of the world and acclaimed by such periodicals as the London *Times, The Spectator, Manchester Guardian, Outlook, Nation*, and many other publications.[51]

In all developments of the period, those that cost money were necessarily neglected. The physical sciences were frustrated by poverty. In most colleges equipped laboratories were not to be found. Clark had to remain contented with its cabinet of minerals until the middle 'eighties when Mrs. E. H. Gammon made a small contribution of apparatus for the sciences. In 1889 Professor Edgar H. Webster from Oberlin, began at Atlanta University the first laboratory work in physics and chemistry done in a Southern Negro college.[52] Atlanta Baptist Seminary followed a few years later with a separate building. The other colleges fared much worse. Spelman girls, of course, studied the sciences in the boys' school, for their equipment in 1900 included only a museum of 500 undefined specimens, a telescope, a stereoptican, a microscope, and a human skeleton.[53] In 1893 the boys' college was proud

---
51. *From Servitude to Service*, 187.
52. Adams, *Atlanta University*, 37.
53. *Catalogue of Spelman Seminary, 1900-1901*, p. 42.

to note a gift of a telescope forty-five inches long, of polished brass.[54]

Libraries fared somewhat better but they too grew with miserable slowness. At the opening of Georgia State Industrial College 250 volumes were on the shelves, mostly through the generosity of Miss Jennie Bill, the daughter of a Connecticut banker. Yet by 1905, fourteen years later, the collection had increased to no more than 600. All the colleges had reading rooms but their book collections amounted to no more than a few hundred or a couple thousand volumes. By 1900 Morris Brown was attempting to serve 500 students with only 1500 books. Societies and individuals alike contributed small handfuls of books and pamphlets, many of which were of doubtful value in a school. The zeal of philanthropists and humanitarians for the welfare of the soul made the shelves ponderously heavy with religious works. Spelman received gifts from both the National Temperance Society and the American Bible Society.[55] At Paine a collection of 1,000 volumes was almost entirely on theological subjects.

Gammon and Atlanta University were exceptions. Each institution received gifts in large batches. The catalogue for Gammon in 1888 noted a gift of 1,000 volumes from the library of a deceased teacher at the Garrett Biblical Institute, and another of 2,000 from Dr. D. P. Kidder. An historical society was set up in the 'nineties to collect books, pamphlets, addresses, articles, and manuscripts particularly on slavery and abolition. Pleas went out also for material on ecclesiastical history, educational movements in churches, and the progress of the Negro in learning, industry, wealth, inventions, and the mechanical arts.[56] The Stewart Missionary Foundation had collected by

---
54. *Catalogue of Atlanta Baptist Seminary, 1892-1893*, p. 22.
55. *Catalogue of Spelman Baptist Female Seminary, 1882-1883*, p. 15.
56. *Catalogue of Gammon Theological Seminary, 1894*, p. 22.

1896 three hundred volumes on African explorations and missions. By 1905, the Seminary boasted a library of nearly 12,000 volumes.

The library of Atlanta University grew likewise. In 1889 Mary Richardson became the librarian. She was a sister of the librarian of Princeton University. Having studied the Dewey System of cataloguing that was just coming into vogue, she classified the Atlanta library, making it one of the first well ordered collections in the South. With more than 12,000 volumes in 1905, the library was surpassed in size among Negro colleges only by Howard and Lincoln universities. In all, the total of 5,000 volumes in Negro colleges in Georgia in 1880 had increased to more than 36,000 in 1905. The trouble lay in the fact that so many of them were unsuited to school work, and they were scattered in too many institutions.

The period also saw certain of the colleges make desperate attempts to extend themselves toward the European ideal of a university that was spreading throughout America. In a few cases master's degrees were served up for post-graduate work done in the institutions themselves; in others, for extra work done in Northern colleges, while the majority of these degrees were purely honorary and included not only master's but doctoral degrees as well. In 1883 the faculty of Atlanta University voted for J. G. Hutchins to receive the degree of Master of Arts.[57] Nearly every year thereafter, one or two or three similar honors were offered. In 1896 the Trustees put in their hand and declared that Master of Arts degrees be granted only to graduates who had completed a regular course of post-graduate study and had turned in a thesis. Honorary Master of Arts and Doctor of Philosophy degrees were excepted and might continue

---

57. **Minutes of the Faculty of Atlanta University, May 29, 1883, p. 206.**

to be granted.⁵⁸ In 1900, George A. Towns, a graduate, was given a Master of Arts diploma for two years' work done at Harvard. At Morris Brown a Master of Arts degree was available to graduates who had earned a baccalaureate degree in a Northern institution. President Walker at Paine specialized on an offering of honorary Doctor of Divinity degrees and presented two or three practically every year to prominent Negro bishops and ministers. In 1900 the Atlanta Baptist Seminary entered the contest and presented an honorary Master of Arts degree to J. W. Lyons, Register of the Treasury in Washington. From then on honorary degrees went out two or three each year to colored ministers, teachers, and school principals. It was all hardly more than a scramble for prestige. No actual graduate study was provided in any institution, for neither faculty nor equipment were sufficient for study on such high levels.

Yet other very sincere efforts were being made to raise standards. As the public schools of the state more and more assumed the responsibility of educating colored children, the need of the private colleges to maintain elementary grades became less pressing. Those aspiring to become colleges gradually discontinued the elementary grades and concentrated on secondary work. In 1893 President Walker announced at Paine that henceforth no students would be admitted who had not completed the grammar grades.⁵⁹ A year later Atlanta University abolished its elementary school. Enrollment dropped from 448 in June to 217 in October. At Paine the plan was not fully executed for many years to come. But at Atlanta University the day of elementary education was definitely over. Enrollment in the secondary branches grew swiftly under this new effort of concentration. And in 1904 the three year high

---
58. Minutes of the Trustees of Atlanta University, May 28, 1896.
59. Minutes of the Trustees of Paine Institute, 1893, p. 122.

school course was joined with the two year normal course in a cooperative merger which lengthened the secondary work from four to five years.[60] While none of the other colleges moved as rapidly, they too were advancing in the same direction toward the ultimate goal of higher learning.

The Negro colleges of Georgia, obviously, were not yet equal to the Northern models they were imitating. They were handicapped by a state school system which made no effort whatever to provide secondary preparation for college. The curriculum of the college departments was from one to two years below that of the New England college. Graduates from Atlanta University were admitted to the senior class at Dartmouth and to the junior class at Harvard. But even this was no small achievement and the teachers were justly proud.

If the standards of the Negro colleges of Georgia were low, it must be remembered that even the white colleges of the nation were little better. After studying American education in the early part of the new century, the General Education Board proclaimed that of 700 institutions in the United States calling themselves colleges and universities, only a few were worthy of the name, and some were even poor as secondary schools.[61] Competition between rival Negro schools for pupils and money had led to low standards of admission and graduation. Thereby progress had been hindered and distrust between whites and Negroes alike had been fostered.[62] As late as 1905 DuBois declared that no more than five Negro colleges in the United States deserved the name.[63] The situation produced a bad flavor in the mind of the white world. People who in the begin-

---

60. Adams, *Atlanta University*, 38.
61. *The General Education Board, An Account of its Activities, 1902-1914* (New York, 1915), 109.
62. L. G. E. Jones, *Negro Schools in the Southern States* (Oxford, England, 1928), 34.
63. *Servitude to Service*, 170-171.

ning had looked to education to solve all the ills of the Negro world fell into moods of disappointment. Their classical tradition had failed to achieve the expected results of raising the Negro race of the South to the level of the white man. Their industrial scheme had collapsed, many not understanding why. Perhaps the black man was a dumb brute, as many people contended, immoral, indolent, slovenly, incapable of rising from the mire of ignorance and poverty. With these dark thoughts clouding the white mind, it is little wonder that Negro higher education passed into an era of neglect. The missionary spirit was all but spent. Crusaders of the second wave had brought a less fervent soul into the field and the Negroes were quick to notice it. The era had carried the dollar sign as its symbol. In consequence, education as a guide to man's yearning to solve the riddle of the universe had proved a feeble instrument.

Surely and steadily, however, the Negro colleges of Georgia had risen from the school huts of Reconstruction. Their ascent had been painfully slow, yet some had moved forward toward the first rims of maturity. The Exposition in Atlanta in 1895 had definitely recognized the capacity of the race for achievement. Racial pride was developing. Conditions of the masses, of rural life, of social welfare, and physical well-being had crept into the consciousness of both races. The liberal arts tradition of higher education had won the battle that for a time seemed destined to subject the black man to the permanent labor of hand without mind. Not for a moment had Atlanta University forgotten the dream of Edmund Asa Ware. Certainly, at the turn of the century, there was no good reason to doubt that the colleges were on the way to being colleges in more than name.

CHAPTER VI

Physical Expansion

INCREASES IN ENROLLMENT

THE BIRTH OF EDUCATIONAL INSTITUTIONS IN THE SECOND wave increased enrollment considerably. During the decade of the 'eighties the number of Negroes in Georgia increased by more than 130,000, making a total Negro population in 1890 of 858,815. This was nearly twice the number of Negroes that were in the state in 1860. By 1893, eight years after Ware's death, Negro enrollment in the public schools had climbed to more than 150,000. In fact, attendance in white schools had increased only 39% in the 'eighties while attendance in the colored schools had advanced over 53%. But the public schools were able to offer only about three months' teaching a year and none of them was capable of fulfilling the Negroes' demand for industrial education. For these reasons, colored students flocked to the infant colleges. In schools like Paine and the Atlanta Baptist Seminary, where poverty prevented trade work from developing, enrollment remained small, hovering around 150 to 200; but at Spelman, where industrial work flourished as nowhere else, more than 600 girls had been lured by 1888. After the completion of the Knowles Industrial Building in the 'eighties, the enrollment in Atlanta University soared to more than 500. During the decade Clark's student body swelled from 167 to nearly 350.

The 'nineties were a decade of less rapid growth, but all the colleges expanded, some attaining a larger student body than they were to have again for many years. In 1891 Spelman reported a record enrollment of 842 girls. From farm and country town, 505 pupils came to Georgia State Industrial College in 1900, not mere children, but 375 of them over fourteen years of age. It took seventeen years for this number to be reached again. The 700 pupils in these embryo colleges in 1880 had increased to more than 2,200 in 1895. There were now, of course, eight institutions compared to three then.

But it was a period of over-expansion and crowded conditions resulted. Frantic efforts to hold the students and give them the kind of education they wanted caused overburdening financial strain. Faculties were inadequate, and in consequence, low standards of admission and graduation allowed students to go forth half-taught to show the world what a hollow thing the education of the black man really was. But expansion did not stop and by 1905 still another thousand had found their way hence, swelling the enrollment in all colleges to nearly 3,500. Spelman was the largest school in the world for colored women. While all the colleges attracted most of their students from Georgia, their fame had spread and small groups came from Mississippi, South Carolina, Alabama, Florida, and Tennessee. A few traveled from the North to gain the social freedom available only in unmixed Negro schools. And an occasional man or woman of adventurous turn found the way in from the West Indies and even from distant Africa, sent hither, no doubt, by missionaries.

Growth in college departments, however, hardly kept pace with this over-expansion. The industrial craze was utterly unfavorable to the ideals of higher learning. Moreover, college preparatory work had experienced almost no increase outside the colleges. By 1900 the state operated 2,800 colored schools under 3,500 teachers. Illiteracy in the state had dropped from about 95% in 1860 to 50% for the colored race, forty years later. But education had not been pushed beyond the grammar grades. The white citizens of Augusta found a way to stifle the public high school in the 'nineties and even the efforts of Senator George F. Edmunds of Vermont to carry the case to the Supreme Court of the land proved futile.[1] At the end of the century, Athens was able to claim the only public colored high school in the entire state.[2] Another handicap to the increase in college level enrollment was the financial inability of most Negroes to continue in school for a very long period. The average colored farm worker was paid but $10 a month plus food and lodging. Most farmers worked for part of the crop.[3] It was a dismal outlook for a father anxious to give his offspring a college education. Even Atlanta University lost its hold on advanced students and enrolled between 18 and 24 each year whereas the 'seventies had produced as many as 30 in the college department. Other colleges mustered no more than five or six a year in the 'eighties, and sometimes, none at all. Few had students in all four classes at any time. The thirty Negro college students in all Georgia in 1880 had increased, within fifteen years, to no more than 45 in 1895.

It was not until the end of the century, after the economic depression had run its course, that any appreciable growth appeared in the higher branches. By then nearly all the colleges had set their four year curriculum on a fairly stable base. By 1902 the Atlanta Baptist Seminary

---

1. Webster, "The Georgia Negro's Fight on Ignorance," 17.
2. *Atlanta University Bulletin*, April, 1899.
3. *Proceedings of the Slater Fund, 1887*, p. 44.

boasted 14 college students while Paine had 16. In this same period of growth Clark increased her college enrollment from 6 to 32 and Georgia State Industrial College reached the high mark in 1901-1902 of 38. Far in the lead was Atlanta University where between 40 and 49 college students appeared in each of the first years of the new century. Between 1895 and 1905 the total number of Negro college level students in the state trebled from approximately 45 to 144.

If this number of 144 was comparatively small, out of a total enrollment of nearly 3,500 pupils, it was not unusual. The University in Athens enrolled only 129 students in 1899-1900 and the attendance of the entire University system was only 279.[4] It was plain, however, that the college departments in the Negro institutions were hardly more than adjuncts to secondary schools. A suggestion by DuBois that the 34 Negro colleges of the South throw all their higher work into about nine institutions located in strategic centers, went completely unheeded, despite its wisdom.[5] The men and women who gave of life and energy for these halls of learning were in no mood to think of giving anything to their rivals. Yet it was not all a matter of jealousy. Often it was a feeling born of affection and faith in the work begun, a determination to carry through the dream sprung from the missionary spirit.

Naturally there was little holding power in these college departments. It was a hard, discouraging grind for students to pour over books whence they would go to preaching or teaching at near starvation wages. Teaching and preaching required little education as they saw it. As soon as the rudiments were learned they were eager

---
4. *Report of the Trustees of the University, 1899-1900*, p. 21.
5. DuBois, *College Bred Negro* (Atlanta University Publications, No. 5), 9, 29.

to be up and about their new professions. Poverty, too, kept them from going on to graduation. At best the colleges were able to turn out only one, two, or three graduates a year. In 1894 President Wright of Georgia State Industrial College reported that only 73 bachelor degrees had been earned in the twenty-eight years since the first had been granted in the state by Atlanta University.[6] This was an average of less than three college graduates a year. But as the century turned, more remained to finish and from 1901 on the colleges totaled twenty or more graduates a year. In 1903 Atlanta University sent out a class of ten, the largest in the history of the state.

BUILDINGS AND EQUIPMENT

The increasing number of students of all grades who flocked into the schools in this period naturally caused a great demand for the means to serve them. Everywhere buildings were needed badly for classrooms, dormitories, teachers' homes, shops, and barns. Old and ramshackle structures of wood served well enough in the days of infancy. None other could be had. But in this new era of materialism, industrial life, and physical expansion which was felt by the whole nation, bigness became a sign of success, a mark of distinction and worldly power. Negro colleges could no longer be content with musty basements, stables, and old farm houses.

Of all the colleges Spelman acquired an adequate plant the quickest. By the late 'nineties the frame dwellings of the old Union barracks stood insignificantly beside four large brick buildings. There was a laundry in which eighty girls could work at a time. Of course, the hand of Rockefeller and his kind was in all things. In 1900, with the return of national prosperity, a frenzy of building got under way so that the next year saw the completion of

---

6. Wright, *Negro Education*, 51.

four more brick buildings—a home for the president, a hospital, a dining hall, and a dormitory. Other structures were improved and modernized. A steam plant was set up. And at the end of the period $35,000 worth of brick, mortar, and wood sat on twenty acres of land.[7]

Even at Gammon Seminary, perched on the southern hills of the city, the sound of hammer and mason's trowel was heard. More than four hundred people, not counting contributors in churches, paid for the completion of the main building. In 1889 a fire-proof library with a capacity of 20,000 volumes was finished. Four homes for professors were added plus ten cottages in which married students lived free of rent. Although Atlanta University had already set up a passable plant, it, too, complained of being crowded. And when it came into the good luck of a large bequest from Mrs. Valeria G. Stone of Malden, Mass., it forthwith used $40,000 of the money for a building. The Knowles Industrial Building, too, had come into being to meet the new craze of trade education which Ware and Bumstead so much disliked. A barn, worth $1,800, stood beside the meadows of hay and alfalfa. A school for practice teaching followed, and in 1905 the beneficence of Andrew Carnegie brought forth a $24,000 library.

Even the Atlanta Baptist Seminary came into its own after many years of struggling beside the railroad tracks in the town. On the death of President Robert in 1885, Samuel Graves was sent to the president's chair. A missionary of similar fortitude and piety, his first act was to call the students together and ask them to pray for him in his efforts to improve the cramped conditions of the puny school.[8] He managed to purchase a few acres on other Confederate breastworks near Atlanta University, and after four years of intense effort, a building was raised.

---

7. *Spelman Messenger*, March, 1901; December, 1901.
8. Brawley, *Morehouse College*, 54.

Indeed, Graves was proud of his handiwork. The new hall had cost $27,000 and was equipped with steam heat, "special" plumbing, boarding equipment, and a huge bell. Into its sixty-two rooms were squeezed dormitories, classrooms, president's apartments, dining hall, kitchen, printing office, and a little chapel. Graves had got the money by hard solicitation from New England, Michigan, and the Negro Baptists of Georgia.[9] When the debts were paid, Graves looked upon his work as done and turned his chair over to George Sale. Then another building went up, this time for $14,000 and named for old "Father" Quarles who had preached his last sermon and gone under the shadows. Then a laundry, a steam-plant, and a president's home rose on the same grounds.

Clark was less fortunate. On April 14, 1892, fire destroyed Chrisman Hall when it was no more than a dozen years old. But it was promptly rebuilt. Other structures had been added for dormitories and shops, and by 1905 the extensive campus, farm, and buildings were worth nearly $200,000. Morris Brown, on the other hand, had a pitiful time making headway. Here, where the Negroes themselves were trying to rise above their own poverty to make a school, building was slow. But the period saw two large wings fastened to the original structure, each with its own name of Turner and Grant to honor bishops.

At Paine conditions were far worse. Through the years of the 'eighties and high into the 'nineties, the old wooden house and stables remained as the only abode and President Walker became desperate. Several times he made efforts to move to an eighty-five acre tract that had been purchased six miles from the city. But there was no money for this dream. At last he gave up and forced the issue of raising money for a building on the present site. After incessant pleading a structure was finally begun in 1898.

---
9. *Ibid.*, 58.

Again money ran out and the work was stopped. But by 1899 a part of the building was usable and Walker moved in. An appeal for furnishings brought in gifts of beds, mattresses, chairs, and dishes. Contributions from individuals included such items as 4 tumblers, 4 napkins, 2 sheets, 20 dishes, 1 pair of pillow-shams, 1 soap dish, a cup and saucer, 1 plate, a knife and fork—the odds and ends of the nation's attics and pantries. The president's wife contributed a stove, utensils, 6 window shades, 2 lamps, and an ice cream churn.[10] After several years the building was completed and named for Atticus Haygood. By 1905 ten frame buildings sat on the twelve acres surrounding the brick structure.

It was to be expected that Georgia State Industrial College in Savannah would lag behind in such developments. The Morrill Act of 1890 had made it understood that none of the Federal money was to be used for the erection, repair, or even preservation of buildings.[11] And the state was not interested. But after five years, philanthropy came to the rescue, roused the state to mild efforts, and by 1901, eight buildings were on the campus, most of them erected by student labor.[12]

At the beginning of the second wave of the crusade about 1880 the property of the Negro colleges of Georgia had amounted to approximately $200,000. By 1905, however, the value of the combined plants was about $1,200,000.

FINANCIAL SUSTENANCE

To some people this considerable facade of Georgian and Gothic walls indicated that the Negro colleges were financially stable, even wealthy. But penury there was, and plenty of it, within these walls. The small schools

---
10. *Catalogue of Paine Institute, 1898-1899*, pp. 30-32.
11. *Federal Laws, 1911*, 8.
12. *Catalogue of Georgia State Industrial College, 1901-1902*, p. 11.

were forced to struggle along with hardly more than enough to pay the teachers. During the whole period of the second wave neither Paine nor Atlanta Baptist Seminary was ever able to find more than $10,000 to spend in any one year. Usually they were fortunate to scrape together five or six thousand dollars annually. Georgia State Industrial College fared better with $24,000 every year in Federal subsidies. But it was not enough for the elaborate industrial and collegiate plan which in one year served more than 500 students. Even Gammon, small as it was, had its struggles for existence all through the 'eighties and 'nineties. In the first year it could find but $1,200. During the 'nineties only about $8,000 a year was available.[13] There was little worry though; for with a handsome endowment of nearly half a million dollars which came into full use at the end of the century, all distress vanished and the seminary found itself with more money than it knew how to use. Spelman, of course, was an expensive proposition. Its many fine buildings and hundreds of students cost $20,000 to be kept together in 1891-1892.[14]

The depression of the 'nineties was a black day for everyone. J. L. M. Curry reported to the Slater Fund that the schools had suffered greatly from this financial plague which rested "like a night-mare, upon the hopes and energies of the South."[15] Corners were trimmed in every institution. By 1901-1902 Spelman had reduced its expenses to $24,000, in spite of additional buildings to maintain.

Atlanta University had fallen into cloudy days long before the depression. Its bright future of the early 'eighties melted quickly after the controversy with the state which deprived the university of $8,000 a year. Standards set by Ware, visionary and optimistic, were costly. In 1887

---
13. *Catalogue of Gammon Theological Seminary, 1899*, p. 3.
14. *Spelman Messenger, March*, 1892.
15. *Proceedings of the Slater Fund, 1895*, p. 5.

a member of the Board of Visitors told the *Augusta Chronicle* that there was not a white school in Georgia possessing such a thorough faculty and equipment.[16] Evidently the public knew little of the labor and sleepless nights Ware and Bumstead put into holding this praise. During the 'eighties, thirty to forty thousand dollars had to be raised each year for operating expenses. As if that were not enough of a strain, the expansion of industrial education in the 'nineties boosted yearly costs to more than $40,000, reaching in one year, 1891-1892, $52,700. The depression, of course, caused retrenchment. But it is to be noted that in 1899-1900 when Mercer spent only $20,000, the University of Georgia, $47,000, Atlanta University had to look for nearly $40,000.[17] Obviously these vast sums, raised mostly by passing the hat, threw a terrific burden on the college. In 1906-1907 expenses were no less than $55,000. There was no way out. The university would neither lower its standards nor toady to the industrial craze for which money could more easily be raised. Debts grew higher and higher and by 1905, $43,000 was on the account books in red.

It was inevitable that income to meet these expenses fluctuated with public opinion. All colleges attempting to offer higher learning to the Negroes depended on the still lingering spirit of Northern humanitarianism and the meagre board and tuition fees of the half-destitute students. Even after twenty-five years of the second wave, only two institutions were free to operate without the yearly aid of society, church, and white benevolence. Gammon became secure in the lap of its rich endowment, and Georgia State Industrial College had yearly subsidies from the Federal government. But for the others, the situation

---
16. *Atlanta University Bulletin*, January, 1888.
17. DuBois, *College Bred Negro* (Atlanta University Publications, No. 5), 51.

throughout the period remained one of constant begging. The humanitarian impulse which had driven Northerners to unprecedented philanthropy in Reconstruction, experienced a notable let down by 1880. The time had come, said many, for the South to assume this responsibility for the black man. The North was getting tired of the whole matter. In fact, many of the early societies had closed their books and called it a day. In the face of this, the Negro colleges were driven to desperate straits. When the new doctrine of industrial education raised its head, carrying with it a popular appeal to the industrial North and even to the New South, the crusaders snatched at it as if it were the last straw by which they could be saved.

Fortunately for the Negro, there were a few of the older generation surviving in the North in whom the spirit of benevolence still lived. By 1882 the inspiration of George Peabody's philanthropy had reached another man of wealth, John F. Slater, a manufacturer in Norwich, Connecticut. At his death he left $1,000,000 to advance the education of Negroes by teacher training, and set former President Rutherford B. Hayes, a Peabody Trustee, to watch over it. Wise management eventually almost doubled the gift. Atticus G. Haygood was taken from his comfortable president's chair at Emory College in Georgia and given the job of spending the proceeds.

In the very first year of his work, 1883, Haygood divided $6,000 of Slater money among Atlanta University, Spelman, and Clark.[18] As the industrial craze spread, the Fund followed, and Atlanta University lost out because of its unwillingness to emphasize trade work. Clark and Spelman thereby came into greater favor, each receiving as much as $5,000 a year while their work in industrial pursuits was compared favorably, if on a smaller scale,

---

18. *Proceedings of the Slater Fund, 1883*, p. 20.

with that at Tuskegee and Hampton.[19] From the training of common school teachers, the Fund branched into educating trade teachers. The Atlanta Baptist Seminary, Paine and Georgia State Industrial College were aided with gifts of $500 to $2,000 a year.

Other aid came from the societies and churches which still lingered in the field. Although Atlanta University had long since gained its independence from the American Missionary Association, it was forced to appeal to it again in 1889 to repair the loss of the $8,000 appropriation withdrawn by the state. For five years, $3,000 was given annually with the concession that the Association nominate six trustees. In the end this second alliance also proved embarrassing and the University renounced the gift in favor of independence.[20] But at Clark, entire support, as well as control, continued to come from its original benefactor, the Freedmen's Aid Society of the Methodist Church. Over Spelman and the Atlanta Baptist Seminary, the American Baptist Home Mission Society maintained its parental influence. In 1886, $35,000 came into Georgia through the Society's treasury, and in 1894, more than $56,000.[21] Although the colleges did not get all of this (for the Society aided elementary schools in the state as well), the boys' seminary depended on the Society largely for its support.[22] By 1896 the Society had sent more than $415,000 into Georgia for Negro education.[23] In 1890, the New England women's division was supporting twelve teachers at Spelman.

The efforts of the Southern Methodist Episcopal Church to support Paine were fraught with difficulty. At first a

---
19. *Ibid.*, *1890*, pp. 10, 20; *1900*, p. 9; Stowell, *Methodist Adventures*, 70.
20. Adams, *Atlanta University*, 36-37.
21. *Spelman Messenger*, April, 1897.
22. *Catalogue of the Atlanta Baptist Seminary, 1898-1899*, p. 14.
23. *Spelman Messenger*, April, 1897.

commissioner was appointed to remain in the field and collect money. Then an attempt was made to have each presiding elder collect three cents per year from every church member in his district. But the scheme failed and a commissioner was again sent into the field. From 1884 to 1892 annual collections by this agent traveling from conference to conference ran between $1,300 and $7,800.[24] Then again President Walker made a change, sending a new commissioner from church to church to plead with each congregation.[25]

The farms, too, were a means of income. In nearly every college vegetables were raised for the dining halls by student labor. By the 'nineties Atlanta University had found itself losing money on this plan, but other schools were more successful and maintained gardens for many years. The catalogue of 1898 for the Atlanta Baptist Seminary recorded a four-acre garden and a barn, a horse, and a wagon. At Georgia State Industrial College more than thirty acres were cultivated. It was this work that provided the so-called agricultural instruction listed under the industrial department.

Other income came from the advertising campaigns of the schools themselves. A steady stream of bulletins, letters, teachers on summer leave, and presidents went North to individuals, churches, and mass meetings. The response was less than in the early days of the crusade, but there could be no letdown in the effort. Taking a cue from Fisk which had come into fame with its Jubilee Singers, Atlanta University sent a quartet of students to the North in the summer. President Bumstead himself campaigned like a theatrical trouper. For him the raising of money was no simple matter. The North was in no mood during the industrial fever to give Bumstead money to raise black

---

24. *Catalogue of Paine Institute, 1894-1895*, p. 17.
25. *Ibid.*, 17.

idlers and loafers on Latin and Greek. But nearly $25,000 had to be found each year.[26] Fortunately, the liberal arts tradition of the University was favored by a few zealots of the old school. All the "great" of the land were appealed to and such names appear in the lists of donors as Charles W. Eliot, Henry L. Higginson, and Julia Ward Howe. Even gifts of $1,000 to $10,000 were recorded, sums which most colleges could only pray for. To Spelman came $200,000 from Rockefeller for the building campaign of 1901.

Many teachers contributed in both money and free services. The missionaries were not usually rich but they counted among their number men and women of substantial Northern heritage, some with sufficient income to allow their humanitarian impulse the luxury of working for the love of a cause. Spelman received contributions of $2,609 in one year, largely from the president and teachers, and such gifts were not uncommon in many schools.[27] The seminary calculated that in the first fifteen years of its history, teachers had donated no less than $70,000 in gratuitous services.[28]

But the signal fact of the second wave rests in the increasing part the Negro was willing to share in this expense. Morris Brown was supported entirely by the congregations of the African Methodist Episcopal Church of Georgia. In the early days at Paine, current operating expenses, excepting teachers' salaries, came from the Colored Methodist Church and the students. At Spelman one-third the operating expenses were paid by student fees.[29] In one year tuition alone amounted to $3,341 and often it was more. In 1897-1898 Atlanta Baptist Seminary received nearly $4,000 in tuition and board toward total operating

---
26. Wright, *Negro Education*, 40.
27. *Proceedings of the Slater Fund, 1903*, p. 29.
28. *Spelman Messenger*, April, 1897.
29. Wright, *Negro Education*, 44.

costs of $7,700. Other small gifts were listed from Negro churches—New Hope Sunday School, $5; Providence Baptist Church, $2.50; Zion Hill Church, $1.10; individual Negroes, $206—all little enough, but the long lists added to substantial amounts every year.

It was in this period, too, that endowments were begun. The half-million dollar fund of Gammon surpassed all others, of course, and was hardly less than a miracle for that day. In 1888 Warren Candler persuaded the Reverend Moses U. Payne of Missouri to give Paine College a permanent fund of $25,000. By the end of the period Spelman had gathered in three small funds mostly for student aid, amounting to $10,800. In the 'nineties a bequest of $20,000 from Josiah W. Cook of Cambridgeport, Massachusetts, endowed the president's chair at the boys' seminary. And Atlanta University was able to boast of $53,900 gradually accumulated into a fixed fund.

To be sure, all this money raising required a large network of beggary. The jealous and discontented population of poor whites could not help but feel the sting of envy at the sight of their own children sitting in wretched schools while money flowed South for the Negro. Here was meat for the demagogues bent on snatching the ballot from dusky voters. So said the *Atlanta Constitution* in 1901, "The hills around Atlanta alone are covered with more high grade opportunities for Negroes than the state has provided for all her children."[30] It was noted as an enviable sign that Spelman was better equipped than any school for white girls in the entire state. Undoubtedly, the mushroom growth of new colleges and the influx of Northern missionaries in the second wave tended to widen the breach between the Southern races. It was intermeddling of a sort that intensified race hatred and increased the

---

30. Quoted in *Spelman Messenger*, December, 1901.

social and cultural isolation of the Negroes for a long time to come.

Here was a kind of strife that promoted criticism. Out of the racial struggle, the lost faith of that generation in the classics, and the collapse of the grand industrial scheme, Negro education as a whole fell into a kind of disrepute that brought the critical eye of philanthropy close upon it. Really, it took no very searching gaze to see that many Northerners had been hoodwinked into "disastrously kind" benevolence. The smooth and sugary tongues of both white and colored presidents who annually made their pilgrimage to the North in behalf of their schools had caused alms-giving to become an indiscriminate ritual. Often the worthless schools prospered while the worthy suffered. In that day of wildcat speculation the thief and the pickpocket plied their trade in all fields. Education was not excepted. The crook campaigned for Negro schools of less than worthless merit, and for some that were entirely mythical. Reports seeped into the Northern states that too many Negro schools existed; that many accomplished nothing; and that even the best produced little for the benefit of civilization. As early as 1895 Curry wrote for the Slater Fund: "Much of the aid lavished upon the Negro has been misapplied charity, and like much other alms-giving hurtful to the recipient. Northern philanthropy, 'disastrously kind,' has often responded with liberality to appeals worse than worthless. Vagabond mendicants have been pampered; schools which were established without any serious need of them have been helped; public school systems, upon which the great mass of children, white and colored, must rely for their education, have been underrated and injured, and schools, of real merit and doing good work, which deserve confidence and contributions, have had assistance, legitimately their due, diverted into improper channels."[31]

Even now, the crowding of five colleges into Atlanta was severely criticized. Rivalry and jealousy hampered the work of the colleges while the drive for students lowered standards of admission and graduation to a point of ridicule. A suggestion from the Slater Fund that Clark and Atlanta universities combine their industrial work was greeted with suspicion and a prompt defeat. Only between the Baptist girls' and boys' seminaries, where there was no need of rivalry, did the spirit of cooperation reach a degree of merit. Under these conditions the North lost much interest in the cause.

The Controversy Over Negro Control

Amidst these shifts of public opinion and support the Negro began to demand a larger voice in the control of his schools. The original board of trustees of Atlanta University had included colored men; but they had exercised little influence in affairs and had been dropped. In 1879, Joseph E. Smith was elected as the first regular colored trustee of the university.[32] By 1904 four of the institution's graduates were trustees, but the board remained predominantly white. The Augusta Institute, of course, had been begun by Negroes. When Spelman organized a board in 1888, William J. White, and William E. Holmes, a colored teacher in the boys' seminary, were both included. Other colleges were similarly represented by one or two colored men. Morris Brown, of course, was entirely in the hands of the black race. As the Negroes rose in education, land holdings, and pride in their capacity to develop a civilization of their own, they began a greater

---

31. J. L. M. Curry, "Difficulties, Complications, and Limitations Connected with the Education of the Negro," *Occasional Papers No. 5 of the John F. Slater Fund* (Baltimore, 1895), 12.
32. *Crimson and Gray*, (Atlanta University), June, 1917.

demand to run their own institutions. The rise of Booker T. Washington to national renown and the recognition of the race in the Cotton States Exposition of 1895, had gone far to augment this feeling of self-confidence. As early as the second year of its life the colored faculty of Georgia State Industrial College had been bold enough to request that President Wright be allowed to attend all meetings of the Commissioners.[33] It was a futile plea and the time came when the Commissioners treated the president as if he were a school-boy.

But the end of the century marked a period of unrest among the Negroes. The increase in the number of lynchings, renewed efforts at disfranchisement, and the exclusion of the black laborer from industrial pursuits produced a spiritual depression in the race unequaled since Reconstruction.[34] Amidst this turmoil, the Negro Baptists of Georgia themselves had split in twain in 1893. When in 1897 the Atlanta Baptist Seminary was re-incorporated into a college, Negro leaders were chagrined that promises of greater Negro control in affairs of the institution had not been fulfilled. Loudest of these voices of anxiety for the future of the race was that of E. K. Love, a colored Baptist preacher of Savannah. Disappointed by his own failure to become a trustee both at Spelman and the boys' seminary, his quarrel descended to a personal brawl. Yet it was not only for himself that he cast ultimatums and threats at the Baptists about him. He spoke for those of his race who saw the foundations of the power they had gained in Reconstruction crumbling under them. The thirty year struggle up from slavery was coming to naught. No less than in Georgia, the scramble for authority went on in the entire South. It was a frenzied effort to save, at

---
33. Minutes of the Faculty of Georgia State Industrial College, November 1, 1892, p. 42.
34. Brawley, *Morehouse College*, 88.

least, the Negro's education in the face of other rights and privileges those trying to disfranchise him were wresting from him. By 1899 Love had rallied sufficient Negro Baptists to his standard to threaten the life of the Atlanta Baptist Seminary by founding a rival college, unless his demands for a voice in control were heard. His many arguments contended that white teachers were incapable of serving the social needs of Negro life; that in this they could only be theoretical and visionary; that the white teachers of the second wave were less consecrated than the early crusaders and their work was neither genuine nor effectual; that such white teachers did not believe in the equality of the races and thus could not create pride of race or produce upstanding men from black students looked down upon as inferiors; that such white teachers induced a spirit of hopelessness and defeat in their pupils; that white control deprived the Negro of a responsibility which, if practiced, would promote self-reliance and self-confidence; and that so long as Negroes remained subjects they would never launch out for themselves to leave their mark on history.[35] Strong as these arguments seemed, the white trustees of the seminary were of no mind to turn their institution over to people hardly able to support themselves.

So saying, Love was forced to carry out his threat and in 1899 his Convention purchased 235 acres near Macon, and Central City College came into being. From the Atlanta Baptist College came William E. Holmes to be the first president of Central. Beginnings were brilliant and by the third year, 365 students were enrolled. Since the institution was opened ostensibly to train teachers and preachers in opposition to the Atlanta school, a college department was set up. But born as it was in this spirit of

---

35. E. K. Love, *Annual Address to the Missionary Baptist Convention of Georgia* (Nashville, 1899), 19-27.

antagonism, without universal sanction or support, the school was pressed to fight for its existence and its work at higher learning remained a petty and pitiful affair.

Although Love had spoken for the most aspiring of his race he had not spoken for all the wisest of them. To many Negroes, the demand for authority had a hollow ring which they knew might be followed by the entire withdrawal of the white man from the colleges. Many saw in it a loss of contact with the white race which could end only in complete segregation from the intellectual and cultural abundance of that other world. As these dangers became evident, the movement for authority subsided into a faint murmur to be revived again only at such times as the Negro was able to gain a foothold without upsetting the main structure of Northern benevolence.

Hostility and Good Will

Thus the second wave of the crusade was an era of conflict within the confines of the educational system itself. A clash of aims—industrial versus classical—a shifting of goals, a discrediting of the educational ideal, rivalry for support, jealousy for superiority, a clamoring for control—all weakened the solid front which the first crusaders had been able to maintain during Reconstruction. True, education had made phenomenal gains, but with each institution pulling away in its own direction, the firm fabric of unity had been rent, leaving gaps for the rising Populist revolt. Again public opinion against Negro education was aroused. From 1899 on, outbreaks of racial violence increased all over the South. In that year a mob in Twiggs County descended upon the Negro school, beat up a few Negroes, and tore up the house of the teacher.[36] Thomas E. Watson ranged the state luring votes from both races by corkscrew methods of playing blacks against

---

36. *Savannah Tribune*, March 12, 1889.

whites and back again, at last emerging as the mass leader of the white clan which subdued the "uppish nigger." And Joseph M. Brown, the Negro's friend, turned in his tracks to cut the black man down to his former low estate. In 1890 Georgia led all states but Texas with a record of eighteen Negro lynchings. In 1892 Georgia passed its "Jim Crow" laws.[37]

To the *Atlanta Journal* the intermeddling of Northern missionaries in Negro schools was still a matter to be fought with scourging pen. For was not Atlanta University "infusing ... the poison of social equality ... all over the country?" And it continued: "Our city is now ring-fired with Negro schools and colleges supported by Northern money, which are doing all they can to make mischief between the races."[38] Again the idea was put forth of taxing the colleges out of existence. Even the strong tie of religion could not bring the Southerner and missionary together. Said the president of the Atlanta Baptist Seminary in 1894: "Between the Georgia Baptists at large and the Northern men and women who are engaged in work in the Baptist schools in Atlanta, there is little sympathy .... We do our work and live our lives apart."[39] At the end of the period DuBois expressed the same sentiment: "Only in a few cases have we been able to get the best class of Southern whites to examine and really learn about our work. The larger part of them either remain indifferent or unfriendly toward us."[40] It was noticed, too, that the eloquent speeches advocating Negro education given by prominent men at college ceremonies rarely found their way into the columns of papers where white voters could read them. The politician had no mind to lose his seat by such exposures. The result was that many of the colleges

---
37. *Ibid.*, January 7, 1891.
38. Quoted in *Atlanta University Bulletin, June, 1890.*
39. Brawley, *Morehouse College*, 68.
40. *Servitude to Service*, 190.

became so discouraged that a general condition of apathy set in from which they were not to be released until the educational revival following the First World War.

But it was not altogether fair to paint the second wave as one of complete hostility. If the "nigger howl" was heard too frequently, it must also be remembered that there were other signs of optimism and hope that such days would not always be. The founding of Paine by men who a short time before had been slaveholders was a bright note of good-will. Although the state had moved grudgingly to set up a college at Savannah, the very move pointed to a better future. Always there were some who spoke well for the higher learning of the colored man—G. R. Glenn, the State Superintendent of Education, Joel Chandler Harris, John L. Hopkins, Henry Grady, Sidney Root— and there were others. Prominent visitors such as former President Rutherford B. Hayes, Julia Ward Howe, Susan B. Anthony, President William McKinley, and General Joseph Wheeler of Santiago fame, all brought messages of Northern friendship. In 1897 commencement exercises at Spelman were made eventful by the presence of Governor W. Y. Atkinson and ex-Governor Northen, while the *Atlanta Journal*, for all its opposition, found space for a colored student's essay. The work of the seminary hospital had won many friends among doctors, ministers, and state officials.[41] Out from Gammon, President Thirkield went to the pulpits of all the important white churches of the city—a signal victory for a Northern missionary to be so received.[42] The faith of Haygood and Curry seemed inexhaustible. From a conference at Capon Springs, Florida, in 1898 had come a still greater contribution, the Conference for Education in the South, which worked steadily

---
41. *Spelman Messenger*, January, 1902.
42. *Catalogue of Gammon Theological Seminary, 1900*, p. 13.

in the first years of the century to arouse the public to join the crusade.[43]

The Crusade Ends

The end of the first wave of the crusade had come in the early years of the 'eighties and had been marked by a definite change of spirit and a passing of old ideals. In this same way the end of the second wave was marked in the first years of the following century by a passing of an old day and the rise of a new one. By 1905 one could not help seeing that a new era was dawning for the Negro college of Georgia. The missionary spirit, the faith that had whipped the crusade into life, the religious impulse, the broad and deep affection for all mankind based on social equality and the brotherhood of man—these profound impulses were all but spent. It took more than a man of humble faith to handle these large educational corporations rising over Confederate earthworks. Executives, business men, educators—these are titles of less heart than missionary—but they were needed in this changing world that had a mania for science and efficiency. In 1906 President Sale resigned from the Atlanta Baptist Seminary. He was succeeded by the first Negro to sit in the president's chair of that institution. A year later, Bumstead retired from the presidency of Atlanta University to return to the quiet of a New England village. Two years later Harriet Giles finished her days in the Spelman Seminary she had helped create nearly thirty years before. Haygood had gone long before. Truly, a generation of men and women who had given their lives to the crusade were beckoned one after another by the fingers of old age and death. The industrial craze had run its course; the classical tradition was being revamped and re-valued; the movement for disfranchisement had won its victories; and the era

---

43. Jones, *Negro Education*, I, 19.

of philanthropy from the mass of people of the North had given way to philanthropy on a larger scale by a few individuals of almost unbelievable wealth. These changes and many others naturally gave rise to another era.

But there was no third wave to the crusade. The crusade was done for and gone. The end of the movement was marked by a definite decline throughout the whole nation in the interest in the Negro. America was concerned with imperial expansion and internal improvements of a physical sort destined to bring the nation to a position of dominance in world affairs. Temporarily at least the Negro became a forgotten man. Forty years of effort in his behalf, with its meagre results, had tired the North, and the South was concerned with other matters.

But the crusade had been more than a noble experiment. The rise of Negro colleges in Georgia had been phenomenal in physical growth alone. The black race had begun to develop a civilization of its own, with pride, race consciousness, and its own leaders in church, education, social welfare, and even business.

CHAPTER VII

The Students and Their Teachers

THE LIFE, WORK, AND PLAY OF STUDENTS IN THE NEGRO colleges of Georgia during the thirty-six years from 1869 to 1905, of course, went through the same variety of changes that attended the rise of colleges, the changes of ideals and ways of life that occurred in the Negro race. But it was not until well into the new century that college life broke from the severe discipline, the religious emphasis, and the perpetual burden of poverty that gave those thirty-odd years a degree of unity.

The students of the first years were nearly all born in slavery. Many had grown to manhood and womanhood as the chattels of white masters. At freedom they were left with scarcely more than the clothes on their backs and an opportunity to go forth a free people to live or die as fate directed them. Those who found their way eventually to schools of higher learning were driven by eagerness to enjoy the white man's world, by aspirations for leadership, by desires to serve their race, or by an urge to escape constant drudgery. Impelled by these forces, the first students trudged mile after mile along the red clay roads of the country from field and village to the doors the Northerners had opened in the cities. A typical example was Richard R. Wright, first president of Georgia State Industrial College. He was born in Dalton, Georgia, a slave. Immediately after the war he attended school in Cuthbert. From there he walked to Atlanta at the side of a buggy in which a white farmer had offered to carry his mother and young sister. Once in the city he attended Storr's School and in 1869 entered Atlanta University as one of the eighty-nine pupils in its first class.[1]

Here is the testimony of a student who migrated from city to city in his efforts to go to school: "My mother and I were sold from my father, who lived in South Carolina, and taken first to Mississippi, and then to Banks County, Georgia. Here when I was six years of age my master started me at work in a stable with the purpose of making me learn the care of horses and become his carriage driver. I was freed in 1865 and then my mother and I walked to Newberry, South Carolina (100 miles) and found father again. We were very poor and my parents had to hire me out for a year. Then they decided to send me to school and I went irregularly from 1866 to 1874. I gained at last a state scholarship in the South Carolina College, but the Republicans after two years were forced out of power and the college closed to them. Finally I entered the Atlanta University."[2]

Even as late as 1894 the Atlanta University Bulletin noted that a student had arrived recently who had walked 560 miles from Vicksburg, Mississippi, hoping to earn his way through school by work at school.[3]

The background of nearly all students was similar—with poverty, toil, and eagerness to learn. A Northern teacher working in Savannah in 1869 wrote to Edmund Asa Ware the following description of a student he wished

---
1. *Crimson and Gray* (Atlanta University), November, 1928.
2. DuBois, *College Bred Negro* (Atlanta University Publications No. 5), 48-50.
3. *Atlanta University Bulletin*, January, 1894.

to send to Atlanta University: "Geo. S. Smith, aged twenty-five, has been to night school only—reads very well in Testament, understands addition, subtraction, multiple, and division, and I do not know how much more. Has studied geography some. He is a carpenter by trade . . . is decidedly above the best of the colored people. He ran away from Macon before the war, went to New York, thence to Jamaica, where he remained until the war was over. . . . He has no means, or not much, but will pay his own passage to Atlanta, and is willing to work his way . . . he may have friends who will help him some."[4]

Another sketch by the same teacher gives an idea of the kind of preparation the schools in the state were able to supply before advancing their students to Atlanta: "Waters, seventeen years old, reads in Fifth reader well, has been through Davis' Pract. Arith., Monteith's Series, and part through Guizot's Intermed. Geog.—writes a good hand, has a little knowledge of Grammar. . . . The boy wishes to become a minister. . . . His father wants him to go to Atlanta two years, and will pay his expenses."[5]

The *Daily Christian Recorder* for 1884 carried the tale of the tribulations of a man who struggled through the mental perplexities of freedom to become a minister. He was M. Edward Bryant, born in Alabama in 1853 of a mother one-quarter Indian and three-quarters African. His father was a white Scotsman who practiced law and played the role of erstwhile politician. Bryant and his mother first belonged to a John Wallack. In 1861 they were sold to Joseph Gillespie at Auburn, with whom they remained until the end of the war. At the time of the surrender Bryant was a lad of twelve years, but he had never heard a sermon, a religious song, or the name of

---
4. Letter to E. A. Ware, August 9, 1869 (in Atlanta University Library).
5. *Ibid.*

God excepting in an oath. After emancipation, his mother sent him to Sunday School. Then in a day school of the Freedmen's Bureau he learned to read and cipher so efficiently in one month's time that he became a popular letter writer for his Negro community. With very little more education, he got busy in church work, taught school several years, and finally became the first principal of the Opelika colored high school. Apparently these advances were not enough and Bryant entered politics, read law, and had the terrifying experience of being hunted by the Ku Klux Klan. The horror of being a hunted man cured him of public aspirations for a time and he went to Atlanta University. He stayed there five years, but not without having his mind wander into free thinking from clandestine reading in Voltaire, Paine, and Rousseau. At last the religious passion of his teachers overcame the struggle for his soul; he was converted and in 1875 was ordained as a preacher in the African Methodist Church.[6]

Said another student of those early years: "I attended the public schools in Augusta, Georgia, and sold papers, brushed boots and worked in tobacco factories. While in College, I taught school in the summer time."[7] And another student described a similar background: "I was born in Greene County, Georgia, and lived on the farm until I was 17. My parents were poor and there were nine other children. I worked hard, saved my money, went to school, and finally entered Atlanta University."[8]

Here is the story of a man of rebellious disposition. "My childhood and youth were spent in Atlanta. Most of my time I was forced to work to support my family. Now and then I went to night school and the summer country school. In 1876 I got desperate and broke away from my family and entered Storr's School. Finishing there in the

---
6. *Daily Christian Recorder*, Philadelphia, May 16, 1884.
7. DuBois, *College Bred Negro*, 45-50.
8. *Ibid.*

spring of 1877, in the fall of the same year I entered Atlanta University and there I remained till I was graduated in 1884."[9]

R. A. Carter, the first college graduate of Paine, described his early years: "I was born in Fort Valley, Georgia, . . . and had the family background of any colored boy of that period. I was reared in Columbia, South Carolina, where I was carried when I was six years old. I attended public school in that city which was taught by white and colored teachers from Yankee land. At 17, I wangled a first grade license to teach in the public schools of S. C. out of a county superintendent who was almost as ignorant and unprepared as I. He was white, however. I entered the South Carolina Conference of the C. M. E. Church when I was twenty years old and matriculated at Paine Institute in 1887."[10]

Even from the North, a few students found their way into Georgia colleges. Said one of his past years: "Sea life for eight or ten years. I traveled much. I attended district school in Massachusetts in winter. My academic training was received at Pierce Academy, Middleboro, Massachusetts; college work at Atlanta University."[11]

Thus they came from homes where parents were farmers, laborers, carpenters, draymen, brick-layers, mechanics, teachers, field-hands, servants, preachers, washwomen—others from homes of their own where they had wives and children to support, or where parents were scattered by slave sales or the chaos of war. They were very often grown men and women, some of them already in their thirties and forties when first they set eyes on the printed page. During the 'eighties students in the upper branches in Atlanta University generally ranged be-

---

9. DuBois, *College Bred Negro American* (Atlanta University Publications, No. 15), 61.
10. Questionnaire sent out by the author, 1938.
11. DuBois, *College Bred Negro American*, 64.

tween 17 and 25 years of age. Those studying for the ministry were often older. As late as 1890-1891 Spelman listed 574 girls between the ages of 16 and 25, while thirty-five women were over the age of 25.[12] At Georgia State Industrial College the majority of advanced students were in their twenties, approaching thirty, and two or three normal students were listed over fifty years of age. Even at the turn of the century, students at Paine were usually between 18 and 30 years of age while a few studying for the ministry were in their forties. In 1897, the year Spelman began a regular college department with two students, forty-three women over twenty-five were enrolled.

Obviously, students were in no condition to pay high prices for education. Tuition in all the colleges remained between $1 and $2 a month during the entire period. In most places ministers paid no tuition at all, while at Georgia State Industrial College all students were admitted free. Board and lodging was by far the largest expenditure of a student. Students in the lower grades were usually from homes in the city, and lived at home. Those in all branches coming from beyond the city lived in college dormitories or in homes in the neighborhood. The cost of board and room was little enough, generally no more than $5 to $8 per month. Atlanta University was for many years the most expensive of all schools, charging $10 per month. As late as 1894 Atlanta University noted that a year's expenses at Yale amounted to $630 while students could attend in Atlanta for no more than $92. Such low costs were not unusual anywhere in the South. In 1882 Emory College reported more than sixty students working their way and living on $8 a month.[13]

Yet these expenses, low as they were, put a tremendous burden on Negro students and their families, who lived in

---

12. *Catalogue of Spelman Seminary*, 1890-1891, p. 50.
13. *Wesleyan Christian Advocate*, January 14, 1882.

poverty. Most of the colleges required from boarding students one hour of free labor a day on grounds and buildings. But additional work was provided as much as possible to permit students to earn part of their expenses. Labor in the laundry, in the printing office, or on the farms was paid for at the rate of five cents to eight cents an hour. Clark reported students earning $2 to $3 per month in this fashion while Georgia State Industrial College claimed that several students were able to earn their entire expenses by farm labor. At the latter, catalogues announced that all would be expected to work and the "dudish" and "sickly persons or weaklings are not desired."[14] Others worked outside the college. When E. R. Carter arrived at the Atlanta Baptist Seminary, he had 50 cents in his pocket. In later years he was able to boast that during his first two months in Atlanta he lived on ginger-snaps and cheese and slept in a piano box, using his coat for covering. From four o'clock to nine in the morning he worked at shoe-making, attended school until two in the afternoon, after which he worked again at his trade until night fall. In the summer students went out to teach, to pick cotton, or to work in former trades, while some found their way to the North to serve as waiters, cooks, carriage drivers, pullman porters, or hands on river boats.

Other aid came from individuals, black and white, Sunday Schools, churches, aid societies, or friends of the students. C. T. Walker, who entered the Augusta Institute in 1874 with only $6, did his own cooking during the first term. When his money gave out three men from Dayton, Ohio, came to his aid and supported him in school for five years.[15]

---

14. *Catalogue of Georgia State Industrial College*, 1891-1892, p. 27; 1901-1902, p. 9.
15. S. X. Floyd, *A Sketch of Rev. C. T. Walker, D.D.* (Augusta, 1892), 2.

Help was given by the colleges themselves in prizes, loan funds, and scholarships. First in the field was the Peabody Fund with student aid to Atlanta University as early as 1869. By 1889 the University possessed an endowment of nearly $30,000 for scholarships. At the Atlanta Baptist Seminary the Ripley Scholarship of $50 a year was given to a ministerial student. Prizes were offered of from $20 to $25 a year to outstanding pupils in normal and college branches. In all schools prizes for debating, essays, orations, and declamations were offered. In the 1890's, a scholarship fund of $5,000 was given Spelman by Mrs. Mary Luther of Monroe, Pennsylvania. Loan funds were available in many places. In 1879-1880 the Atlanta Baptist Seminary aided 41 pupils with small loans. At Gammon cottages were built by the carpentry department of Clark so that married students might live free of rent.

From the North came boxes and barrels of clothing, shoes, and bedding for student use. At the Atlanta Baptist Seminary, the "Grand-Raps," as the boxes from Grand Rapids, Michigan, were called, were looked forward to with as much eagerness as the student looked forward to his next meal.

But such philanthropy was small in comparison with the great need. Although many of the students in Atlanta University and a few in other schools were soon coming from prosperous homes, the majority in all colleges continued to arrive little above destitution. Only in rare cases could students in college departments afford to remain beyond the freshman or sophomore year. It was the practice in most places, however, never to dismiss a student for failure to pay his bills. During the summer or the year following, payments dribbled in, two, three, at best ten dollars at a time from wherever the student had gone to work.

Yet the daily activities of the students kept them too

busy to become very depressed by their hard lot. Reared in a background of bare necessity, they were content with little money and simple comforts. On the whole, college life was a happy, delightful period of carefree association. The students were hustled out of bed at five or six o'clock in the morning. They washed in tin basins and some took up the fastidious practice of brushing their teeth. Then came breakfast to be followed by an hour of study or devotions. In some cases the horror of a study period on an empty stomach was experienced before breakfast. The rest of the morning was given over to classes. After dinner, other recitations were held or students went off to trade shops, farm labor, or the usual "duties" about the buildings and grounds. As sports and athletics gained a reputation for decency later in the century, part of the afternoon was allowed for these activities. Supper about six o'clock was followed by evening prayers and a study period which lasted two to three hours. At nine-thirty or ten o'clock lights went out, and students were forced to climb into bed regardless of their inclinations.

Living conditions varied in each institution. At most places the usual dormitory rooms prevailed, each accommodating two or three students. Before the completion of Haygood Hall at Paine late in the 1890's the little school was so crowded that beds were rigged up in the halls, and smaller boys were lined up in triple formation, three in a bed.[16] Boys at Georgia State Industrial College were herded on the barracks plan in one huge dormitory. There the martial spirit found a rendezvous in the formation of a military corps. Army discipline was installed in the barracks under the vigilance of advanced students, who took great delight in lording it over their shuffling soldiers. Faith in the home as the guardian of all human virtues held sway at Spelman where students lived on a family plan,

---

16. Minutes of the Trustees of Paine Institute, 1895-1896, p. 134.

being divided into groups under the eye of a matron.[17] Everywhere students were their own janitors, sweeping and cleaning buildings and their own rooms, even making the mattresses they slept on. Usually a clean tick was issued from the laundry every sixty days. Sweet-smelling rice straw was stuffed into the tick until it bulged to a thickness of about two feet before being slept on. Girls at Spelman were obliged to do their own laundry work, washing at five-thirty in the morning, and ironing in the afternoon. In the early days all water had to be carried from outdoors to the laundry where it was heated and then rationed out for laundry and rooms. Until plumbing was installed, Atlanta University boys carried fifty to sixty buckets of water a quarter of a mile every day. Saturday was general house cleaning day: stoves were blacked, floors and windows washed, furniture polished, and all things arranged in order according to New England concepts of cleanliness and Godliness.

This melange of constant activity and arduous tasks was interrupted by social gatherings at meal time. Each meal was a school in itself, as well as a social event and a means of adding energy for those long, hard days. Lessons in etiquette, discipline, and home management were given three times a day. The older students often presided over tables with dignified parental pose. In Atlanta University the white teachers ate with the students, one or two at a table, carving and serving the food while they kept open a lynx eye for breaches in table manners. All the students stood behind their chairs and at a nod from the presiding elder sat down simultaneously. At Spelman the girls stood until each had recited a verse of Scripture and an all-embracing invocation was pronounced. At Atlanta University ten or twelve girls sat along one side of a table while an equal number of boys gathered in embar-

---

17. *Catalogue of Spelman Seminary*, 1900-1901, p. 42.

rassed stoicism on the other. If the faculty were small, older students who had demonstrated a capacity to accommodate themselves to polite society sat at the ends of the board to officiate. The carver asked each of his charges what was wanted and the girls were served first, usually with dainty helpings. When the boys' turn came after many minutes of waiting, they roared "some of each" and fell to until the time came for a second helping.[18] In most places, however, the social equality practices of Atlanta University were tabooed and if teachers remained in the dining room at all, it was on police duty to keep order. The impeccable New Englander, of course, could not imagine a meal without a napkin and all students were required to furnish their own. But it was not always easy to convince the dusky students the value of such embellishments. Forthwith frequent campaigns had to be inaugurated to press the napkin into service.[19]

In co-educational schools the classrooms and dining halls were practically the only retreats for cupid and the romantic arts of courting. Elsewhere, association between boys and girls was forbidden and guarded over by a reign of law swift and uncompromising. Campuses were usually divided into two parts with an imaginary line between them more impassable than the Alps. Girls and boys sat in different sections in the chapel and in the study hall; they used separate stairways in the buildings. Walking or even speaking together on the campus might bring the culprits under the harsh hand of discipline. This segregation was an exasperating trial, claimed James Weldon Johnson, at Atlanta University where there was a bevy of good-

---

18. *Spelman Messenger*, April, 1886; J. W. Johnson, *Along This Way* (New York, 1933), 66-67; E. B. Emery, *Letters from the South on the Social, Intellectual, and Moral Condition of the Colored People* (Boston, 1880), 14.
19. Minutes of the Faculty of the Atlanta Baptist College, No. 10, 1902, p. 33.

looking girls from the best colored families of Georgia, attractive in dress and ranging in complexion all the way from milk-white to ebony.[20] Dancing, of course, was a thing of the devil to the Puritans who came in from the North country. But "sociables" were arranged for intermingling two or three times a year. The students from Spelman and the Atlanta Baptist Seminary fraternized occasionally at joint entertainments and an annual lawn party.[21] A boy wishing to call on a girl at any other time might appear in the reception room at Spelman and after convincing the chaperon of the nobility of his soul was allowed a quiet twenty minute interview with his fair one. But a boy was permitted to call only once a month. On the other hand, a girl could receive the heart throb of a different caller every week if she could entice enough different men into her orbit.

In Atlanta University a suitor had to go through the rigmarole of getting a pass-slip signed by the president or dean for his monthly twenty-minute visit. Naturally, the rules were not always kept. But in this association of the sexes the influence of the New England divines was supremely manifest. It was no less than amazing the way students, used to the informality—indeed used to the immoral practices during slavery—which changed slowly among the masses over the years, became instilled with an idealistic concept of womanhood and developed a moral code more stringent than the professed chivalry of the Old South. James Weldon Johnson declared that in his college days in the 'nineties a veritable Sir Galahad idea of women was prevalent among the boys. Sexy talk was tabooed even in the confines of their own rooms.[22] Rules or no rules, however, surreptitious courting went on in

---
20. Johnson, *Along This Way*, 75.
21. Minutes of the Faculty of Atlanta Baptist Seminary, March 30, 1903, p. 41.
22. Johnson, *Along This Way*, 68.

this romantic mode at every opportunity. Saturday rather than Sunday was the day for best clothes. Once turned loose for a Saturday afternoon of visiting in town, both male and female would likely turn up at the same place, visiting mutual friends. Under the pressure of Puritanism, these accidents were suspiciously frequent.[23]

Activities beyond the usual routine of study, labor, eating, and love-making were squeezed into student life also. Leisure and idleness had no place in the philosophy of the founding fathers. Life was a serious matter; minutes and hours were God's gift to man to be used for divine service and the upbuilding of an earthly kingdom. Humor was not banned; a dry, stolid kind was good for mankind; but the laughter of light hearts and empty heads was an emotional expression to be frowned upon as a serious menace to the future of civilization. The relation of the student to his Maker was the alpha and omega of faculty enterprise. These colleges were no place for the dull in spirit, and abundant efforts were exercised to strengthen faith. Daily devotions and Sunday preaching services called for compulsory attendance.

Additional blessings were bestowed by campus organizations of Epworth Leagues, Baptist Young People's Unions, and Christian Endeavor Societies. Everywhere, lively groups of Young Men's and Young Women's Christian Associations looked to the welfare of their fellows. At Atlanta Baptist Seminary Wednesday evening was the time for Young People's Meeting, Thursday for Prayer Meeting, and Saturday for Bible Reading. At Paine, a Week of Prayer was held every year. At Spelman the spirit was nourished every night: on Monday, the Social Purity Society held forth; Tuesday, Christian Endeavor; Wednesday, the Congo or Free Mission Circle; Thursday, General Prayer Meeting; Friday, Sunday School Lesson

---

23. *Ibid.*, 69.

Study; and Saturday, Hall Prayer Meeting. As if this were not enough to secure one's entry into the golden land, catalogues announced that "Semi-monthly a stirring social purity meeting is held, and rousing missionary and temperance meetings are held monthly."[24]

Surely it was a crusty-hearted student who remained untouched by the electric charges of this religious current. Such was the spirit in the Augusta Institute that ministerial students were tempted into Sunday preaching in city pulpits more than President Robert deemed good for them. And they were lured into missionary work in the community to such an extent that one evening a week had to be turned over to hearing reports on their trials and victories.[25] The Sabbath was usually brought to a close with a vesper service or, as in Atlanta University where students were indulged with an authentic New England tea after which they sat reverently while prayers were said, psalms that had been memorized during the day were repeated, and hymns were sung until bed-time.[26]

Here was no mere religion of form. It was a spiritual crusade measurable not only in meetings and eloquence of testimony but also in emotional depth and profound faith. In all schools the Bible was a required textbook. Morning, noon, or night the presence of the Omnipotent could never be evaded. The very atmosphere was charged with this spirit. Every institution welcomed students regardless of denomination but the simple teachings of Christianity were impressed upon everyone. Naturally the staid New England teacher would not countenance the emotional outbursts characteristic of plantation ritual, and it took some time to instill the quiet order of Christian peace into many breasts. But everywhere efforts were

---

24. *Catalogue of Spelman Seminary*, 1897-1898, p. 41.
25. Brawley, *Morehouse College*, 29.
26. *Atlanta University Bulletin*, November, 1891, p. 2.

made to lead the pupils to the "glorious fountain." During three months of 1885 Spelman recorded no less than sixty conversions.[27] In the first twenty-five years of its history only six college degrees were awarded but 1,291 girls were led into the "Kingdom."[28]

It is justifiable to question just how many of these conversions were genuine. By the 'nineties religious zeal had subsided somewhat in Atlanta University, but a student noted that anyone not displaying sufficient fervor received fewer preferences from the faculty. Obviously, this requirement was bound to promote a certain amount of hypocrisy, and the suspicious student-reporter believed that more pupils were bored in the Sunday services than were willing to admit it. Some went so far in offending the faculty as to attend only those meetings that were compulsory.[29] On the whole, however, religion was a sincere and highly acceptable part of every student's experience. James Weldon Johnson later boasted of gaining an unholy distinction in Atlanta University for his agnostic leanings. His reasoning left his fellows aghast and startled all who believed that card-playing and smoking were inventions of the Evil One.[30]

But if religion was the most vital feature of college life, there were also other activities to promote cultural development. No college, of course, black or white, went long without music. Vocal and instrumental instruction found a place in every curriculum. By 1880 Atlanta University was proud to advertise a collection of four organs and two pianos on which instruction was given, and practice allowed an hour a day for $2 a month.[31] Even before that date the faculty voted to give special attention to musical

---

27. *Spelman Messenger*, March, 1885.
28. *Proceedings of the Slater Fund*, 1905-1906, p. 33.
29. Johnson, *Along This Way*, 80.
30. *Ibid.*, 30.
31. *Catalogue of Atlanta University*, 1880-1881, pp. 23, 24.

teaching in old standard hymns and tunes, a few Sunday School hymns of superior merit, temperance hymns, the best old slave songs and chants.[32] Piano recitals and concerts were common in most places. Choirs poured forth the entrancing melodies of the classics as well as the sombre strains of devotional songs. Brass bands blared martial tunes and even Georgia State Industrial College was favored with $140.45 from the legislature for a set of band instruments.[33] At Spelman the girls made revengeful thrusts at their white masters of the South by marching out of chapel to the victorious bars of "Marching Through Georgia."[34]

Even more notable than music was the quantity of oratory and debate that emanated from the many literary societies on every campus. Students roared and flung their arms with all the zeal of a parliamentary struggle. In Atlanta University the Ware Lyceum and the Phi Kappa Society battled for polemical supremacy. In 1880 the Atlanta Baptist Seminary organized the Ciceronian Lyceum. The Young Men's Literary Association rose primarily to rival it. At Morris Brown similar societies reared eloquent heads, one named Gaines and the other Florida Grant. Even at Gammon, ministerial students orated and debated over the theological, literary, and moral issues of the universe. At Georgia State Industrial College the "Greeks" joined hands and tongues with the Philosophian Society for the lower branches, and Phi Kappa for the proud orators of the college department. Not to be outdone, the girls organized the Phyllis Wheatley Lyceum to promote literary and physical culture pursuits.

An endless stream of similar societies rose and fell in all the colleges. Indeed, oratory and debating were serious

---
32. Minutes of the Faculty of Atlanta University, October 8, 1878.
33. Minutes of the Faculty of Georgia State Industrial College, April 23, 1896, p. 89.
34. *Spelman Messenger*, January, 1892.

matters. In the earliest years subjects were of a sombre hue involving history and the problems of the race. At the Atlanta Baptist Seminary students argued such topics as Migration to Africa, The Pulpit versus the Bar, Columbus versus George Washington for Praise, and Benedict Arnold versus Aaron Burr for Blame.[35] Later other subjects became more popular and included woman suffrage, coeducation, American literature, politics, and the ever-present race problem. During commencement week of every year the rhetorical fanfare reached its fullest flower. At the first commencement of Georgia State Industrial College in 1892, the main feature was a bout between the conflicting educational theories of the day, "Resolved; That in the present stage of their development the colored people need men with an industrial more so than men with a classical education." Apparently feeling their lonesomeness, the boys resolved further, "That young ladies should be admitted to the Georgia State Industrial College."[36] The following year it was resolved: "That the annexation of the Hawaiian Islands to the United States is desirable."[37] And a year later it was argued: "That Toussaint L'Ouverture . . . was a greater statesman and general than Napoleon Bonapart."[38] Commencement at the Atlanta Baptist Seminary in 1881 produced the full program of six classical declamations, one debate, and three orations.[39] In Atlanta University Henry Lincoln Johnson spent his wrath on the manual training he detested by debating violently against it. The celebration of holidays, especially Emancipation Day, was occasion

---

35. Brawley, *Morehouse College*, 120-121.
36. Minutes of the Faculty of Georgia State Industrial College, October 11, 1892, p. 41; *Savannah Tribune*, June 4, 1892.
37. Minutes of the Faculty of Georgia State Industrial College, March 21, 1893, p. 49.
38. *Ibid.*, March 27, 1894, p. 64.
39. Brawley, *Morehouse College*, 49.

for the full flight of speech. Although political discussions and demonstrations were discouraged in most places, Atlanta University allowed such enthusiasm to run its course once every four years as Republican presidents were elected. The victory of Benjamin Harrison in 1888 was celebrated by a torch light procession led by a brass band, which the students followed around the campus. Boys dressed in plug hats and loud clothes exhausted themselves in the making of speeches, the waving of brooms, and the beating of skillets.[40]

In a less dramatic way, public examinations once or twice a year provided an outlet for student energy. Visitors, both white and black, came to inspect the grounds and buildings and attend the oral exercises. At Spelman a "Temperance Day" was celebrated wherein girls were examined for their knowledge of the "nature and effects of alcohol and a hearty determination to avoid it," while the exercises were interspersed with "lively temperance songs and recitations."[41] Students from the country at Georgia State Industrial College formed themselves into a Farmers' Association to study farming and foster the agricultural spirit.[42] Nowhere, however, did dramatics catch a foothold to any extent until after the turn of the century. The theatre, if not an invention of the devil, was an evil to be frowned upon in the early days. But what was once a sin gradually ceased to be so, and the drama was taken in as cultural blessing. Shakespearean plays reached the boards of Atlanta University under the inspiration of Mrs. Alonzo F. Herndon of the faculty. In 1905 Atlanta Baptist College began a notable tradition of classical productions with *Julius Caesar*.

While these activities were filling the already crowded hours of student life, some students spent their talents

---
40. *Atlanta University Bulletin*, December, 1888.
41. *Spelman Messenger*, May, 1885.
42. *Catalogue of Georgia State Industrial College*, 1901-1902, p. 9.

in such literary pursuits as school papers. The bulletins and early advertising sent into the North in the early days had not been student publications. But during the 'nineties the urge to write expressed itself in the establishment of papers and magazines in nearly every college that had a printing press. At Clark the *Courier* was got out twice monthly by faculty and students. Morris Brown issued *The Aurora*. In 1895 students and teachers in Atlanta University began *The Scroll*, a serious paper with stories and articles on affairs of the college and the problems of the race. Students in the Baptist seminaries combined on *The Athenaeum* wherein questions were expounded concerning Y. M. C. A. Work, The Art of Teaching, Student Life at Chicago, The Pressing Needs of the Negro, and like serious topics. And by the 'nineties the girls at Spelman had got their hands into the pages of the *Messenger* with articles ranging all the way from the "Story of the Sweet Potato" to "The Effect of Oxygen on the Human System." Short stories pointing a moral made popular reading. Jokes and the light humor of the twentieth century, of course, found no welcome in these pages. Yet intellectual curiosity of a high order was evident in articles on history, education, and college affairs.

It was not until the second generation of crusaders took the helm that athletics were admitted to any school. By 1889 Bumstead saw fit to indulge his wards with baseball, and the fad spread quickly to all colleges. In 1896 football was introduced with games against Tuskegee and Claflin.[43] During the late 'nineties, the Atlanta Baptist College announced that a gymnasium had been set up in the lower story of the laundry, a cubby-hole thirty feet square, and it merely awaited the generosity of friends to provide equipment.[44]

---

43. Adams, *Atlanta University*, 104.
44. *Catalogue of Atlanta Baptist College*, 1898-1899, pp. 7-8.

Although these physical arts seeped into most of the schools, they were tolerated more than encouraged by the faculty. There was no coin in the school purse for novelties of this sort even where the Puritan masters sanctioned sports. But students took to athletics like ducks to water, dressing their best on Saturday for the afternoon games of football and baseball. Here once a week the hand of discipline relaxed and students were allowed to vent their muscular tension in shouts and screams.

During the summer months the great body of normal and college students went forth to teach in the common schools of the state. Even in its first years, Spelman sent out between two and three hundred girls a season.[45] All the schools participated. The work was not easy, especially in the early days when county boards of education looked suspiciously at the rise of Negro education. Salaries ranged from $25 to $50 a month, but they were not always paid, sometimes not more than half the sum being given when the job was done.[46] Any student suspected of fostering ideas of social equality and civil rights was speedily purged of his iniquities or packed out of the country. Threats of violence were usually enough to disperse such summer teachers; or if the student persisted, a little man-handling or the burning of the schoolhouse were convincing arguments for them to mend their ways.[47] It was in this wise that R. R. Wright, while teaching in Hannahatchee, Georgia, in 1875 received an invitation from the Ku Klux Klan to "leave the county in 24 hours or we will give your d--n carcass to the buzzards, because we understand you are in favor of the Civil Rights Bill."[48] But such action was not universal. Even the students sent out from

---
45. *Catalogue of Spelman Seminary*, 1886-1888, p. 36.
46. *Atlanta University Bulletin*, March, 1895.
47. *Ibid.*, June, 1890.
48. Letter from R. R. Wright to P. N. Chase, August 21, 1875 (in Atlanta University Library).

Atlanta University were urged to eschew politics and spend their efforts to impress the people to buy land and build homes.[49]

Besides conducting the common schools, summer teachers were expected to use their tumble-down shacks for church and Sunday School. They were evangelists as well as educators, going into the country laden with temperance tracts and Sunday School papers, although they carried a volume of Cicero and Virgil for their own edification.[50] Such was their Christian zeal that the students returning to Spelman in the autumn of 1886 reported more than 300 conversions.[51]

The whole scheme of summer teaching was designed, of course, to provide teachers for the rural schools and at the same time provide students an opportunity to earn money to continue their education. But as the colleges turned out greater numbers of regular teachers and the school system of the state became stabilized, the practice ceased to be a necessity and was discontinued.

Over all this college life lay the stern hand of discipline. The purifying codes of early monasteries, of the Reformation, of Puritan England, of New England divines, of American revivalists, and of Victorian reformers contributed to a complex network of rules which hounded the dusky students of the South from dawn to moonlight. And to make the laws complete, the black codes of the slave days and of Reconstruction were dipped into for restrictions to keep rebellious souls out of trouble among themselves or beyond the bounds of the campus. Such was the temper of the day. Even white students were dangerous in the early days of our Republic and many a faculty member in distinguished seats of learning had

---

49. *Servitude to Service*, 178.
50. *Atlanta University Bulletin*, June, 1883.
51. *Spelman Messenger*, November, 1886.

experienced the democratic ruthlessness of their pranks. In all colleges of whatever color a reign of law was considered necessary. If white boys took a delight in dumping pails of water on the heads of their masters, what might be expected of black boys? The evils of human "cussedness" were soul-trying to the crusaders from the North country and it was not to be expected that they came otherwise than armed with the laws of their own schools. Nor was it odd that they added rules to cover the weaknesses of slave culture, a culture in which morality, responsibility, and staunch character were said to have no part. The Negro was a child to be made a man. And it was because of this that a spirit of affectionate paternalism was put into the book. This feeling of moral obligation was the difference between the codes of the white and black schools.

The rules were similar in all the colleges in Georgia. Students were forced to attend daily prayers and public worship on Sunday. Boarding pupils were not allowed to leave the campus without permission, and after six o'clock at night they were expected to be in a building. No one was supposed to visit another's room without permission. They must not visit friends in the city or receive visitors on the Sabbath. In some cases visitors from the city could be received only with permission from the faculty, and then no more than once a month.[52] Under no circumstances must students leave the campus on Sunday excepting for religious work. It was also urged that no student arrive in the city on the Lord's Day, for the college would not receive him then. In 1883 the faculty of Atlanta University suggested that college students be allowed to leave the campus one evening a month, visit rooms, and to attend one Sunday service a month in the city without asking permission. But this was too novel

---
52. *Catalogue of Central City College*, 1900-1901, p. 7.

a venture and the only suggestion adopted was that allowing the college students to visit one another's rooms.[53] In order to further maintain the spirit of the Holy Day, mail was not distributed until Monday.

Other rules to promote moral strength prohibited students from bringing any spirituous or fermented liquors on the campus, or drinking any such in a barroom or store. In most places students were required to sign a pledge to abstain from all intoxicating drink and tobacco, whether during school or vacations. Nor might they possess or carry a gun, knife, or other deadly weapon, send or accept a challenge to fight a duel or be a second in a duel, possess indecent pictures, read lascivious or irreligious books, swear, lie, be obscene, play unlawful games, quarrel, strike or insult a fellow student or other person, or be disrespectful to their teachers.

To promote good habits, the "law" forbade loud talking during school hours, the reading of newspapers in class, sleeping during study periods, tardiness at recitations, and disorder in the dining hall. All students were required to be in bed with lights out at a prescribed hour. Those in the upper branches were permitted the privilege of studying in their rooms rather than in the study hall, but they were obliged to remain quietly in their rooms and were compelled to study, but not later than the study hour. In 1879 the faculty of Atlanta University made the bold suggestion that college students be given the freedom of coming from their rooms to recitations in pairs, that they be allowed to whisper on the way, and return in the same manner.[54] Promptness was no small matter and to encourage this habit at meals, Atlanta Baptist College took to lock-

---

53. Minutes of the Faculty of Atlanta University, January 2, 1883, p. 199.
54. *Ibid.*, February 4, 1879, p. 148.

ing the doors of the dining hall three minutes after the last bell had rung.[55]

A miscellany of other rules existed. Hazing was unlawful and culprits found guilty were punished swiftly. In most places, students were forbidden to participate in any political activity, meetings, or mass meetings, or to make political speeches. At Georgia State Industrial College the commissioners saw to it that no public speeches of any kind were made unless first read by the faculty, and the faculty, surely, was aware of the grave responsibilities of working for the Empire State.[56] Hunting was not allowed without special permission. Nearly all institutions required one hour free labor a day, and at Savannah students were fined 5c for each hour's absence from appointed tasks.[57] While there was a hide-bound rule forbidding students from receiving boxes of food and provisions from home, pupil and parents were told forcibly not to upset the diet in the dining hall by such sentimental expressions of affection. "Send no boxes of food, without enclosing money for doctor's bills," was the way Clark put it.[58]

For nearly half a century this code marked the straight and narrow path for Negro students in Georgia. The humanitarian leanings of the New England crusaders softened rigorous penalties somewhat, but in the schools where the scepter of authority was wielded by Negroes or the state the parental impulse was brushed aside for the more terrible spirit of the Inquisition. The code lost ground very slowly and remained almost intact until after the first World War. Yet some bars were let down, as ex-

---

55. Minutes of the Faculty of Atlanta Baptist College, April 6, 1903, p. 42.
56. *Catalogue of Georgia State Industrial College*, 1896-1897, pp. 43-49.
57. Minutes of the Faculty of Georgia State Industrial College, February 21, 1893, p. 48.
58. *Catalogue of Clark University*, 1883-1884, p. 30.

emplified in Atlanta University where, by the 'nineties, the faculty satisfied itself by merely frowning when boys and girls were seen walking together on streets outside the campus,[59] or as at Clark where the turn of the century brought larger freedom to male students sixteen and over whose exemplary behavior classified them as "privileged" and allowed them to be off the campus from four to five-thirty P.M. on school days and from two to five-thirty on Saturday.[60]

Dress of the students also came under the lynx eye of Puritanical masters. Boys presented little difficulty, however. Their sombre suits, usually shabby, emulated the ministry and nothing more than this dignity was desired. Yet Georgia State Industrial College saw fit to dress the men in military uniforms. They were dark blue costumes of a heavy wool that cost the students about $8 a suit.[61] But this example was not followed by most of the colleges. On the other hand, the love of finery among the girls offered a greater problem. Under the headline of a sensation the *Savannah Advertiser* of 1872 pointed a mocking finger at Atlanta University where the "*creme de la creme*" of colored female society displayed stimulating costumes. "They dress in the highest styles of fashion, wear the highest bustles in the city, and where beneficent nature has obliterated the spindles of niggerdom by a liberal supply of calk, display an immensity of leg with a liberality that may justly be termed profusion. These gushing creatures, *en passant*, are taught the highest branches, including dancing, French and 'pyahner.' "[62]

But this charge was downright ridiculous. To the missionary of that day dancing was hardly less a vice than

---

59. Minutes of the Faculty of Atlanta University, October 8, 1890, p. 274.
60. *Catalogue of Clark University*, 1903-1904, p. 17.
61. *Catalogue of Georgia State Industrial College*, 1901-1902, p. 44.
62. *Savannah Advertiser*, June 2, 1872.

STUDENTS AND TEACHERS 141

adultery. And as for the fashions in dress, even the earliest catalogues proclaimed that finery would not be allowed.[63]

The faculty in any school had no intention of permitting their poverty ridden charges to spend money on any but the plainest and simplest of garments. Everywhere dark clothes were prescribed for daily wear. The laundering of white dresses was considered too expensive. Girls at Spelman were allowed the luxury of white waists with dark skirts on Sunday, while at Clark, white dresses could not be worn between November first and April fifteenth, or during the remainder of the year excepting at public entertainments.[64] Silks, velvets, nets, georgettes, chiffons, or satins were banned at all times. Spelman required students to bring with them dark wash dresses, dark petticoats, dark aprons, dark skirts, one pair of high shoes, and strong cotton stockings.[65] French-heeled shoes and thin, gayly colored hose were forbidden. Jewelry was evidence of evil spirits and anything beyond a simple pin or ring was not countenanced.

The observance of this multitude of rules was not difficult for the majority of those ignorant folk who went to the schools in the earliest years. With those Freedmen, accustomed to generations of slave discipline, good conduct was still a matter of submission to the white man. They knew no other way. White teachers marveled at their pupils' openness to suggestion, their willingness to work for moral development, and their submissiveness to authority under kindness and confidence.[66] Docility was a habit learned in the days of slavery.

But neither the zeal nor laws of the crusaders were successful in completely stamping out the rebellious spirit

---
63. *Catalogue of Atlanta University*, 1873-1874, p. 27.
64. *Catalogue of Clark University*, 1886-1887, p. 36.
65. *Catalogue of Spelman Seminary*, 1913-1914, p. 14.
66. Mayo, *Southern Women*, 98.

of mankind or dimming the attractiveness of vice. Punishment of the guilty usually followed mild forms involving demerits, suspensions, public reprimands, lock-ups, penal labor about the buildings or farm, or, as a last resort, dismissal. While the birch twig continued to be the board of education for tiny children unable to understand the language of logic, whippings had no part in the law of the upper branches. This sparing of the rod, however, was not entirely approved by parents reared in the terror of the plantation. What was good enough for them, apparently, was good enough for their children. The bad conduct of John Turner in Atlanta University in 1876 roused his father to suggestions of punishment as terrible as that any slave ever experienced. While the distressed father beseeched Ware not to expel John, he cried out, "If he comes here, I will beat him to death. . . . I am almost in rags" from trying to educate the children and "for two weeks there has been nothing in my house decent to eat on there [sic] account. . . . Mr. Ware take john and hit him fifty lashes on the bare back, tie him up by the thumbs, feed him on bread and water a month, but if it is possible to save him for heaven do it, my wife is bathed in tears." And if John were expelled, he wailed, "I will try to kill him . . . he is getting mannish, take it out of him by a public whipping. . . . If I was there, I would hit him a hundred lashes."[67]

But the New Englander's stomach for such brutality had long since perished. It was the practice of Atlanta University to give demerits for such misdemeanors as absence from morning prayers or Sunday service, absence from recitations, dropping things on the floor, laughing at others' mistakes at random, leaving the grounds after supper, talking above a whisper in the reading room, or

---

67. Letter from W. M. Turner to E. A. Ware, January 4, 1876 (in Atlanta University Library).

putting in the wash clothes not properly marked.[68] Similar black marks were awarded in most schools for untidiness in dress, disorderly rooms, and bad deportment in classes and dining halls.

Despite the natural docility of the students the dockets of criminal cases that came before the faculty reached enormous proportions over the years. For taking food from the dining halls, girls received not only the benefits of a public reprimand, but in some instances, the additional penalty was imposed of being locked up for two days.[69] In the case of Annie Varnell, only a severe reprimand was inflicted for writing a note to a boy, but George Towns was suspended for two weeks for a similar offense.[70] Suspensions for stealing, smoking, or lying were frequent. In this way the hand of the "law" caught up with two boys who had made off with a chicken from the college farm.[71] Fighting or drawing a knife brought the same penalty of suspension, and despite the rule against weapons, many boys were discovered to be well-armed.[72] Suspension also was meted out to two students who were secretly married, while all those who knew of the engagement or the marriage and concealed it were reprimanded before their fellows.[73] Girls who gossiped and used profane language were humiliated in the same fashion. Absence from grounds beyond the time allowed was punished either by confinement to the campus or by suspension.

During the 'eighties, Atlanta University found it expedient to lock up anyone so rascally as to fight, lie, or receive

---

68. Minutes of the Faculty of Atlanta University, October 24, 1873, p. 309.
69. *Ibid.*, November 13, 1884, p. 213.
70. *Ibid.*, October 12, 1872, p. 58; October 22, 1888, p. 245.
71. Minutes of the Faculty of Georgia State Industrial College, April 1, 1913, p. 237.
72. Minutes of the Faculty of Atlanta University, October 29, 1888, p. 246.
73. *Ibid.*, May 28, 1872, p. 58.

a note from a boy or girl. Even for disorderly conduct in class a boy was locked up and then persuaded to apologize publicly for his crime.[74] In all the schools cases were recorded of cheating on examinations, hazing, indecent talk to girls, and sneaking out at night. The great transgression of dancing in the college chapel also brought culprits to the bar.[75]

For students who failed to respond to these character building penalties, additional labor was found to convince them that, after all, righteousness was the best policy. In one instance, the refusal of a boy to accept a mild punishment resulted in the request that he saw two cords of wood. But the lad could not be induced to abuse himself by such toil and eventually he was forced to accept suspension.[76] At Georgia State Industrial College young William Patterson was set to work on the farm for a week without pay for disobedience and insurbordination.[77] Here also four boys were provided with 100 hours of penal labor for misconduct toward girls.[78]

Even the spread of pernicious ideas among the students was met with discipline. When the boys at Georgia State Industrial College became exasperated with the steward of the boarding department and took it upon themselves to present a petition to the president demanding the steward's removal, the faculty declared that students had no right to organize and anyone attempting such a social revolution would be punished. Even Gammon was forced to keep open a quick eye for evil theories. Anyone there

---

74. *Ibid.*, January 6, 1880, p. 164.
75. Minutes of the Faculty of Georgia State Industrial College, March 3, 1905, p. 356.
76. Minutes of the Faculty of Atlanta University, November 27, 1883, p. 208.
77. Minutes of the Faculty of Georgia State Industrial College, February 8, 1899, p. 151.
78. *Ibid.*, March 11, 1913, p. 233.

STUDENTS AND TEACHERS 145

caught advocating such an idea as anti-prohibition was sent off with indignant haste.

But in spite of this network of rules and zealous teachers, the "spirit of evil" moved about in elusive fashion. Unfortunately few records have been left by the successful criminals of those days who smoked behind the barn or had their tryst of love in the shadows of surrounding forests. Gambling or card-playing of any kind, of course, were inventions of the devil, punishable very often by uncompromising dismissal.[79] Yet James Weldon Johnson successfully eluded the teachers of Atlanta University in many a game of whist or seven-up. With shades drawn, a hat over the keyhole, and the crack under the door chinked, the boys responded to their roguish instincts by a merry night of talk in muffled voices around the gambling table.[80] It was also possible at Atlanta University in those years for boys who had fifteen cents in their pockets to run the gauntlet for a late night snack. After lights were out they took off to the house of old Watson, the college herdsman. His cottage lay in a remote corner of the campus and was known as "Little Delmonico's." The herdsman's wife was a good cook and for fifteen cents in cash, no credit, a supper of fried chicken, biscuits, and milk could be had; and no one ever asked where the milk and chickens came from.[81]

Concern For the Future

Nothing is more significant in the first two generations of Negro college life than the seriousness of the student mind. As the dreams of the forward-looking black man of Reconstruction faded into empty hopes, the status of his race became uppermost. It was not the carefree Negro

---
79. Minutes of the Faculty of Atlanta Baptist College, April 26, 1909, p. 120.
80. Johnson, *Along This Way*, 77.
81. *Ibid.*, 77.

of plantation days who wanted an education. The happy and the indolent remained at home wrenching existence from the soil he knew so well. It was the climber who went to school—and stayed. With the solemn caste of thought of the New England crusader imposed upon him and the low state of his race ever before him, the struggle for freedom and life took on a sombre tone. The race problem was not in the curriculum, but the atmosphere was charged with it. It was talked, debated, written, and orated.[82] The destiny of the student was wrapped in it. While the playing of pranks or crimes or games took moments, the currents of the sober mind consumed hours.

But to most students college life provided the most pleasant existence they had ever known. Here was the sincere friendship of white men and women who, as teachers and guides, gave confidence and affection in return for obedience and effort. The missionaries were revered to a point of sentimentality. The writings of early students and graduates fairly gush with praise. To those with a philosophical turn, even the long hours of meditation on the status of the race and the seriousness of life produced the pleasure and beauty that attend tragedy.

After leaving the colleges, students scattered from the plains of Texas to the busy cities of the North. Yet most of them remained among their own people of the South. A survey of college graduates made in 1900 showed ninety per cent of them still in Southern states while fifty per cent of those who had come in from the North remained in the warmer clime.[83]

The profession of teaching absorbed most graduates. By 1902 Bumstead noted that sixty per cent of all living normal and college graduates were teachers.[84] Some became

---
82. *Ibid.*, 66.
83. DuBois, *College Bred Negro*, 14.
84. Letter from H. Bumstead to Wallace Buttrick, September, 1902 (in Atlanta University Library).

principals of schools, others rose to be college professors and presidents. The ministry absorbed many.

Few fields of labor beyond these were available to the educated Southern Negro. But the lists of occupations later followed also included a sprinkling of newspaper editors, postal clerks, mail carriers, Y.M.C.A. agents, government employees, bank tellers, and musicians. Industrial colleges turned out some who went into printing, construction, carpentry, brick-masonry, blacksmithing and shoe-making. Certain others went into small businesses for themselves, or became clerks and bookkeepers. The higher professions requiring more study were obviously beyond the reach of the majority, yet some went on to be doctors, dentists, and even lawyers.

The era of materialism soon had its effect. The students who followed those of the first two generations came with different ideals, less for service, and more with the hope of economic equality. It changed the philosophy of college life, produced lighter hearts, lifted athletics to prominence, made the making of money the end and aim of education, stimulated race consciousness, and eventually divided the black race into classes based on wealth and position as distinct as the counterparts of the white world. The spirit of the crusade had all but vanished.

The Teachers

Crusaders from the North began the Negro colleges of Georgia and the South. For a generation they reigned supreme, establishing their law, imposing their ideals, laboring to destroy the philosophy of the South that education should be provided only for the superior few. Their army was small but their influence was great. They spread hope and put heart into millions of black people and spread fear in the camps of white supremacy. Such was the power of their ideas. The Southern dream of an ideal society in which gentlemen of leisure and taste could enjoy the "good life" was laid low. Unwittingly the missionaries were part of the dynamic social theory of progress that had been gathering force for a hundred years. They believed in progress—in the continual improvement in the lot of mankind on this earth by the attainment of knowledge and the subjugation of the material world to the requirements of human welfare. Had they known they were laying the foundations for the age of materialism they would have stopped dead in their tracks, astounded. Their problem was with the soul, earthly and eternal happiness. But the very idea of education for all was a democratic thesis for materialism.

Certainly the pioneers meant well. They struggled through the long days of toil, beset by destitution and opposition, without the comradeship of their own race. And many remained even after their first illusions had been lost.

The crusaders who stayed on formed the nucleus of the second generation. Of the notable quartet in Atlanta University, only Ware had died, and the Baptists had lost President Robert. But a new generation of men and women came on the crest of the second wave. The Negro teacher was among them this time and by the end of the period at the turn of the century all but three colleges were of mixed faculty, and those three—Georgia State Industrial College, Morris Brown, and Central City—were entirely Negro.

All faculties had grown apace. By the end of the century Georgia State Industrial College had grown from three to fourteen members while Atlanta University had increased from six to thirty-odd. Spelman had nearly forty. Expansion elsewhere was similar.

Yet the increase in numbers was not accompanied by more training. The majority of the teachers were not college graduates. They came from academies and normal schools. Of thirty-one teachers in Atlanta University in 1891 the catalogue listed only four with bachelor's degrees, two with master's and one Doctor of Divinity. With four instructors in the college department at Spelman in 1900, only one had a bachelor's degree. In Atlanta Baptist College, two teachers in the upper branches had no degrees. While a shower of master's symbols soon began appearing after faculty names in catalogues, the profusion of honorary degrees given out by the colleges themselves forbids one to take these marks of advancement too seriously. Undoubtedly, some were well earned but time has obliterated the record. The need of high scholarship, however, was not considered pressing in these institutions where the college department was only a minor adjunct to a secondary school. In no institution were men of advanced training able to confine their efforts to college subjects. Normal and high school courses were served by all alike.

But as higher learning got under way as the goal of the colleges, presidents began a search for talent. The quality of faculties was raised by graduate work in Northern universities, and by the end of the century graduates of Harvard, Colgate, Brown, and Toronto were speaking in the classrooms of Atlanta Baptist College. In 1889 Myron W. Adams appeared at Atlanta University as the first Doctor of Philosophy to teach the Georgia Negro. Later DuBois came with the same title.

The admission of Negroes to the faculty was a significant note. The use of advanced students to assist in teaching was universal in the early days. In 1874 William E. Holmes began instruction in this fashion at Augusta Institute and remained on the faculty for a quarter of a century. In Atlanta University Edgar J. Penny taught gardening for a year after graduation in 1876 and four years later, Rebecca Massey came from Oberlin to teach music. But the first colored teacher of college grade subjects there was John Young, who taught Latin and mathematics from 1886 to 1890. He was followed by George Towns, and in 1897 W. E. B. DuBois appeared on the scene.

In 1876 William Crogman began a career at Clark destined to lift him into prominence among Negro scholars. Born in the West Indies in 1841, he grew to follow the sea and began his education in Massachusetts at the behest of the mate of his vessel who saw more than brawn in the dusky sailor. It mattered little that he was already a man of twenty-five. Within ten years he had wandered South and in 1876, at the age of thirty-five, had found himself in the first class to graduate from the college department of Atlanta University. From there he went to Clark and taught for forty-five years, serving as president meanwhile, in a day of white presidents.[85]

Yet at Paine the admission of a Negro to the faculty caused an uproar. When in 1888 President Walker recommended the name of John Wesley Gilbert, the faculty revolted. But Gilbert was a notable man. He had studied at Brown and had even found his way to the ancient cities of Greece where the classics he loved had once flourished. As soon as the trustees of Paine approved the appointment, the faculty split in twain. To one teacher the evil of the "revolutionary measure" constrained him, as a respectable white man, to hide himself, and he resigned in a flurry of indignation.[86] But the decision of the trustees held. By 1894 Spelman included three colored women. Drawn into the current, Atlanta Baptist College hired John Hope, John Hubert, Benjamin Brawley, and C. H. Wardlaw. And within a few years the colored teachers

---
85. Stowell, *Methodist Adventures*, 73-75.
86. Peters, "Geo. Williams Walker" (a leaflet issued by Paine College, n.d.).

at both the Baptist College and at Clark outnumbered the white ones.

Naturally, the Negro colleges of the day were not conducive to scholarly achievement. Even had men existed with training and the will to plumb the riddles of the universe, conditions would have given the urge scant nourishment. With almost no equipment, libraries that were only poor imitations, and the burden of long hours of teaching augmented by the duty of playing father to the students, there was neither means nor time for creative effort. Thus it was not until late in the second generation that anything was done at all. Yet five men, all of them Negroes, eventually were able to lay claim to being creative scholars. At Gammon was J. W. E. Bowen, sometime president of the seminary, a doctor of philosophy, and historian. With such works as *The Struggle for Supremacy Between Church and State in the Middle Ages* and *The History of the Education of the Negro Race* to his credit, he entered the distinguished chambers of the American Historical Association with acceptable dignity. Essays and sermons flowed from his pen—social, philosophical, and religious. Amidst the rise of race consciousness that was stirred by the Populists, Bowen delved into the background of the black man with such articles as "The American and African Negro," "The Comparative Status of the Negro at the Close of the War and Today," "University Addresses," and "Plain Talks to the Colored People of America."[87]

Across the road at Clark, William Crogman was working in the same vein. He wrote sparingly, but a collection of addresses issued in 1896 as *Talks for the Times* established him as a prophet of progress. Believing in the brotherhood of man he struck boldly at the white world that refused to accept the colored man of learning and culture

---

87. D. W. Culp, ed., *The Twentieth Century Negro Literature* (Naperville, Ill., 1902), 29.

as a social equal. He opposed all teachers, white or black alike, who reminded the Negro race of its lowliness. He preached self-reliance and independence as the only paths to manhood and responsibility. Taking a cue from Henry Grady's doctrine of a New South, Crogman became a champion of the New Negro, advertising the virtues in the background of the race, popularizing achievements, and chiding all his fellows who refused to be spurred onto the rolling wheel of progress.

Of less note was the work of Charles H. Turner and John Wesley Gilbert in the realm of natural science. But despite handicaps of poor laboratory equipment Professor Turner sent out from Clark a commendable array of articles on biology that found a haven in the pages of the nation's learned journals.[88] While the fame of Gilbert at Paine rested mostly on his success as an inspiring teacher of classical languages, he also found time for excursions into archaeology. During the 'nineties he supervised excavations in ancient Eretria and also joined with John Pickard in drawing maps of the once-proud cities that stood over the blue waters of the Mediterranean.[89]

By far the greatest contributions of creative labor, however, came from the fertile imagination of William Edward Burghardt DuBois. Born three years after Appomattox in Great Barrington, Massachusetts, he had a mixture of French, Dutch, and Negro, but "thank God, no Anglo-Saxon," blood. He was a product of the second generation of colored students, getting a bachelor's degree from Fisk in 1888 and another from Harvard two years later. Then with a master's degree from Harvard he sojourned in Germany two years, returning afterward to the old Yard at Cambridge to win recognition and a doctorate with an exhaustive dissertation on the *Suppression of the African*

---
88. *Ibid.*, 163.
89. *Ibid.*, 191.

Slave Trade. By the time he appeared at Atlanta University his academic ability had again been proved by a sociological study for the University of Pennsylvania on the *Philadelphia Negro.* He was only twenty-nine. Immediately he set to work as the editor of the sociological studies already begun as *Atlanta University Publications.* Exacting in his demands and impatient with stupidity and indolence, he was at first anything but popular with his students. But in short order his pupils became proud of him.[90] In 1903 DuBois issued a collection of fourteen essays titled *The Souls of Black Folk* that ran through thirteen editions and established him in the ranks of American literary artists. In this work he banged away at the white world that suppressed his race. Venom was in his pen. He warred on the blood and ashes of what he considered injustice. For less, many Negroes had been strung up, and it was a miracle that this heretic went unmolested in the hotbed of Atlanta's wrath that knew how to express itself in race riot. But escape he did, and such writing was only a prelude to eloquent outbursts that were to make DuBois the patriarch of American Negro scholars.

The social life of the teachers had changed but little over the years. The same ostracism experienced by the first teachers was felt by missionaries of the second wave. Firm in their belief that they would not be accepted by Southern whites, the crusaders came resigned to a life apart and looked only for the companionship of one another. Even Walker at Paine, Southern minister and man of culture though he was, serving the Methodists of his own land, encountered hostile thresholds. Congregations walked out when he rose to preach in churches about Augusta. And many Negroes doubted the motives of this man of the master class who extended them the hand of friend-

---

90. Adams, *Atlanta University*, 61.

ship.[91] For all their high breeding, the Bumsteads and Adamses found only one door in Atlanta open to them, that of a German family. While some few joined white churches of their sects, most teachers attempted no social inroads. Atlanta University continued to maintain its own church. There the leading social event of every week was a Saturday night gathering of teachers and their families at the home of the president. There social equality was still a fundamental principle of life. Students and teachers ate the same fare at the same tables. But on other campuses the color line was noticeable. At Spelman teachers ate and lived apart, and in the Atlanta Baptist College, William Holmes had his own cottage off the campus, visiting or being visited on business, but intermingling in no way on a social basis.

---

91. Peters, "Geo. Williams Walker."

PART TWO

Transition to the Modern College

CHAPTER VIII

Decadence and the Upturn

IT WAS APPARENT TO MANY OBSERVERS THAT NEGRO EDUCAtion turned into the new century under the handicap of wavering aims. Assuredly, the Negro college in Georgia had risen steadily from the rickety corn-cribs of Reconstruction and the days of the "Blue-Back Speller." A promising system of universal education had spread over the entire state. But there was no doubt that uncertainty of purpose was hurting this progressive looking movement. Certainly the experiment to bring about racial equality had failed and the Negro had been stripped of the ballot. The final bitter scene was staged in the gubernatorial fight of 1906 between Clark Howell and Hoke Smith wherein political mud was slung amidst the pitiless "nigger howl." The year culminated in race riot in Atlanta. Although the militia was called out to suppress this mob terror and throw up protecting barricades about the colleges, it was a frightening experience for the entire race. The few who had gathered in Atlanta University before the fall term huddled in South Hall at night and kept up a fearful watch.[1] And the end of violence was not yet. In

---

1. Adams, *Atlanta University*, 37.

the years that followed the confidence of the rural Negro was shaken by further lynchings, a slaughter of nine at Palmetto, abuse for even trivial offenses. What hope was there for the rural Negro? Beset with poor police protection, bad roads, and inadequate school facilities, farm hands began a trek to town which in a decade swelled to a pilgrimage.[2] Under these unsettled conditions the Negro college was forced to shift its steps, but it knew not where to turn.

Moreover, there were many other troubles which upset the aims of the colleges. The collapse of the industrial scheme had created doubts in the white mind sufficient to dry up much Northern philanthropy. The rise of mass production, exemplified especially under the masterful hand of Henry Ford, soon showed that hand-training was little good as preparation for factory work.[3] Of course, the conflict between the classical and industrial factions had been more talk than actual conflict. There was no surplus of Negroes able to read Greek, no overcrowded professions. But the war of ideas had shattered the foundations of educational thought, leaving the colleges in confusion.

Additional handicaps to the progress of the colleges lay in the failure of the state to promote sufficiently the lower orders of education. As late as 1910 only 43 per cent of the Negroes between seven and twenty years of age were in school in Georgia and there was no compulsory school law. While illiteracy had dropped tremendously since emancipation, it was still more than 36 per cent for the Negroes of the state. Of the more than four thousand colored teachers in the public schools, 70 per cent had less than an eighth grade education.[4] The state had not even taken pains to provide schoolhouses. As late as 1912, 63

---

2. Jones, *Negro Education*, I, 99.
3. *Journal of Negro Education*, II, 3 (July, 1933). A survey of Negro Higher Education, Yearbook No. II.
4. Jones, *Negro Education*, I, 71.

per cent of the buildings were not owned by public authorities. Most of them were rural churches, lodge halls, and deserted cabins. County boards of education owned but 208 colored schoolhouses worth an average of $166 each, while the 1,544 others privately owned were valued at an average of only $106.[5] In cities like Atlanta and Augusta seating capacity was available in public schools only for a part of the population, and that by holding double sessions morning and afternoon.

The discrepancy between expenditures for the education of blacks and whites had come to the forefront of race discussions and had begot some bitterness. While the average salary for white teachers in the state was no higher than $318 a year, Negroes were forced to be content with the less-than-half salary of $119.[6] Still more repugnant to the colored teacher was the per pupil appropriation for salaries which gave whites $9.58 compared to $1.76 for the Negroes.[7]

But even if elementary education had worn a brighter face in those years, higher learning could not have developed to proper proportions without the high school. Yet the high school was almost a foreign institution to Georgia soil. The early decision to limit state educational efforts to "elementary branches of an English education only" was not repaired appreciably until 1912 when the restriction was removed.[8] True, the turn of the century had brought forward a great secondary school movement backed by the University of Georgia so that by 1914 seventy-eight four-year and a hundred and thirty-two three-year high schools were serving 25,000 pupils. But these were of no use to the Negro. Even at this later date, the high school in Athens and a handful of secondary students

---
5. *Ibid.*, 32-33.
6. *Ibid.*, 34.
7. *Ibid.*, II, 10.
8. Dabney, *Universal Education*, I, 252.

in a trade school in Columbus comprised the only public efforts of this kind in the state for the black race. And in neither public nor private schools was secondary work adapted to the needs of the pupils or well planned to prepare teachers according to the aims of American education of the time.[9] In brief, the whole educational program within the borders of the Empire State in 1910 was so bad that only Mississippi, Alabama, and North and South Carolina ranked below it.[10]

The Negro colleges themselves were at a low ebb of spiritual fortitude. Competition for students and support had produced rivalry unbecoming and harmful to the colleges. So bad was this feeling in Augusta that neither Haynes nor Walker Institutes would send their students to Paine. In Atlanta the fight for supremacy was even more keen. Moreover, trustees were now of little help. The generation of guardians of the new century could not be interested in the crusade of their fathers' humanitarianism. Although prominent names continued to grace the boards of the institutions, they were names only. Many persons allowed their names to be used to satisfy a friend or the head of the college, but there was little concern in management, and it was often difficult to get a quorum for a meeting. Afflicted by such public apathy, Negro education nearly starved to death in the years approaching the First World War. Nor were the relations with Southern whites much better. Atlanta University, particularly, found it difficult to win the good will of the community. The ruthless slashings of DuBois' eloquent pen were naturally resented by the white world. And the University breathed a sigh of relief when in 1910 this radical cockspur packed

---

9. Jones, *Negro Education*, I, 41.
10. *Annual Report from the Department of Education of Georgia*, 1912, p. 29.

his ideas and left. After all, he had become an embarrassing ornament.

Fortunately, it was no secret that Negro education was close to the valley of despair. Peabody agents had sniffed the atmosphere of decadence. The guardians of the Slater Fund had seen the weaknesses of Haygood's plan, which scattered appropriations in driblets among too many institutions; and though the good bishop refused to be called down, declaring he knew more about the education of the Negro race than the whole pack of easy-chair grumblers of the North, efforts made to study the situation in a cool, calculating, accounting method resulted in Haygood's successor, J. L. M. Curry, concentrating the disbursement of funds on the basis of better knowledge. Then in 1900, DuBois had published a survey of Negro college education which had thrown a white light on the problem.

As these reports circulated throughout the land a small army of agents was sent into the field to turn the lights of research on the educational system of the South. But the missionary was not in the ranks this time. In his stead came a body of educators skilled by professional experience in the doctrines of learning. It became a day of associations, interracial boards, and powerful philanthropic funds set up by the tycoons who had reaped rich harvests in the era of fabulous materialism. Carnegie, Rockefeller, Rosenwald, Anna Jeanes, Phelps-Stokes, and Sage were names that symbolized the new century. By their philanthropy a movement was begun that paved the way for the modern system of education. Encouraged, Negro institutions began weaning themselves to the tune of "There, little high school, don't you cry; you'll be a college bye and bye."[11]

The activities destined to draw Negro education out of the "valley" in Georgia were varied. As early as 1901 President Wright of Georgia State Industrial College called

---
11. Trevor Bowen, *Divine White Right* (New York, 1934), 236.

together heads of colleges, and the National Association of Teachers in Colored Schools was organized.[12] In the same year, the Conference on Education in the South shot out a root that became the Southern Education Board designed to stimulate public opinion in favor of all education. A year later John D. Rockefeller dipped a palm into the greatest treasure chest of the age and came up with a million dollars to found the General Education Board for the "promotion of education within the United States of America, without distinction of race, sex, or creed." And so successful was the venture that within seven years $52,000,000 had been turned over to the trustees.[13]

But even before the General Education Board had turned out a rule book of requirements to be met by colleges, the Carnegie Foundation had begun the process of standardization that eventually regimented many colleges and universities of the nation into a straight path. In 1905 agents of the steel king began gathering data and setting standards to determine which institutions merited retirement pensions for professors. Measuring sticks calculated the length of courses, preparation of teachers, entrance requirements, the quality of equipment, income, organization of departments, and criteria of graduation.[14] Colleges that failed to become accredited hurried to meet the standards.

So great was the impact of the new movement to lift education in the South from its low estate that by 1910 it had almost become a campaign. In that year DuBois wound up his work in Atlanta University by a second survey of *The College Bred Negro American*. His findings were not sentimental but they were less harsh than a more comprehensive study soon to follow. Atlanta Baptist College and Atlanta University were given good ratings by DuBois,

---
12. *Crimson and Gray*, (Atlanta University), November, 1928.
13. *The General Education Board, An Account of its Activities, 1902-1914*, pp. 3, 15-16.
14. Jones, *Negro Education*, I, 57.

DECADENCE AND THE UPTURN 163

and Clark and Paine came in fair seconds. But behind them came Georgia State Industrial College, then Morris Brown, limping in with the humiliating verdict of "poor" in every judgment.[15]

Still the influence of Booker T. Washington was abroad trying to bring harmony to the two races. Under the magnetic influence of the brown-faced orator came Julius Rosenwald, made rich in the marts of trade. In 1914 Rosenwald began building schools for the farm children of Alabama, and from there his project spread to crossroads all over the South.

In truth, transition was under way. Even the Federal government joined the campaign. In 1906 the Adams Act increased aid for agricultural experiment stations, in which colleges of agriculture received a share. A year later the Nelson Amendment increased the land-grant appropriations and liberalized conditions on which funds might be used. And in 1914 the Smith-Lever Act gave annual appropriations for agricultural extension teaching in each state.[16] Nor did the government lag in turning the light of research on the land-grant colleges it had established. It was an evil day for the legislators of Georgia, for the survey of 1915-1916 showed the little college in Savannah loitering behind all other land-grant institutions in apparatus, equipment, and library.[17]

The haste of the Negro colleges to climb on the bandwagon of the campaign produced more virile leadership among the institutions. The 1910 survey by DuBois showed defects that called for immediate remedies. Thus in 1913 white and colored representatives from eight colleges, including Benjamin Brawley and Myron W. Adams from Georgia, met in Knoxville and organized the Association

---
15. DuBois, *College Bred Negro American*, 22.
16. B. F. Andrews, *Agricultural and Mechanical Colleges, 1915-1916* (Washington, 1917), 3-4.
17. *Ibid.*, 33.

of Colleges for Negro Youth. At the second meeting a year later standardization was the main theme. While little more was done after the argument than to set a hundred and twenty hours of credit as the requirement for the bachelor of arts degree, discussions mulled over entrance requirements and secondary school ratings, thereby beginning the first serious attempts of the Negro colleges to standardize themselves.[18]

In the meantime, certain of the Negro colleges stood by and watched the progress of the campaign with some fear. The microscope of research revealed weaknesses that were not pleasant to behold. Protests went out from Paine against the judgments passed by DuBois. Pointing a proud finger at its faculty, composed of graduates from the University of Alabama, Emory, Wesleyan, Vanderbilt, Columbia, Brown, the University of Georgia, and Hampton, Paine appealed in vain for a "fairer" verdict.[19]

To Atlanta University the endeavors of the wealthy foundations were a campaign of destruction. Particularly the General Education Board stood before it almost as an evil monster. With its unflinching creed of social equality, the inability of the University to get along with Southern whites nearly brought about its undoing. The Rockefeller Board was in no mood to antagonize the white South by proffering succor to a foe. Moreover, the Board was "perplexed" by the number of Negro colleges in Atlanta. The duplication of work was criticized, and it was considered a wiser precaution to lend permanence to those colleges which possessed sturdy church backing rather than to an institution like Atlanta University, whose props could be knocked out at any moment.[20]

---
18. Johnson, *Negro College Graduate*, 292-295.
19. *Catalogue of Paine College*, 1911-1912, p. 15.
20. Letter from Wallace Buttrick to Edward T. Ware, November 6, 1907; H. Bumstead to Edward T. Ware, July 15, 1916 (in Atlanta University Library).

DECADENCE AND THE UPTURN 165

But the problem was deeper than that. It was quite natural that the oil czar, stout Baptist that he was, should favor Baptist institutions. With his Board led by Dr. Wallace Buttrick, who was not only a Baptist but a representative of the American Baptist Home Mission Society and a trustee of Spelman as well, the colleges of the church were in high favor. Under this situation the rivalry of Spelman and Morehouse (the name to which Atlanta Baptist College was changed in 1913) with Atlanta University became sharper. An attempt at coordination between the three schools in 1908 failed utterly.[21] By 1912 the hitherto prosperous University was in such tightened straits that a merger with Fisk seemed the only solution. But the proposal to abandon the costly plant and move to Nashville was more than the trustees could stand and twice it was voted down.[22]

The result was that the competition between Atlanta University and the Baptist colleges continued. To Bumstead the condition was untenable, calling for battle. But no longer at the helm, the aged gentleman sat in the confines of New England retirement on his Carnegie pension, sending a stream of letters to his successor. A proposal to make the University solely a school for teacher training brought forth fiery objections from Bumstead. And when the new president of Morehouse had the temerity to suggest that the University become a technological school, the old crusader became enraged. To Bumstead all such suggestions were malicious attempts to give Atlanta University the "bum's rush" out of education.[23] Writing with old time missionary fervor, he exhorted his successor to remember the ideals of the founders, to maintain the vision of Edmund Asa Ware and train leaders for the larger en-

---
21. Adams, *Atlanta University*, 67.
22. *Ibid.*, 67.
23. Letter from H. Bumstead to Edward T. Ware, July 15, 1916 (in Atlanta University Library).

deavors of Negro life. To do otherwise would be selling a birthright.[24] After begging on its knees for fourteen years at the door of the General Education Board with no avail, thought Bumstead, it was high time the University got busy and raised a large endowment before the other colleges beat it to it.[25]

But the spirit in Atlanta was less heated. To the presidency of Atlanta University had come Edward Twitchell Ware, son of the founder and one of the few children of crusaders who had returned South to take up their parents' labors. A graduate of Yale in the class of 1897, he had spent several years raising money for the college in its darkest days. He was blessed with the foresight of his father, knew the value of compromise, and wished to antagonize no one. At his side, moreover, was the staunch support of Myron W. Adams who, as dean of the University, wanted the policy of bitter rivalry to be changed to a spirit of cooperation.[26]

As this struggle was going on for the favor of the wealthy, a survey of conditions in Negro education was being made that was to revolutionize the whole system of Negro education. The research of the philanthropists and of DuBois had been limited, telling little of the merits of these institutions of the South into which $3,000,000 was being put annually. The need for a "Who's Who" of schools was self-evident. The court conviction of a colored man out of Brunswick, Georgia, who for seven years toured the country armed with letters from prominent men and collected money for a mythical "Naval Industrial School for Colored Youth," was only a sample of the fraud possible in indiscriminate benevolence.[27]

---

24. *Ibid.*, July 27, 1916.
25. *Ibid.*, July 22, 1916.
26. Letter from M. W. Adams to Edward T. Ware, September 5, 1916 (in Atlanta University Library).
27. Jones, *Negro Education*, II, 1.

DECADENCE AND THE UPTURN

Accordingly, the Phelps-Stokes Foundation proceeded to bring order out of the chaos. This Foundation had been established by the will of Mrs. Caroline Phelps-Stokes of New York in 1910. Finding itself non-plussed in the distribution of its aid, the Fund joined hands with the United States Bureau of Education and immediately set about an elaborate survey, consuming three years of labor at an expenditure of more than $46,000.[28] At last in 1917 the findings of the survey were published by the Federal Bureau of Education in two ponderous volumes. Nearly every colored institution in the nation, public and private, had been visited from one to three times. The staff had probed into plants, equipment, faculties, students, curriculum, departments, apparatus, policies, income, expenditures, accounting systems, methods of control, organization, location, and the needs of the states and local communities. Hardly a stone was unturned.

At first sight of the report colleges were dismayed, for judgments were harsh. Only Fisk and Howard were classed as colleges. The remainder of institutions that for years had prided themselves on being colleges and universities were classed as secondary schools, and many of those were of doubtful merit. To many the report was a downright attempt to destroy Negro education by smothering it under ridicule.[29] Many leaders of Negro education were surprised and awakened.

The verdict on Georgia was comparable with most states, and in some cases better. Institutions were classified according to groups beginning with colleges at the top, in which Georgia failed to appear. In the second group comprising secondary schools with less than 10% of the enrollment in college courses, Atlanta University and

---
28. *Twenty Year Report of the Phelps-Stokes Fund, 1911-1931* (New York, 1932), 106.
29. Johnson, *Negro College Graduate*, 295-296.

Morehouse appeared. While the curriculum and the thorough work of the faculty of Atlanta University came in for high praise, the survey recommended that teacher training be made the central work of the school and that manual training, gardening, and agriculture be given greater attention; and college work should be carried on in cooperation with other schools to avoid duplication and small classes.[30]

At this, the rage of Horace Bumstead was almost boundless. With the years closing about him he proclaimed that the university of his love was as good as Fisk any day. Why, even the normal course was of college grade![31] But Edward T. Ware was in the presidency, looking at the ideal of the early small college with less respect than his predecessors. The Phelps-Stokes verdict failed to excite him and he shook his head sadly in approval that the report was true. Atlanta University was not, after all, a university![32]

Morehouse also was commended as one of the higher ranking Negro institutions of the South, thorough and devoted in its work. But there, too, the school had tried to extend itself beyond its powers. The training of ministers and teachers should be its aim. Courses should be strengthened in the physical sciences, and practical arts should be emphasized to promote the economic and social welfare of the race. College work should be done with the other colleges.[33]

Below these in the third group were ranked Clark, Morris Brown, and Paine, secondary schools making feeble attempts to teach a few collegiate subjects with neither

---
30. Jones, *Negro Education*, II, 215.
31. Letter from H. Bumstead to T. J. Jones, November 9, 1917 (in Atlanta University Library).
32. Letter from Edward T. Ware to H. Bumstead, December 17, 1917 (in Atlanta University Library).
33. Jones, *Negro Education*, II, 219-220.

teachers nor equipment for efficient work.[34] In all the state only 149 Negro college students could be located. Yet Georgia was exceeded in the nation only by Tennessee and the District of Columbia. The teaching of trades and vocations, especially farming, in a state 80 per cent agricultural was perpetually suggested. Only Georgia State Industrial College was equipped to teach industries and farming beyond the usual round of home economics and manual training. And even there the catalogue was brazen enough to announce that "work in this department in no way intereferes with prosecution of the regular literary studies."[35] Agricultural instruction was fairly nil. The failure of Gammon to make provision for the study of rural problems in the preparation of ministers also was noted. Yet a liberal (arts and sciences) college education was defended in concentrated form at strategic centers for the education of teachers, physicians, and leaders of moral uplift. For a better distribution of facilities it was recommended that Georgia State Industrial College move to a more central part of the state, and to relieve the congestion of Atlanta, Morris Brown should carry out its intention of shifting to Macon. While Howard and Fisk should develop as universities for the upper reaches of the race, college centers should be concentrated in a few cities, such as Atlanta, Richmond, and Marshall, Texas. The rivalry in Atlanta should be destroyed and the plethora of ineffective college departments should be federated on the Toronto University plan of affiliation. Institutions of lesser note, bogged down in group three, should be developed into junior colleges. Such were the main recommendations.

Here was direction for the future. Out of these examinations into the ways of education came the plans by which the institutions groped their way through the transition

---
34. *Ibid.*, I, 59.
35. *Ibid.*, II, 200-201.

first from secondary schools of uncertain status into embryonic colleges, emerging finally, in a later period, into acceptable institutions of higher learning. The rise of the great philanthropic funds, research, widened public interest, and new blood—all these set the stage for the educational renaissance that was in the offing. But before the plans of the Phelps-Stokes survey could be realized, the First World War had begun and it was not until after that great drama was over that the suggestions of the surveys could be carried out.

A Few Signs of Progress

As the forces of widened educational interest and plutocratically blessed investigations were clearing the path for the oncoming rise of the modern college, the Negro institutions themselves were looking forward. Undoubtedly advances were negligible. In fact, the era between 1905 and 1919 was the most passive period on the colored campuses of Georgia. But here and there a few signs of progress were visible.

In 1903 Paine Institute had centered its gaze on the future by changing its title to Paine College. Ten years later Atlanta Baptist College found a name to praise and christened itself Morehouse in honor of the Reverend Henry Lyman Morehouse of New York, benefactor and Corresponding Secretary of the American Baptist Home Mission Society. New blood also appeared. The retirement of Bumstead, of course, had brought young Edward Twitchell Ware to the presidency of Atlanta University. The retirement of George Sale from Morehouse the year before, 1906, had lifted John Hope to the presidency. But being the first colored head of the college was not Hope's only distinction. A Georgian, born in Augusta in the chaos of Reconstruction in 1868, his life was an American success story. As a boy he struggled for an education, working his way, and was in the first college class at Paine. But his star rose higher, taking him to Worcester Academy where he jumped over the barricade of his color to become editor of the student monthly, class historian, and commencement speaker. At Brown University, too, he continued his success by giving the class oration at graduation in 1894. From then on he taught in Baptist schools, finally emerging as the head man in Atlanta. His slogan became "A Greater Morehouse." As his chief aide, Hope selected Benjamin Brawley, a graduate of Morehouse, who after study at Harvard and the University of Chicago returned to his alma mater to become professor, dean, and historian. It was these two who developed a better curriculum and raised Morehouse to the high standards that previously had been sadly lacking. In 1910 Dean Lucy Hale Tapley, of New England origin, ascended to the presidency of Spelman. And a year later Morris Brown also was served with new blood in the election to the presidency of W. A. Fountain. Paine tried three different presidents, while the turnover at Clark went on as usual until the trustees settled on Henry Andrews King, who remained for more than the usual span of years.

Advances were noted in the rise of admission requirements also. Atlanta University increased its high school course from three to four years. Clark and Morris Brown began dropping elementary grades. By 1914 both Atlanta University and Morehouse were demanding four years of high school or the equivalent of fifteen units required in standard institutions for admission to the college department. In these institutions and at Spelman, the same requirements were held for admission to the Higher Normal or Teachers' Professional course.

In all places curricula were revised to provide more freedom by the adoption of the elective system. In accord with the DuBois study of 1910, ancient languages suffered mortally while French, German, English, history, sociology, and the natural sciences were promoted. Under Hope at Morehouse, the elective system developed quickly, and to a lesser degree the idea spread to all colleges.

The period also saw greater interest in the past civilization of the Negro. With the social studies of Atlanta University going on until cut short by lack of funds in 1917, race consciousness and pride found expression in regular college courses. At Spelman and Morehouse, Brawley began a course on Negro American history in 1912. Other colleges followed the example, while Atlanta University offered several courses in both the history and social life of the black race. Even Gammon saw fit to come down to earth by relaxing its requirements of Greek and Hebrew in favor of the English Bible and the English language in courses designed to meet current needs of the colored masses.

The liberalizing spirit of the young century was manifest also in the student body. While the reign of law continued to regulate the twenty-four hours of every day, a certain relaxing of the sceptre permitted older students more freedom of behavior. By 1907 the faculty of Atlanta University was giving college students the privilege of being off the grounds two afternoons per month in addition to the usual Friday night holiday.[36] Two years later it was recorded that college students were not confined to their rooms or grounds at all, and that they, and they only, might use the front door of Stone Hall.[37] Even girls partook of the new liberalism and those in the college department were soon permitted two short trips a week off campus by day, if the journey had been approved by the preceptress.[38] So, too, religious piety received a setback as the years rolled toward the brink of world catastrophe.

36. Minutes of the Faculty of Atlanta University, January 3, 1907, p. 138.
37. *Ibid.*, March 18, 1909, p. 171.
38. *Ibid.*, February 7, 1911, p. 197.

At Georgia State Industrial College President Wright lamented the indifference of both the faculty and students toward the age-old tradition of public worship.[39] And under the rising temper of war fever, Edward Ware moaned to Bumstead about the spirit of laxity in discipline among the students.[40] At Paine the faculty was dismayed at the insurbordination of the students and noted "stealings, fightings, and gross immoralities" beyond the usual amount.[41]

It was the inevitable change of new times. With the increasing popularity of athletics, the student mind shifted toward the more temporal amusements of the world, and to levity. Football, baseball, basketball, and even track came in for greater emphasis. The religious and moral tone of college magazines and papers gave way to athletic notices and news of the internal affairs of the college. The *Athenaeum* of Morehouse and Spelman became virtually an athletic bulletin ballyhooing the victories of the teams. Choirs were abandoned for glee clubs. In 1911 Kemper Harrell came to the faculty of Morehouse fresh from study in Chicago and Berlin and began a notable career in the development of music at both the boys' and girls' Baptist schools. His glee clubs and orchestras became famous, beginning a vogue of annual tours that brought honor to the institutions. Debating also branched into more popular channels. In 1905 Professor George A. Towns of Atlanta University inaugurated intercollegiate contests with Fisk, later including Howard and other colleges beyond the borders of the state. In 1915 public speaking received an additional impetus with the establishment of the Herndon Prizes, endowed by Alonzo F. Herndon, a colored businessman of Atlanta. Here were signs that the Negro race itself was developing its own upper class and philanthro-

---

39. Minutes of the Faculty of Georgia State Industrial College, September 26, 1913, p. 251.
40. Letter from Edward T. Ware to H. Bumstead, May 13, 1918.
41. Minutes of the Trustees of Paine College, June, 1913, p. 189.

pists. In accord with the liberalizing spirit, the classical orations and declamations of Commencement Week were submerged for exercises in a lighter vein. After 1913 the big feature of commencement at Morehouse became the production of an original comedy reflecting some phase of the college's life.

It was in this period, too, that the Negro members of the faculties became dominant. Everywhere the teaching staffs had grown, being one of the causes of financial duress, yet reducing teaching load and promoting the efficiency of instruction. Between 1905 and 1918 the staff at Georgia State Industrial College increased from 14 to 22 members, while Atlanta University added nearly a dozen teachers. Although the faculties of Gammon, Spelman, and Atlanta University remained predominantly white, the colored membership increased so that by the end of the period the colored teachers throughout the colleges of the state outnumbered the whites 118 to 94.

The worst feature of the college's physical development during this period was the financial strain that ensued as a result of the general public apathy toward Negro education. Paine lost one president after another in the turmoil of a growing debt. At his resignation in 1917 President Atkins sent the trustees into pandemonium by declaring that the Southern Methodist Church was showing no interest in the Negro.[42] Money for teachers' salaries was hard to get. For a short period Clark and Gammon tried to economize by operating under a single president. So bad was the situation at Central City College in Macon that college work was abandoned altogether. When the two Baptist Conventions patched up their split in 1915 (out of which Central City had been born in 1899) the little college was carrying a debt of $25,000. It was even suggested that the property be turned into a home for the

---
42. Minutes of the Trustees of Paine College, January 5, 1917.

DECADENCE AND THE UPTURN 175

aged. By 1918 Atlanta University also had gathered unto itself a debt of $57,000.

But the Negro colleges of Georgia continued looking forward in spite of their difficulties. Under John Hope, Morehouse raised two brick buildings, Sale and Robert halls, at a combined cost of $70,000. The fruits of Carnegie and Rockefeller were delivered to the door. By 1917 Morehouse had $7,000 worth of scientific equipment. The library was enlarged slowly, and gifts of books were recorded from such sources as William Dean Howells, Richard Harding Davis, Edwin Markham, James Whitcomb Riley, and Charles Evans Hughes.[48] In 1917-1918 Spelman completed the Bessie Strong Nurses' Home and the Laura Spelman Rockefeller Memorial Building where household arts were given a rebirth. Paine got its second brick building, Bennett Hall, at a cost of $25,000. Gammon dedicated a refectory. Morris Brown built Flipper Hall, a boys' dormitory, spending $18,000 for it. And both Clark and Georgia State Industrial College came in for new dairy barns. Although Morris Brown and Georgia State Industrial College had suffered from fire, the damage at each place was repaired quickly. The college at Savannah secured, in fact, a second Meldrim Auditorium far superior to the original. Even endowments had increased at some places—by nearly $20,000 at Spelman, by $35,000 at Clark, and by almost $90,000 at Atlanta University.

Out of these movements within the colleges and the force of ideas from without, the pattern for the course of things to come was being shaped. The Negro colleges of Georgia had cut their teeth. Out of one war they had been born. And after the flames from another had died they were to rise to maturity.

---

43. Brawley, *Morehouse College*, 115.

Chapter IX

An Awakening State

Post-War Social Ferment

AMERICA CAME OUT OF THE FIRST WORLD WAR IN 1918 seething with social and intellectual unrest. Inevitably the social order, if constant change may be called order, was being transformed, moving at a faster tempo, becoming more diversified. A great inquiry into the ways of man was being pursued. In all this turmoil society was investigated as never before. Social welfare work that had been struggling for a hundred years as a hobby of humanitarians now became a profession. The social investigators probed into community health, relief, unemployment, crime, education, housing, and living deficiencies of all sorts.

Naturally the racial problem of the South came in for attention. Racial strife had burst forth again. The demands of industry during the war had called the Negro from cotton field to factory, making him more important as a factor in national man power. The swarming of the race into cities was accompanied by the usual problems of disease, crime, and ignorance. Homecoming Negro soldiers seemed no longer content with the dull toil of rural life. Economic possibilities spurred them to increased efforts to compete with white labor. White soldiers returning found black workers in their jobs. Racial consciousness stiffened on both sides; Negro leaders had banded together to guide their people toward economic equality. From the colored press poured hundreds of books, papers, and articles symbolizing a race become vigorous and dynamic. Naturally, the white South was alarmed and again as in earlier periods lynchings became more common, while trade unions discriminated against colored laborers. Abuse, insult, and violence, revealed particularly in the revived mystic order of the Ku Klux Klan, were heaped on the heads of Negroes in many places.

But the incoming tide of social welfare came to the aid of the Negro. Indeed, the Negro had become a powerful social factor, which even the South could no longer neglect. The idea began to flourish that the welfare of the entire South was tied up with the improvement of this race. Better race relations were a necessity. Of course, the foundations for comity had been in the making for years under the hands of such philanthropic funds as Slater, Peabody, Jeanes, Rosenwald, Phelps-Stokes, and the General Education Board, to say nothing of a more liberal attitude among Southern whites.

In the new drive for interracial cooperation, Georgia and Atlanta became the hub of leadership. Here State School Commissioner M. L. Brittain, J. L. Dixon, Fort E. Land, and even the staid pages of the *Atlanta Constitution* had already ceased attempting to prove that the South was fair to the Negro. Injustices of the past were admitted, particularly in the field of public education.[1] Now that a reign of terror was stirring the passions of white labor into another period of violence, other champions appeared. White churches and the press called for a halt in mob law. In Atlanta in 1919 the Commission on Interracial Coopera-

---

1. Walker, "Attitude of Georgia Toward the Education of Negroes," 65-67.

tion was organized. Originally an agency to create favorable conditions for returning Negro soldiers, the Commission spread to become a national influence for conferences between leaders of both races. Other conference groups sprang up like mushrooms. In Columbus, Julian Harris applied the columns of his *Enquirer-Sun* to a battle against racial lynching and injustice, receiving for his pains a Pulitzer prize plus threats from the Ku Klux Klan, and a 20 per cent loss in circulation.[2] And in 1921 Governor Hugh M. Dorsey lashed the perpetrators of malicious deeds with an exposure of 135 cases of mistreatment, lynchings, peonage, exile, and physical cruelty that had been brought to his attention within the two years of 1919-1921. He advocated not only a militant public opinion against this inhumanity, but proposed as well that the full strength of law be adjusted to cope with the outrage.[3]

The Atlanta School of Social Work

In this period of social unrest, a new educational endeavor was born in Georgia—the Atlanta School of Social Work. Since 1915 social welfare interest for the Negro had been developing. In 1920 the National Conference of Social Workers meeting in New Orleans stressed the need of trained colored workers to go among their own people. Atlanta was fertile soil for a training experiment, for here was the hub of interracial leadership. Here too were the facilities for Negro social work—the Atlanta Associated Charities, Anti-Tuberculosis Association, Urban League, Leonard Street Orphanage, Neighborhood Union, Gate City Free Kindergarten Association, and a plethora of colored colleges—all eager to cooperate.[4] Inspired by the New Orleans conference, a small group of white and col-

---

2. *Spelman Messenger*, October, 1926.
3. H. M. Dorsey, *A Statement from Governor Hugh M. Dorsey as to the Negro in Georgia* (Atlanta, 1921).
4. *Proceedings of the Slater Fund*, 1920-1921, p. 39.

ored workers returned to Atlanta and, under the parentage of Morehouse College, opened the school. Courses were given in economic and social theory, medical-social problems, social case work, community organization, rural problems, clinic study—and within ten years forty-five courses were available. Begun as college study, admission to the regular curriculum soon demanded the completion of two years of undergraduate work. By the end of the decade nearly all study was related directly to the needs of Negro life—recreation, industrial problems, rural life, crime, housing, and a myriad of social difficulties. The Red Cross, Atlanta Community Chest, individuals, and Northern philanthropic foundations rallied to its support.

In 1927 Forrester B. Washington followed E. Franklin Frazier to the directorship of the school, and a few years later old Quarles Hall on Morehouse campus was turned over to the new enterprise. Quickly the role of headquarters for Negro social work was thrust upon the school. Institutes, round-table conferences, and research investigations were conducted. Surveys were carried on concerning Negro business, industrial opportunities, real estate holdings, and manifestations of racial discord. And out from the school went graduates to become case workers, medical workers, probation officers, Urban League secretaries, settlement residents, institutional managers, day nursery heads, employment secretaries, school attendance officers, government administrators, and workers in education, health societies, religious social service, community centers, travelers' aid bureaus, and Y.M.C.A.'s.

Thus the currents of social change eddying about the country were evident in Georgia's Negro colleges. As the needs of the national order diversified, the educational system of the Republic was drafted into new fields and the public demanded that schools widen their functions to incorporate more than the general tradition of preparing the mind to guide man's soul to the end and aim of life. To study the culture of the ages was not enough. The daily problems of society must be faced and solved. The school became a social laboratory for the study not only of literature, but of masses, of minds, of human behavior. Education, in fact, became one of the most dominant factors of the post-war social renaissance. Schools and colleges sprang into new life overnight. Enrollments doubled and trebled, buildings in stone and marble were virtually flung up, and finances soared on the commercial boom. The effect on the South was immense. The great philanthropic foundations of the North were reorganized, and they energetically supported the project of universal education. Indeed, the state of Georgia had been infected by interracial cooperation; and with Walter B. Hill, Jr., in the saddle as supervisor of Negro schools, the educational system went forward swiftly.

But the picture was not all complimentary to Georgia. Although the Elders-Carswell law, enacted in 1920, compelled local governments to bear more of the burden of educational expense, the state continued to lag near the tail-end in the national march. And it was complained that the whites received most of the benefits that did arise. Even if the per pupil expenditure for colored teachers' salaries rose from $1.76 in 1912 to $5.54 in 1922, it was a pittance compared to the $23.68 given to white teachers. North Carolina gave its colored instructors $15 while even Florida provided $13. As late as 1930 colored leaders were indignant that white children received more than five times the educational expenditure for dusky youngsters. No wonder no more than half the colored population ever passed beyond the second grade of school, said the Negro leaders.

It was the high school movement of the post-war years, however, that provided the most significant impetus to higher education. In 1905 the state had within its borders only twelve public four-year accredited high schools for both blacks and whites. But by 1928, 360 had sprung up.[5] True, white children had nearly eight times as many of these schools as the Negroes; but the 47 colored high schools of 1930 were a far advance from the two of the earlier period. As the steady march of social reform moved on bolstering and creating elementary and secondary schools, colleges found it less and less necessary to continue these lower branches that held them down. At last the college was free from the necessity of preparing its own students.

During the decade of the 'twenties and the early years of the 'thirties every Negro college in Georgia abolished elementary grades. Atlanta University had done this years before and the remainder now followed, leaving the task to the state. Then high school grades were dropped also. In 1924-1925 the college department of Morehouse, for the first time, became larger than the academy. A year later more than half the students of Atlanta University were of college rank. With the establishment of the Booker T. Washington High School in Atlanta in 1924, these colleges gave up the work for good, and in the early 'thirties, Clark, the last of the lot, let secondary education vanish. Georgia State Industrial College responded at the same time. At Paine the process was slower, for not until 1937 was a public Negro high school refounded in Augusta.

THE JUNIOR COLLEGE MOVEMENT COMES TO GEORGIA

Hand in hand with the development of high schools another movement, that of the junior college, began to flourish. It was part of the growing effort to close the gaps of the educational structure, to put an integrated relationship through education from level to level. The Phelps-Stokes survey had advised several nebulous colleges to concentrate on this intermediate effort of junior college

---
5. Webster, "The Georgia Negro's Fight on Ignorance," 18.

work. In fact, certain Negro institutions of Georgia accepted the advice and made sporadic attempts to satisfy their benefactors. Spelman, Morris Brown, and Clark all suffered the junior college idea to take hold in the early 'twenties. But the ambition of these colleges was for the more eminent standard of four-year courses and the experiment was abandoned. But as the doctrine spread successfully throughout the nation, three colored institutions in the rural sections of the state—at Fort Valley, Albany, and Forsyth—took the hint and labored toward providing two years of college study beyond their secondary tradition.

At Fort Valley the High and Industrial School became the Fort Valley Normal and Industrial School. It was an institution that seems never to have been founded, growing out of small town schools that opened and closed at irregular intervals from the days of Reconstruction to the turn of the century. In the era of the Freedmen's Bureau, a Union soldier named Captain Daniel Lucey had appeared on the scene and opened a school for the Freedmen in the upper story of a colored church. From then on spasmodic attempts were made in shacks, lodge halls, and churches, shifting from public to private support as the funds of the state and the appearance of itinerant teachers permitted. In the 'nineties, J. W. Davidson, a graduate of Atlanta University, produced the first permanent establishment. In 1895 he organized a board of trustees, got himself elected principal for life, and acquired land and a brick building.[6] And so fetching were the ways of the young teacher that he aroused the interest of Anna T. Jeanes in the cause of Negro education, securing from her a building and the first considerable donation to the cause of Negro education, an

---

6. Minutes of the Trustees of Fort Valley High and Industrial School, October 2, 1895; *Catalogue of Fort Valley Normal and Industrial School*, 1933-1934, p. 13.

AN AWAKENING STATE

interest that eventually was to inspire her to a rich endowment in the enlightenment of the black race.

But despite Davidson's election for life, his years of success were numbered and in 1903 the trustees pushed him from his pedestal. Apparently finances had become muddled. For within a year after opening, the trustees were forced to rent out a room of the school for a printing office at $5 a month and let out the hall on the ground floor as a skating rink.[7] By 1901 the little school was near bankruptcy.[8] To remedy these sad affairs, George Peabody, a trustee, and Wallace Buttrick of the General Education Board brought in from Biddle University one of the most notable colored men Georgia had ever produced. Hoping to create an industrial school modeled on Tuskegee, they secured the experienced services of Henry A. Hunt. Already Hunt was a mature man of thirty-eight. He had been born in Hancock County, Georgia, in 1866, had graduated with honors from Atlanta University in 1890, had plied his carpenter's trade, taught school, and had become well established as director of trades and business manager at Biddle University in North Carolina. For all his Atlanta University heritage he was more interested in farmers than in Greek scholars. To Hunt, agriculture was the only way out of distress for the Georgia Negro. Even at Biddle the old line classical tradition of his learned gentlemen masters had disgusted him for its lack of attention to the daily needs of life. The mantle of Booker T. Washington was upon him.

But encouragement was hardly to be found in Fort Valley. Hunt inherited a school of 145 students running on a budget of $840 a year. His wife has described their findings: "The water standing around the house.... The

---

7. Minutes of the Trustees of Fort Valley High and Industrial School, March 25, 1896, p. 6.
8. *Ibid.*, June 7, 1901.

rooms so large, so empty, so bare. The old log barn. The old laundry shack right alongside the principal's home. Anna T. Jeanes Hall dormitory partially completed. The three-room school building across the road. The deep cellar . . . filled with water. The beginning of another building. The school grounds, a sand bed, millions, billions, trillions of pebbles, but trees, shrubbery, lawns—where, . . . were they!

"The big pond between the School and Central of Georgia railway so near. Men, women, children, paddling in the water, riding in bateaux, shooting the bull frogs. At night the croak of the frogs, the yell of drinkers, gamblers on the railroad banks, green slimy puddles of water, mosquitoes, malaria, typhoid. Summer-time, few gardens, green pork, no screened markets, flies, gnats, sore-eyed babies, no nurses, no colored doctors. Girls and boys loitering along to school—eight, nine, ten o'clock—any hour. Excused at noon to go home to carry dinner. Four months, three, two, in school during the year. Christmas Eve to January first—firecrackers, drinking, shooting, swearing, fighting, going to jail. The new educated Negro, looked at so hard, so silently, with the eyes of suspicion, doubt, fear."[9]

Immediately, however, Hunt put himself to the task of erecting a Tuskegee-Hampton type school in the midst of this dismal scene. Trades were introduced and enrollment increased by hundreds. With student labor and the benefactions of Peabody, Harkness, Rosenwald, Rockefeller, Carnegie, Huntington, and Jeanes, buildings went up over a campus of ninety acres. In 1913 while finances were in a tenuous state, the American Church Institute of the Episcopal Church assumed parental care. As the years of the renaissance after the War went by, the plant de-

---

9. *Down Where the Need is Greatest* (New York, n.d.), 23-26.

veloped to a value of nearly half a million dollars while the $480 budget found by Hunt rose to $80,000.

During the prosperous years of the early 'twenties, the normal course was extended one year beyond the high school. Then came the junior college idea installed for the training of rural teachers. The first class opened in 1927-1928 with thirteen freshmen. In addition, a liberal arts course was offered to prepare ambitious students for future study in colleges and advanced professions, and finally the junior college expanded to include vocational courses in agriculture, home economics, and building trades.

As John Hope in Atlanta became the Moses of the urban Negro of Georgia, so Henry Hunt became the patriarch of the rural masses. With extension programs, institutes, community service, health campaigns, and a vigorous crusade for social and economic betterment, Hunt and his school at Fort Valley became symbols of the potential powers of the race.

Meanwhile the government of the state had branched into a junior college experiment at Albany in South Georgia. Nearly a generation before the First World War Joseph W. Holley had gone into Dougherty County and established the Albany Bible and Manual Training School. Holley was of the second generation of Freedmen. Born in 1874 in Winnsboro, South Carolina, he came into the name of his parents' old white masters. By a stroke of good luck, his parents put him into the employ of the notable New England family of Hazards, whose head, old Rowland, took such a liking to the youngster that he sent him to be educated in Revere Lay College and Andover Academy and left a death-bed injunction for the Hazard heirs to look after the promising colored boy. Sensing the boy's gift of words, the Hazards tried to steer him into a career of journalism, but the tug of the ministry out-pulled them and he was sent to Lincoln University to complete his studies. There in the final year a copy of DuBois' *Souls of Black Folk* fell into his hands and the vivid descriptions he read of conditions of evil and destitution in Dougherty County at the turn of the century had moved him to compassion at the desolation of this former "Egypt of the Confederacy." There, wrote DuBois, in the days of the Old South had flourished one of the richest slave kingdoms of the cotton empire. The Smiths, Gandys, Boltons, Lagores, Lloyds and their kind had lived in "earldoms" holding sway over 90,000 acres of rich land tilled by 6,000 Negroes. The Civil War had demolished the "royal" structure. Then the county became the huddling ground for Negroes who massed together to create the protection of numbers. By the 'nineties the competition of cotton raising with the West had sapped the vestiges of strength from the region. With the descent of cotton to 4c a pound in 1898, hope for salvation had vanished. Negroes labored in the fields for 30¢ a day without board, living again almost as enslaved peasants. Land lay under the pall of debt; the rich soil washed into gullies; rows of decrepit slave cabins, cheerless and stark, were conspicuous only for their dirt. Illiteracy and the dull mood of apathy were everywhere. Ignorant of the world, of government, of individual worth, of life and opportunities, the masses toiled daily with no knowledge of standards of a better existence. Marriage customs were akin to the codes of slavery. Eight or ten people lived in one or two rooms of rotted cabins. And Negroes outnumbered whites four to one.[10]

Moved by these descriptions Holley met Booker T. Washington and on a bench in New York's Central Park unfolded his plans for a school. The oracle supplied the needed encouragement. Promptly the self-appointed mes-

---

10. DuBois, *Souls of Black Folk*, 113-154, *passim*.

siah besieged the Hazard sisters, Ann, and Caroline, the president of Wellesley, for the money for his project. With $2,000 in his pocket he descended on the desolate waste of Dougherty County. By 1903 he had organized his board of trustees and opened a school in the Union Baptist Church of Albany. Within a year forty acres of land and a building had grown out of more Hazard philanthropy. But there was no ambition for higher education. Confronted with the task of wiping out ignorance and illiteracy the institution grew and prospered content with elementary grades supplemented with a few secondary courses and normal training.

In 1917 the legislature of Georgia made its first appropriation to the school. By that time the research and cooperative appeals of educational foundations had begun to swing public sentiment of the South into the avenue of racial cooperation. A bill was passed creating a State Agricultural, Industrial, and Normal School for Negroes, and the institution at Albany was selected as the most appropriate facility. But it was not the intention of the state to assume full responsibility for support. Beginning with a meagre appropriation of only $5,000, by the late 'twenties annual sums of more than $25,000 from the public till were providing 60 per cent of the school's revenue. Junior college instruction was inaugurated in liberal arts, teacher training, home economics, and agriculture. The preparation of teachers for these fields was the major aim.[11] Finally, agriculture was dropped from the curriculum, and with the name of the school changed to Georgia Normal College, the institution took a place in the reorganized University System of Georgia as one of the regular units of the state higher educational structure.

---

11. *Catalogue of Georgia Normal and Agricultural College*, 1926-1927, p. 9; A. J. Klein, *Survey of Negro Colleges and Universities* (Washington, 1929), 336-337; Thomas, "Legislation as it Affected Public Education for Negroes in Georgia," 46-47.

At the same moment the junior college idea was enriching the soil about Albany, a similar experiment on a smaller scale was begun by the state a few miles to the north at Forsyth. There the conditions of Negro rural life were scarcely better than in the neighboring region of Dougherty County. Racial clashes were frequent, but no messiah marched in to sweep the blight of ignorance from the masses. Yet a school teacher had sauntered undramatically into the vicinity in the person of William Merida Hubbard, a young colored graduate of Fisk and Cornell, who was seeking a healthy spot upon which to settle his sickly bride. Although experienced as a teacher, Hubbard was then involved in the practice of photography and had no idea of beginning a school. But at the behest of a colored preacher and a couple of neighbors, he was moved in 1902 to begin the instruction of five Negro youngsters under a barter agreement that allowed him to set up a photographer's gallery in the Kynett Methodist Church. It was a shabby, forlorn building with holes in the floor and more wind inside than out. But the white population of the town came to the rescue of the little enterprise, and as the years rolled by it flowered into the Monroe County Training School, backed by Northern philanthropy and Federal subsidies. In the early 'twenties the expansive energies of the state educational program spread out to include the school with annual appropriations. But it was not until 1929, after a destructive fire and rebuilding, that the state moved into complete control and introduced the junior college idea. With instruction in agriculture already well established, that and the training of rural teachers eventually became the objectives of the school. The name of State Teacher's and Agricultural College was given it and the institution became incorporated as one of the three Negro colleges in the University System of Georgia.

Indeed, the state of Georgia was awakening. The educational body was stretching to the throb of energy, new blood, and the spirit of the zooming 'twenties. The crusade of social reform, interracial cooperation, commercial expansion, and driving forces of the enlivened American mind were sweeping away the obstacles to intellectual bondage that had given Georgia and the South the opprobrium of a mental desert.

In fact, the birth of junior colleges was surpassed by an even more important development by the state—the revolution in Georgia State Industrial College in Savannah. The Phelps-Stokes survey had revealed in an array of dark data the lethargy and inefficiency of all Negro land-grant colleges. In no case were the original aims of the Federal Morrill acts being followed, and the college in Savannah lagged in obscurity even behind the feeble institutions of other states. To remedy these evils, the United States Commissioner of Education called all presidents of Negro land-grant colleges to a conference in Atlanta in 1919. The demands of Washington for compliance with the Federal law were spread on the table. A year later, a citizens' conference was held in Atlanta to consider the requests of the government. Reorganization and expansion of the collegiate work in accordance with the Federal law were resolved.

But more than gestures of amity were necessary to spur the state into action. As Commissioners in Savannah and the legislators in Atlanta failed to respond with tangible improvements for the college, investigators arrived from Washington. For even after thirty years only $2,000 was given annually from the state treasury toward the support of the institution, while $24,000 was provided by Federal subsidies. In 1919, however, the legislature had made a gesture at quieting Washington's demands with $50,000, and later more, to reconstruct Meldrim Auditorium that had suffered destruction by fire. But when, after a lapse of years, the building was still unfinished and poor management had permitted exhorbitant outlays in material to be wasted and left to rot, Federal officials became angry. In the State Capitol itself the supervisor of Negro schools, Walter B. Hill, Jr., was a firebrand in his own right. He, too, chastised the state for its indifference. In 1921 President Wright resigned. Finally in 1923 a Federal survey of the institution was sent to the State Capitol showing needs and accompanied by threats that unless the legislature got busy all Federal aid for education in Georgia would be abolished.

The survey was clearly unflattering. Here in a state with a larger Negro population than any other state in the union, there was scarcely any public facility for higher education of the black race. At Georgia State Industrial College there were only eight students of college grade in May, 1923. More than half the elementary and secondary pupils were from Chatham County. The Federal government was supporting a county school! The faculty was of a low order, most of them graduates of the institution itself and largely devoid of higher training. Salaries were too low for good teachers and the president was only half paid. The farm was a penal department just now emerging for the first time into a faint semblance of a scientific agricultural branch of learning. Buildings and equipment were decrepit and the entire value of the plant was only $193,000. College instruction was haphazard, five instructors, some with inferior training, teaching all subjects in all grades, higher and lower, and attempting to offer a four-year college course leading to a baccalaureate degree. The library of 400 volumes was stored in a basement and never used. The practice school, designed for teacher training, had one instructor and sixty-five pupils crowded into a dingy cellar. Only the trades were well taught. The Board of Commissioners was fossilized, unsympathetic to Negro education, and unprogressive. Some never attended board meetings. Yet the authority of two or three Commissioners held affairs in a death grip. Proud in their smugness that the college was "neither a pauper nor a beggar" the Commissioners made few efforts to enlarge appropriations from the legislature. Even offers of financial aid had been repulsed with haughty pride. Such was the apathy of the rulers that the General Education Board refused further aid for the summer school. The Commissioners had no plan for expansion. And in their paternal sway, the president of the college was treated like a school boy, without authority to buy a broom or even leave the campus without permission.[12]

The suggestions for reform offered by the survey were virtually commands bolstered by threats. They called for the self-perpetuating board of superannuated Commissioners to be abolished in favor of a board appointed by the governor; Meldrim Auditorium should be completed and a substantial building and repair program inaugurated; and the small annual appropriations of the state should be increased about $30,000.[13] The Bureau of Education in Washington took oath to keep its eye on these developments of the college and warned that neglect by public officers would be answered by a recommendation to withdraw the annual allowance of $50,000 of Federal land-grant subsidies. Then whites as well as the blacks would suffer.[14]

With affairs thus forced to a crisis, the governor, two years later, abolished the old Board of Commissioners and appointed five trustees headed by a progressive Savannah lawyer, A. Pratt Adams. Within a year Wright's suc-

---
12. L. E. Blauch, "The Georgia State Industrial College" (Mimeographed report, United States Bureau of Education, June 15, 1923), 2-23, *passim*.
13. *Ibid.*, 30.
14. *Ibid.*, 32.

cessor to the presidency was brushed aside and Benjamin F. Hubert was called from the headship of agricultural and vocational education at Tuskegee to take the helm of the college.

In 1927 Adams and Hubert made a sally on the legislature, and as a result the annual appropriation was raised to $50,000 a year. Income for the college jumped from $34,000 to $86,000 in one year. The General Education Board and Julius Rosenwald responded to the demand for buildings and the value of the plant was increased by nearly $300,000. Emphasis was placed on college work. Home economics and vocational education were expanded. With the doctrines of Booker T. Washington in Hubert's bones, trades were rejuvenated and placed on a college level. The faculty was recreated on a higher plane. And advertising, for the lack of which the school had remained obscure and starved for college students, went out to all corners of the state quickening the desire of men and women to take advantage of the facilities now offered by public effort for higher education. Although only 53 college students were enrolled at the beginning of this program in 1927-1928, no less than 447 were on the campus ten years later.

At last Georgia had become an awakened state. Although the advances of white education had been even more rapid, the Negro masses of the commonwealth had achieved a recognition of social worth. Racial cooperation was becoming a symbol of cultural achievement.

Chapter X

Affiliation and Merger

THE AWAKENING OF GEORGIA TO A REALIZATION THAT higher education of the Negro was to be henceforth a function of government was partially an outgrowth of a developing spirit of social cooperation as opposed to traditional American individualism. At last in the third decade of the century the cooperative spirit bore tangible results, first in the revolution of state educational efforts for the Negro and promptly thereafter among private colleges in the creation of the Atlanta University Affiliation.

But the road to harmony had been arduous. No sooner had the missionaries of New England laid the broad foundations for an educational system in Reconstruction days than the crusaders unlocked their hands. The bonds of the common cause were dissolved and, often in opposite directions, the leaders of the colleges strove for the survival and supremacy of their particular institutions. With the coming of the second wave of the crusade, bringing on its crest another group of schools and the expensive features of industrial education, the competitive scramble for the favors of Northern philanthropy rose to a new high.

Very promptly the evils of indiscriminate benevolence were revealed. As early as the 'eighties the trustees of the Slater Fund were aware of the lack of unity, but their efforts to concentrate aid were squelched by the objections of Atticus Haygood. With the appointment of J. L. M. Curry as agent in 1891, however, the policy of concentrating appropriations was taken up again. For their unwillingness to coordinate industrial training in 1895, Clark and Atlanta Universities were cut from the lists of recipients. The crowding of five colleges into Atlanta also brought forth criticism from philanthropists and educators alike. Under this overabundant system of schools, low standards, small libraries, insufficient equipment, and a scramble for support and supremacy were inevitable results. The cooperative spirit must be nourished, said the agents of Slater, Jeanes, Rosenwald, Phelps-Stokes, and Rockefeller. And as they held the whip hand over Negro college economic life, their suggestions were listened to with an ever growing attitude of respect.

But it was no easy matter to induce the colleges to give up their cherished prerogatives. College work, for all its infinitesimal size, was the pride and joy, the symbol of distinction of every institution. Only between Spelman and Atlanta Baptist Seminary was any of this work coordinated. Under President Sale the men's college provided all work of higher learning for the women across the road; teachers were exchanged between both schools, and a semblance of unity came into being. But so long as Miss Packard and Miss Giles were in control of Spelman, the fear of being subjugated to the dominance of a man's world remained a barrier between the institutions. At one time Bumstead was on the verge of suggesting that the two Baptist colleges unite to satisfy the demand for fewer institutions in the city. But lest the suggestion be too attractive and create a college more powerful than Atlanta University, Bumstead gave up the idea.[1]

---

1. Letter from H. Bumstead to Edward T. Ware, February 26, 1908 (in Atlanta University Library).

In 1908 attempts at cooperation had advanced far enough to bring about friendly conferences between Atlanta University, Spelman, and Morehouse, but no action rose from the conversations. Yet by this time Edward T. Ware had replaced the unflinching Bumstead, and John Hope had become president of Morehouse. Both saw the need for a new spirit of amity and coordination. By 1914 Ware began to prophesy a large center of higher learning in Atlanta, formed from the cooperation of all the colleges.[2] In the same year, Philip Weltner, an Atlanta attorney, taught a course in business law, with classes alternating between Atlanta University and Morehouse, enrolling students from both. Slowly but steadily the stiff cross-currents of jealousy and alumni loyalty were dissolving before the cooperative spirit.

It remained, however, for the years following the First World War to see the actual fact of affiliation. By then there was no help for it. Economic forces were too swift and strong to be stemmed by bull-headedness. Although a $76,000 legacy from Charles Drew of Providence in 1920 brought Atlanta University out of debt after more than thirty years under the pall, evil days were soon upon it again, for the General Education Board withdrew sustenance.[3] Faced once more with the dilemma of debt, the University was forced to bend to the will of philanthropy. Of course, it was easier this time. In 1919 Myron Winslow Adams had replaced the invalid Edward T. Ware in the president's chair. Although Adams had come to the University in 1889, proud possessor of a doctorate and the New England tradition, and had served as dean, he was not a reactionary of the old guard. His gift was a capacity for keeping abreast of the times. He abhorred the old policy

---

2. President's Report to the Trustees of Atlanta University, May 26, 1914 (MS. in Atlanta University Library).
3. Adams, *Atlanta University*, 71.

of bitter rivalry and immediately he set about discussing a merger with Clark. Nothing came of it immediately, but again in 1926 the faculty records reveal conversations for cooperation with Spelman and Morehouse.[4]

In the end, affiliation was brought about by the perseverance of Northern philanthropy. The trend of the period was all toward mergers. And with the mind of the nation focused on higher education, the development of colleges became the center of interest. In the early 'twenties, the General Education Board promoted the endowment of Morehouse to more than $300,000. By such methods Northern philanthropists gathered more power into their hands. College enrollment was growing; expenses were rising; denominational boards could not answer the demands; the student was unable to increase, proportionately, his expenditure. Thus philanthropists came into command.[5]

It was the need for libraries in several colleges in Atlanta that finally precipitated action. By 1928 pleas for books and library buildings in the growing colleges were making a clamor at the doors of the General Education Board. The Board answered that it would be glad to build a *joint* library. In recent years Adams and Hope had fostered the cooperative impulse and in 1926-1927 a limited interchange of class work was carried on among Atlanta University, Morehouse, and Spelman. In 1927 new blood in the person of Florence Matilda Read flowed into the presidency of Spelman, and a year later the cooperative efforts of the two Baptist colleges went a step further by the merging of the summer schools. Now with the proposal of a joint library the path was cut for affiliation. The three campuses were only a few blocks apart.[6]

---

4. Minutes of the Faculty of Atlanta University, January 5, 1926, p. 30.
5. Holmes, *Evolution of the Negro College*, 195.
6. *Ibid.*, 194-195; Adams, *Atlanta University*, 67-70. See also *Annual Report of the General Education Board*, 1929-1932.

Actually the whole movement was an outgrowth of the new policy of the General Education Board to encourage the development of three or four university centers for the Negroes of the South. Acting quickly on the suggestion, President Adams of Atlanta University called for committees from each institution in the early months of 1929 and by spring a plan for merger had received unanimous adoption. Under the new arrangement of the Atlanta University Affiliation, as the system was called, Spelman was appointed to conduct undergraduate study for women, Morehouse for men, and Atlanta University was designated to perform graduate and professional study on a university level. Spelman and Morehouse colleges continued as previously under their own boards of trustees and their own management, but the board of Atlanta University was reorganized to include representatives of each college, plus trustees elected at large. The trustees of Atlanta University, of course, were looked upon as lords of the household and John Hope was elected president of the Affiliation. Thus eighty-seven acres of land and twenty-eight buildings were coordinated into effective service. Resources were pooled in fact, if not on paper. Faculties were reorganized, abolishing many of the old guard, and reconstructed on a higher level. Beginning its graduate work gradually, the new Atlanta University opened in September, 1929, offering fifteen advanced courses in biology, chemistry, economics, education, English, French, history, home economics, Latin, mathematics, and social science.[7]

Immediately a large building program got under way. By 1932 the promised library was completed at a cost of $450,000 and endowed with $600,000. Within its beautiful Georgian walls was space for 600 students and shelf-room for 175,000 volumes. It became the hub of the sys-

---

7. *Spelman Messenger*, October, 1929; *Atlanta University Bulletin*, May, 1930.

tem for higher learning for the Negro in Atlanta. Then with another million dollars, given anonymously to aid unemployment in the depression, an administration building, dormitories, and a president's residence were erected. Grounds were landscaped and beautified into a campus rivaling, and perhaps surpassing, the finest plants in the state, and laboratories were built and equipped.

To insure the permanence of the Affiliation, endowment campaigns were hurried through despite the lean years of financial chaos that troubled the nation. With the General Education Board continuing its role of godfather, intent on developing university centers for the Negro at strategic points of the South, the Affiliation went out for big donations—Spelman, three million, Atlanta University, three million, and Morehouse, six hundred thousand. Vast sums in comparison with the past! But the plutocracy of the North was still available. By 1934 seven and a half million dollars were permanently in the coffers of the new system and total assets were more than ten million dollars.[8]

Once the merger had been accomplished, the remaining colleges of the city, then left out, began to converge on the central system. The advantages of the scheme were obvious even to those institutions of irascible tradition in whom the spirit of cooperation was slow to flower. In 1928-1929 the Atlanta School of Social Work put a foot in the door of coordination by interchanging courses between the school and the colleges. And a decade later, in 1938, the Atlanta School of Social Work entered formally into the Affiliation as a graduate school, offering master's degrees on the completion of its two year course.[9]

---

8. Holmes, *Evolution of the Negro College*, 194-195; *Annual Report of the General Education Board*, 1930-1931, pp. 16-18. While the financial statements of the respective institutions usually are not published, they are available in the offices of the Affiliation.
9. *Bulletin of the Atlanta School of Social Work*, 1929-1930; *Spelman Messenger*, August, 1938, p. 5.

With the accomplishment of the building program in the early 'thirties, Morris Brown abandoned its plant on Boulevard and moved into the old campus vacated by Atlanta University. Although not part of the Affiliation, Morris Brown reaped the advantages of closer cooperation in economy, larger facilities, and proximity to the new library.

Only Clark and Gammon were then segregated from the combination. In 1936, however, the General Education Board took steps to include Clark in the merger. With pledges of land and $750,000 from the Board, plans were made to move the college from the southern hills of the city to a spot opposite the new campus of Atlanta University. A campaign for a half-million dollar endowment was begun, and by 1939 four-fifths of the money had been secured.

The Second World War that broke out in Europe in 1939 and then flowed east and west until it engulfed America in 1941 might well have put a stop, as the First World War had done, to these progressive developments had not the cooperative spirit already achieved such great momentum. In actual fact, however, the years of war speeded the process of coordination. In 1941, for example, Clark moved into a handsome new plant directly across the street from Atlanta University. The presidents of all seven Atlanta institutions were soon meeting in a general educational policy-making body called the Conference of Presidents, and faculty members of the various institutions were assembling in departmental meetings which cut across institutional lines. Gradually more and more senior college and graduate courses were opened in each institution to students in other institutions, and interchange of teachers became common even to the extent of joint payment of salaries. Classrooms, laboratory facilities, and even athletic field facilities were used on a cooperative basis. Even the academic calendar for all seven institutions was soon coordinated, and such activities as the annual baccalaureate service, purchasing, adult education programs, and musical and dramatic organizations for the students were operated jointly by some, even though not all the colleges.

After the war two other steps were taken indicating that even more cooperation was yet to come. In 1947 the Atlanta School of Social Work gave up its corporate charter to become a professional school integrally a part of Atlanta University. In 1948 the trustees of Gammon Theological Seminary (lonesome at the south side of the city since the moving of Clark) voted to relocate the institution near the Atlanta University Center.

At last the Negroes of Georgia had come into the possession of a modern university. It was the triumph of three generations. The vision of Edmund Asa Ware to lift the minds of Negroes into the high atmosphere of learning at its best was being realized. No longer could the critical eye of savants look down on the Negro colleges of Georgia as wretched secondary schools. The University Center in Atlanta rivaled the best educational opportunities of the state, surpassing those for whites in some respects and surpassing some white establishments completely. By 1946-1947 the Center, including all seven institutions, was able to boast of a well coordinated plant valued at more than $5,000,000, a combined endowment approaching $12,000,000, an annual income of approximately $1,800,000, library facilities with nearly 135,000 volumes on the shelves, and an enrollment of nearly 3,500 students.

Signs that even more cooperation was in the offing were conspicuous, and the temptation to prophesy that some day all Atlanta's Negro institutions of higher learning would be completely organized under one corporate roof was a temptation that was well-nigh irresistible.

Outside Atlanta the same trend toward mergers and

affiliations was visible. The transformation of Holley's college at Albany into a state institution in 1917 and the gradual absorption by the state government of Hubbard's school at Forsyth in the years between 1922 and 1932 were incidents within the same general movement. The many surveys of education in the era showed plainly, however, that the state-supported system of both white and Negro education needed revamping. The 1932 action of the legislature, which reorganized all the state institutions into a "university system" under a centralized Board of Regents, went far toward correcting some evils. Despite these developments, however, Negro education in general and the Negro colleges of the "system" in particular were far from being adequate to meet the needs of the colored population of the state.

The depression of the 'thirties and the accompanying New Deal atmosphere, which even Georgia could not escape, highlighted these weaknesses. Figures showed that of the 250,000 colored families in Georgia in the late 'thirties, three-fifths of them lived in rural areas on a cash income of approximately $4.00 per week. The remainder lived in cities on no more than $8 per week. The Negro was still a social outcast and a political nonentity. It was no wonder that Negro college students had a deficient background. Their eleven years of schooling were mostly wretched. There were still only seventy-six high schools to serve a population of more than a million. That the state was not doing its share to support Negro education was apparent.

In 1938, therefore, the College of Education in the University of Georgia produced a survey of higher education for Negroes in Georgia that appealed boldly for greater public responsibility.[10] The report declared that the Negro

---

10. "Report of the Study on Higher Education of Negroes in Georgia" (Athens, 1938). A survey by the University of Georgia College of Education.

colleges of the state system should busy themselves correcting the defects of civilization by attacking such problems as health, poverty, and citizenship. To this end they should have five objectives: to prepare teachers, to train agricultural and home-life leaders, to give instruction in trades available to colored workers, to educate adults, and to give a high cultural education to a selected group of qualified Negroes.

The survey also noted that the state's present instruments for achieving these goals were worthy of little praise. The State Teachers and Agricultural College at Forsyth was declared to be so inadequate that it ought to be abandoned to the county and its movable property transferred to Hunt's school at Fort Valley. The Fort Valley Normal and Industrial School, moreover, should be brought into the University System where its superior facilities and eleven years' experience in junior college work could be utilized—a suggestion, by the way, which was quite agreeable to both Hunt and the controlling authorities of Fort Valley.

Although the outbreak of World War II, to say nothing of disagreement over some of the recommendations of the survey, prevented all the suggestions from being carried out, some steps to fulfill them were taken. In 1939 the institution at Forsyth was abandoned by the Board of Regents and its facilities were merged with those at Fort Valley. The Episcopal Church's guardianship of the Fort Valley school ceased and the institution became a four-year, degree-granting college under the name of Fort Valley State College. The major aim of the college was to train teachers for rural schools.

As a result of the same survey the Board of Regents in 1939 transformed the college at Albany into a four-year, degree-granting institution and in 1943 changed its name to Albany State College.

But in spite of the fact that these developments caused the University System of Georgia to include three fairly acceptable degree-granting colleges for Negroes, the Supreme Court of the United States was not satisfied. As a result of the decision in the Gaines case of 1938 and subsequent similar decisions ordering the states to provide educational facilities for Negroes "equal" to those available for whites the state government began a program in 1944 of subsidizing individual Negro citizens who desired graduate and professional training not available in the Negro colleges. By February, 1947, the state had distributed $49,728.00 among 1,291 such students, all but 77 of whom had proceeded to Atlanta University.

That the task of the state was far from complete, however, was evinced by the fact that as late as 1948, and in spite of ever increasing appropriations to the three Negro colleges, not one of them had achieved an "A" rating with the Southern Association of Colleges and Secondary Schools. How long it would be before critical educators could point with pride to the state-supported institutions of learning in the Empire State was anyone's guess.

CHAPTER XI

Characteristics of the Modern College

AMERICAN EDUCATION EMERGED FROM THE CHAOTIC years of the First World War searching for new objectives. During the three decades that followed, the aims of the liberal arts tradition to lead man to a cultural plane of life were abandoned as goals that were insufficient. Society and its problems became the base of the new doctrine that was being born. According to the new theory the individual must be taught to become "adjusted." First, he must learn to earn a living; second, he must learn to play; and third, he must be socialized, culturally and humanly, and be prepared to make his contribution to the sum total of material progress. His cart was hitched to the star of mechanical progress—better health, better houses, better motor cars. The way of life of the Greeks was considered of little moment to this young citizen of the earth's most prosperous nation. And whatever the effects of the Great Depression, the New Deal, and World War II, there was little evidence at the middle of the twentieth century that these great and historic convulsions had done anything more than intrench still further the crass and bold materialistic aims of the American educational system.

Naturally, the Georgia Negro found a place in the new social order. The dollar sign became his cloud and pillar of fire and it led him to cities of the South and North where opportunities for material prosperity seemed more abundant. His colleges also were quickly absorbed into the new atmosphere. Industrial education was all but gone, to be sure. But it now became apparent that the trade-school movement of the earlier years had been but a forerunner of vast vocational programs that were soon to make the work in trades and simple handicrafts seem extremely primitive. Business and the professions were new goals for an army of ambitious youngsters; and, although these fields did not open sufficiently to absorb all the Negroes who wanted in, most college graduates continued to strive for the white collar that symbolized middle class achievement. Science also was taken up with greater zest now that it had become more utilitarian. At last agriculture reached scientific status and the study of home economics, social work, library science, the fine arts, and economics rose to eminence.

The three decades from 1918 to 1948 were particularly notable for the trend toward standardization that resulted from a continuous series of surveys of educational institutions. The suggestions of the Phelps-Stokes survey of 1916 for the improvement of Georgia Negro education had been suffocated by war. But once peace had returned to the land, bringing on its heels an intellectual awakening, colleges made use of the reports and began to change their procedures. Other surveys followed to inspire and guide educational leaders. In 1923 the Federal government probed again into the Georgia State Industrial College, causing a veritable revolution.[1] Five years later all Negro

---
1. L. E. Blauch, "The Georgia State Industrial College."

institutions of higher learning were surveyed for progress, and a year later land-grant colleges were again scrutinized.[2] Then the University System of Georgia was examined. The Methodist Church made its own survey. *The Journal of Negro Education* campaigned diligently for higher standards. Philanthropists delved into all things, sometimes presenting embarrassing questions and making demands before benefits were forthcoming. All during the 'thirties and 'forties surveys continued, forcing standardization and spurring many forces into action to create the panorama of the modern college. Accrediting agencies were bowed to and colleges rushed to meet the standards, which in conformity with the age of the salesman, were based too often on criteria of quantity. In the early 'twenties the Negro colleges of Georgia were still unworthy of the name of "college." But by the end of another decade, nine institutions were devoted solely to the tasks of higher learning.

To the naked eye the most significant development during the years 1918 to 1948 was the expansion of the physical plants of the colleges. The great philanthropic funds, the state legislature, the New Deal, and a series of building campaigns enlarged campus grounds and facilities often by as much as three or four times their earlier size. By 1947 the total value of Negro plants in Georgia amounted to more than $8,000,000 and in practically every institution new building programs were again under way. Perhaps the fact that the three state-supported institutions—the "poor cousins" of the Negro college family—possessed nearly one-third of this total property and each year were getting more was the most cheering part of the development.

The effort of the state-supported institutions to catch

---

2. A. J. Klein, *Survey of Negro Colleges and Universities* (Washington, 1929); A. J. Klein, *Survey of Land-Grant Colleges and Universities* (Washington, 1930).

THE MODERN COLLEGE

up with the privately-controlled colleges was visible also in the figures on cost of operations. Of the nearly $3,000,000 being spent annually for operation by the late 'forties, for example, the state-supported schools were expending about one-third. Nor was the increase in the state's share due solely to increased enrollments and fees, for the legislative appropriation to the state-supported institutions increased from $55,000 in 1929-1930 to $426,000 in 1946-1947. In the latter year, moreover, the Board of Regents instituted the same salary scale in the Negro institutions that prevailed in the white institutions.

Needless to say, however, the days wherein the Negro college was forced to "scratch" for funds were not yet over. As the years rolled by and millionaires and philanthropic funds declined in number and the return from endowments decreased, most of the colleges found themselves in the usual tight pinch. The college at Macon (which changed its name during the 'forties from Central City College to Georgia Baptist College) remained perpetually on the verge of bankruptcy and closure. Although Gammon remained the nation's leading Negro theological seminary, the decline of income from its once handsome endowment was felt severely. The years after World War II showed, moreover, that the nearly $12,000,000 endowment of the cooperating institutions in Atlanta was not enough for post-war development.

Paine luckily found two new sources of income during the 'forties: Race Relations Day offerings collected in Methodist Churches and the United Negro College Fund that was organized in 1944 by Negro institutions which saw the wisdom of a joint fund raising campaign. Most of the private institutions continued to rely on endowment campaigns, however, and the booming years after World War II found Clark, Morehouse, Atlanta University, and the others inaugurating movements (assisted by the General Education Board) to raise from $600,000 to $3,000,000 each, most of which was intended to further their endowment funds.

Another mark of physical expansion in the panorama was the tremendous increase in the number of college students. Released from the burden of elementary and secondary grades, colleges moved forward on all fronts to gain a place with institutions devoted solely to higher learning. In 1918 there were only 220 students of college rank in the Negro schools of Georgia. Within ten years the number of Negro college students in the state increased seven-fold, to more than 1,400. During another decade the figure doubled, totaling over 2,800 in 1938; and by 1946-1947 the number stood at nearly 6,000.

The state-controlled colleges had accounted for almost none of the increase in enrollment during the 'twenties. But once the state was awakened, public colleges moved ahead rapidly and between 1928 and 1938 increased their college enrollment five-fold. By 1948 the public college at Savannah had the largest enrollment of any Negro institution in the state. By 1932 Atlanta harbored more colored college students than any other city in the South, excepting the District of Columbia. Certainly Georgia was a leading state in the higher learning of the black race. Even by 1928, 10 out of every 10,000 Georgia Negroes were in college, while Florida had only four, Alabama five, Louisiana seven, and Mississippi three. Only North Carolina surpassed Georgia in this proportion.[3] Obviously this was a small number in proportion to the large Negro population of the state. But the movements for social cooperation, better race relations, increased economic opportunity, and the awakened intellect of the people were making holes in the dikes that stemmed the waters of enlightenment.

---

3. A. J. Klein, *Survey of Negro Colleges and Universities* (Washington, 1929), 245-246.

The ensuing years disclosed evidence that these advances were enriching the scene in Georgia. Seventy per cent of the graduates of the colleges remained to live and work in the state. In 1932 Atlanta alone had 567 colored graduates in its population.[4] In addition to filling the usual fields of the ministry, medicine, and education, the modern college was turning out social workers, home demonstration agents, business men and women, lawyers, editors, and a few rare phenomena known as scholars. It was part of Georgia's sad destiny, however, to lose many of the best graduates to the North, principally to Illinois, Ohio, Michigan, and New York. While more than three-quarters of the names in *Who's Who in Colored America* belonged to Southern-born Negroes, only 39 per cent had remained in the South.[5] Thereby, the modern panorama was shorn of a good deal of brilliance.

But there was more in the current picture than physical expansion. Fields of scholarship were also enlarged. A certain freedom of investigation crept into these strongholds of New England Puritanism. The old curriculum was tossed out or revamped to fit a philosophy of education based on economic progress. The soul of black folk was not forgotten, but major emphasis was placed on leading the Negro to his place in the financial sun of a devotedly materialistic nation.

The materialistic trend expressed itself in the private colleges in a high fever for the study of business and economics. By the middle 'twenties Morris Brown was teaching the principles of money, credit, and banking. But by 1929 it was evident that Negro colleges were missing fire with courses patterned on Wall Street. Once the financial crash of 1929 shook their faith in the American economic structure, the colleges based commercial courses more on

---
4. Johnson, *Negro College Graduate*, 25, 34.
5. *Ibid.*, 45, 49.

the needs of Negro life.[6] Suddenly it was realized that even the process of earning a living called for a knowledge of business principles. And if the race was to achieve any economic progress, it must look into this hitherto closed book of business management. Immediately Atlanta University strengthened its department of economics. In accordance with this effort, the Carnegie Foundation gave $100,000 to endow a chair of business administration. By the late 'thirties the field of business was the major interest of freshman classes entering Morehouse. In 1943 Fort Valley began offering a major in business administration, and three years later Atlanta University opened a School of Business Administration. At Clark, moreover, considerable emphasis was being placed on consumer education. True enough, the field of business was still somewhat narrow for the educated Negro, but the fact that the colleges were no longer satisfied to see their graduates work for the crumbs of a livelihood was evident.

The awakened spirit of social uplift for the masses made welfare courses popular. Better preparation for medical and dental colleges was made possible by increased equipment and laboratories for the study of the sciences. Social consciousness was roused by courses in criminology, urban sociology, social pathology, race relations, and the family. Soon Negro colleges were swept into the current of the New Deal. To meet these demands the Atlanta School of Social Work offered studies in social legislation, public welfare administration, and management of social agencies.

The renaissance streamlined all curricula. Survey courses designed to broaden the student's general background were created for the first two years of college study. Contemporary civilization study reduced attention to the past and tried to make the present more meaningful. At Clark a critical survey of the Bible was inaugurated to steer young

---

6. Bowen, *Divine White Right*, 298.

minds through the dangerous canyons between religion and science. The social sciences were rebuilt to give the colored race a greater place in the story of civilization. The contributions of the Negro in music, literature, politics, and education were used to promote race pride, and the Negro was made conscious of his strength and potentialities.

With the creation of a central library in Atlanta, courses in library science were at last made available to colored students. So great was the demand for librarians, in fact, that in 1941 Atlanta University inaugurated a School of Library Science which by 1948 was able to boast of graduates serving in 23 states and in Japan.

Since, however, most of the colleges were still primarily teacher-training institutions it was quite natural that all these developments were really only supplementary to improvements in the curricula concerned with training teachers for the elementary and secondary grades in liberal arts and specialized teachers in home economics, agriculture, and industrial arts and mechanics. The changes in those areas of study are too numerous to mention here, but by the late 'forties it was quite clear that the great bulk of the undergraduate work in the Negro colleges of Georgia fell neatly into one of the five following fields: education, home economics, arts and sciences, agriculture, and business administration. Most of the colleges had thus far tackled only two or three of those fields, however, and it was unlikely that many of them would be engaged with all five in the near future.

A bright spot in the modern panorama was seen in the beginnings of graduate study. At last in 1929 Atlanta University began the first actual efforts on a graduate level for Negroes in Georgia. It was three-score years since Edmund Asa Ware had first seen this vision. Now his dream for a university was being realized. In 1935 the Atlanta

School of Social Work also raised admission requirements to four years of college study, and by 1939 the school was able to offer work leading to a master's degree in social welfare. In the meantime, the Methodist Church raised requirements for ministers to college graduation and other churches followed suit. Gammon took quickly to the new standards and four years of college preparation were soon demanded for admittance to the regular course of study. Beginning in 1944 Gammon also proceeded to raise its women's program in the field of Religious Education from the undergraduate to the graduate level. In 1946, moreover, the state Board of Regents, perhaps prematurely, voted to begin graduate work at Fort Valley, offering master's degrees in education, home economics, and agriculture.

True enough, graduate work developed slowly and its scope remained limited. Within ten years after initiating graduate work, however, Atlanta University had twenty-seven faculty members offering sixty-five advanced courses in biology, chemistry, economics, business administration, education, English, French, Latin, history, mathematics, sociology, and home economics; and in that first decade of experimentation 186 master's degrees were granted. Since the training of teachers was the primary aim of Negro graduate work it was natural that in those first years most of the degrees were taken in education. But a few in history, English, mathematics, economics, and sociology were included. As graduate study progressed, however, the School of Social Work blossomed into the most popular of all Atlanta University schools, eventually surpassing even the School of Education in enrollment and the number of master's degrees granted annually. Of the 162 master's degrees granted in 1947, for example, 62 were granted by the School of Social Work as compared with only 54 granted by the School of Education. The

Graduate School of Arts and Sciences ran a fair third with 44 degrees and the new fledgling school of Business Administration granted only 2. No matter how calculated, however, the granting of more than 1,000 master's degrees by Atlanta University in the years from 1931 to 1948 was a notable achievement.

In all this study it was plain that the Negro and his relation to the world about him were the chief objects of scrutiny. Theses were concerned, for example, not simply with history or labor but with Negro history, Negro labor, Negro literature, and the social, political, and economic aspects of race relations. Of 22 theses approved by 1939 in the department of sociology at Atlanta University, nearly all were studies of race relations. Resentment against the white world was more evident in many studies, moreover, than is generally desirable in the objective realm of academic scholarship, and it was quite apparent, particularly in the sociological studies, that Dr. DuBois had returned to the cloisters of the University and was radiating his bitterness with his usual eloquence and thoroughness. Aside from this weakness and the limitations on subject matter forced on the Negro college by lack of facilities, the graduate work of the Negro institutions of Georgia was of such scholastic merit and high standard that no apologies had to be made for it and the white institutions of the state could hardly boast of surpassing it.

It was also during these three decades of the modern scene that the fine arts were at last given official recognition as fields of study worthy of a place in college curricula. In the new affiliation music was the first of the fine arts to be recognized. Professor Kemper Harreld was still there at the end of the period improving the quality of his glee clubs and orchestras and operating a modernized and ever-enlarging department of music. In the 'thirties he organized the Harreld String Quartet. In 1937 the Carnegie

Corporation improved facilities with the gift of a music library of records and books. And every year a series of concerts brought to the campus some of the best artists of America and Europe. The leading musical event of every year was the Christmas Carol Concert given by the joint choirs of Spelman and Morehouse. Both races flocked into the beautiful setting of Sisters' Chapel on Spelman campus to hear the fine expressions of Negro spirituals and the folk songs of foreign lands. In due time full-fledged departments of music appeared also at Paine, Albany, Fort Valley, and Savannah.

But music was an old tradition in Negro colleges. Perhaps it was the coming of the other fine arts, of painting and sculpture, that gave the panorama its fascination. It was in 1931 that John Hope returned from Europe bringing in tow a noted Negro painter, Hale Woodruff, to give the University its first real teacher of these arts. In 1934 Elizabeth Prophet was brought in to teach sculpturing, modeling, appreciation, the history of art, and architecture. Creative talent of students was turned loose in all directions. Art exhibitions were promoted and students and teachers displayed their wares in the new library. Other displays came in quick succession every year, such as the Harmon Exhibits of Fine Arts by Negro Artists, the Berry exhibits of water colors, and loans from the Whitney Museum and other leading galleries throughout the nation. Lectures by writers and artists became part of the ordinary course of events; training was given at Spelman in the art of the dance, and by 1937 nine faculty members were teaching the fine arts in the University.

During the 'forties the state-supported colleges also proceeded to broaden their art program to include something more than simple handicrafts. The gift of an "art set" of several hundred reproductions and an art reference library by the Carnegie Corporation enriched the scene at

Fort Valley; and while no college outside Atlanta developed an art department comparable to those in the Affiliation, the teaching of design, ceramics, art appreciation, and art teaching methods was developing in all the state-supported institutions.

A similar emphasis was put on the drama. Since 1905 Morehouse had followed an annual tradition of one full-length classical production. But the late 'twenties made the drama a fine art. At Spelman, provisions were made for a little theatre. In 1928 Anne Cooke came in as the first regular director of dramatics and a few years later a graduate of Baker's Workshop at Yale was brought in as assistant. The University Players were organized. Then to crown these dramatic efforts, in 1934 the Atlanta University Summer Theatre was established with a full-time acting company of students and faculty members. Nothing like it had ever happened in the South before and it was the only one of its kind in a Negro college anywhere. Study was available in acting, directing, stage production, theatrical designs, speech, and movement. Also as dramatics developed in the public schools, the teacher-training institutions of the state were, in a few cases, exerting themselves to offer courses in theatrical production, even if on a very modest scale. Obviously the Georgia Negro was experiencing new vistas in the world of creative imagination.

Libraries felt the same zest for new life. Although no library of national rank was yet possible, the joint collections of the Atlanta Universy Affiliation were increasing rapidly. By 1938, 60,000 volumes were on the shelves. Clark had increased its collection to 13,000. And even Georgia State Industrial College, which a few years before had been accused of hiding a mere 400 books in a dark basement, had managed to begin a collection by acquiring 6,000 volumes. Most notable of all advances were those at Paine. There a well-selected collection of 15,000 books especially suited to college study was accumulated in the years of the 'thirties. Everywhere collections on Negro life and literature were emphasized. Of course, these libraries were small, but the 36,000 volumes in all Georgia Negro colleges in 1905 had swelled by 1938 to 137,000 volumes and by 1948 to more than 200,000 volumes. The prosperity of the era was having its effect.

Another note on the modern scene was the reaching out of the colleges to the community. The national social welfare renaissance was behind the movement. Most prominent were the efforts to improve rural life in the state, to develop appreciation for the country, to inspire love for the soil and the realization that the Negro could be independent only if working on land of his own. The rural life conferences of the old days were fanned into large social campaigns. As early as 1921 Gammon was offering its preacher-students courses in rural life and sociology that covered diseases, economics, family life, migration, crime, club work, and the place of the minister in an agricultural society.[7] The public colleges and the school at Fort Valley fostered home gardening, farm management, and improvements in the home and the church. The health clinic at Fort Valley served the community. At Georgia State Industrial College efforts were spread throughout the state to develop community life, social gatherings, home ownership, and better methods of agriculture. Adults were taken into the program. To President Hubert the only hope of the Georgia Negro was in the country—and the depression emphasized his argument. With the economic duress of the city Negro, and closed trade unions depriving the town dweller of his independence, rural life seemed the only solution. In the 'twenties Spelman began a rural institute and, after Affiliation, Atlanta University

---

7. *Catalogue of Gammon Theological Seminary*, 1921-1922, p. 27.

revived the effort to train teachers and leaders in the economic and social problems of rural service.

At Paine a unique experiment in community welfare appeared with the establishment of a children's library which for the first time made books available to colored youngsters of Augusta. Subjects ranged from *Li'l Black Sambo* to the English poets, and nearly 500 children registered in the first year. In 1930 Spelman opened the first colored nursery school in the nation to train college students in parent education, child development, pediatrics, and to serve as a research institute for the study of child care, psychology, and home economics. Fort Valley began radio broadcasting in 1936 and by 1943 that endeavor had developed into a permanent weekly series. In 1942 Atlanta University began a People's College which in its first year enrolled more than 400 porters, clerks, domestics, businessmen, professors' wives, and others in 35 courses; and in later years it progressed to radio programs, film forums, workshops, and rental libraries to include many persons who never appeared in a classroom. On a small or large scale, in fact, every college in the state was soon engaged in some kind of adult education program for Negroes unable to attend college.

Extension work was part of the same movement. In nearly all colleges courses were available for those not able to attend as regular students. In 1933 the University System of Georgia opened its Extension Division to Negroes. By 1938 nearly 2,000 persons each year were taking regular college courses in the state system in education, English, and the social and physical sciences. In many colleges courses were available to nearby school teachers on afternoons and Saturdays. As early as 1914, Georgia State Industrial College had branched into extension work with one agent working under Federal supervision. In 1921 the college at Savannah became the headquarters for colored extension service for the state. Within three years twenty-four agents were in the rural areas of Georgia urging the fulfillment of an improved country society. By the late 'thirties the clubs organized by the several agents were enrolling 25,000 colored persons a year.[8] In 1947, moreover, Gammon added a Department of Rural Church and Religion and began offering extension courses.

During the same period summer schools appeared on the scene. In 1913 the Fort Valley High and Industrial School had opened the first summer school in Georgia for colored teachers.[9] But it was not until after the First World War that a statewide movement got underway. In Atlanta, Morehouse opened the first summer school in 1921. Work developed quickly to a college level, and by 1933 all the colleges in Atlanta had joined in a united summer session under the auspices of the new Affiliation. In 1937, 758 students were in attendance from twenty-two states and the Virgin Islands. Among the lot were 265 graduate students.[10] The public colleges responded to the same movement. In 1922 Georgia State Industrial College began summer instruction for colored teachers and during the ensuing years the junior colleges followed suit. By 1946-1947 the summer school had become such an established institution that approximately 5,000 students were enrolled. Of this number nearly 3,000 were attending summer sessions in the state-supported institutions, the remainder being in Atlanta University or in the small summer school operated at Paine.

It was natural that in this new era a new generation of leaders should appear. Only three institutions, in fact, survived the Great Depression of the 'thirties with the

---

8. *Spelman Messenger*, November, 1924; *Savannah Morning News*, October 13, 1927.
9. *Catalogue of Fort Valley High and Industrial School*, 1928-1929, p. 25.
10. *Crimson and Gray* (Atlanta University), July, 1937.

same leaders that had guided them through the period of the First World War. Holley continued at Albany, Hubbard at Forsyth, and Hunt at Fort Valley. But even these presidents were eventually forced to give way to the new age. The death of John Hope in 1936 and of Henry Hunt in 1938 deprived Georgia of the two most distinguished and worthy Negro educational leaders the state had ever had. The retirement of William Merida Hubbard in 1939 at the merger of the Forsyth and Fort Valley colleges and the retirement of J. W. Holley from Albany in 1943 brought to an end the days of founder-presidents.

Among the new generation there were Matthew S. Davage and James P. Brawley at Clark; the Fountains (father and son) at Morris Brown; Florence M. Read at Spelman; E. C. Peters at Paine; Samuel Archer, Charles D. Hubert, and Benjamin Elijah Mays at Morehouse; Willis King, John W. Haywood, and Harry V. Richardson at Gammon; Rufus Early Clement at Atlanta University; Horace Mann Bond and Cornelius V. Troup at Fort Valley; Benjamin F. Hubert and James A. Colston at Savannah; and Aaron Brown at Albany. More significant, perhaps, than the appearance of new blood was the fact that long before the three decades were over every one of the colleges except Paine and Spelman were being led by Negro presidents.

It was inevitable, also, that the spirit of change should take hold of the student body. Yet all through the 'twenties the Puritanical rules of the New England fathers remained as the supreme law of every campus. But there was no way to stem the tide of new standards of morality that were sweeping the country. By the early 'thirties colleges in metropolitan centers were forced to wink at practices of smoking, courting, and card-playing. Confinement to campus made a belated exit from the rule book and retiring hours vanished from all the catalogues.

In many colleges there arose fraternities and sororities, designed primarily to permit older students to lay the cudgel on their younger brethren. Athletics achieved social supremacy. And in a short span of years the way of life of the colored student was scarcely different from that of his white fellows.

It was natural that the social movement of the times should be abundant with the subject of race relations. Gradually the white world began to realize that the barrier between the races could not be so tightly drawn as in the past. The Negro had shown power of development. His achievements in business, agriculture, education, religion, literature, science, and the arts were receiving profound tributes of respect.[11] Although the legislature of Georgia contributed only $55,000 toward Negro higher education in 1930 compared to $1,300,000 for whites, even this slight increase was significant of better recognition and during the 'thirties and 'forties the proportion of funds expended by the Board of Regents on the Negro institutions increased from 4 per cent to 12 per cent of the total funds allotted to the Regents. Still more notable were the interracial experiments launched at Paine where President Peters' experience in the Orient produced a new attitude. Out of his insistence for better relations, racial equality, bold and bald, appeared on the campus. Through the department of sociology, campaigns were inaugurated to stir local colored people to the polls. And although the Methodist Church refused to sanction the activity, it was willing to accept the effort as an experiment that might turn a light on the eternal problem.

Such was the panorama of the Negro colleges of Georgia in the years 1918 to 1948. The abandonment of the institution at Forsyth had removed one school from the

---

11. *Twenty Year Report of the Phelps-Stokes Fund*, 31.

scene. The struggle for survival of the college at Macon also seemed to jeopardize another despite a brief revival that had occurred under J. H. Gadson in the early 'twenties.[12] But aside from these casualties the Negro colleges of Georgia were, for the most part, well-established and flourishing institutions. In the troubled years of the twentieth century no man could predict with accuracy the eventual fate of the colleges, of Negro higher education, or of civilization itself. But at last it seemed as if the dreams of the founding fathers of the Negro colleges of Georgia had achieved a provident fulfillment.

---

12. In 1949 the Georgia Baptist College at Macon underwent financial reorganization and continued junior college work under a newly-elected president, Peter G. Crawford.

Appendix

CHRONOLOGICAL TABLES

ATLANTA UNIVERSITY (Atlanta)

1865   Classes held for ex-slaves in Jenkins Street Church and railroad box-car.
1866   Storr's School established.
1867   Atlanta University formally chartered under sponsorship of the American Missionary Association; Edmund Asa Ware founder and first president.
1869   North Hall completed. First normal class assembled with 89 students.
1871   South Hall completed.
1872   College department opened with 12 students.
1873   First normal class students graduated.
1876   Six graduates from college department received first bachelor's degree ever granted Negroes in Georgia.
1882   *Atlanta University Bulletin* established.
1885   Death of Edmund Asa Ware; followed 1885-1888 by succession of three acting-presidents—Thomas N. Chase, Horace Bumstead, and Cyrus W. Francis.
1887   Georgia State Board of Visitors discovered children of white teachers in student body; State withdrew $8,000 annual Morrill Act subsidy.
1888   Horace Bumstead elected president.
1889   Myron W. Adams appeared as first Ph.D. to teach in a Georgia Negro college; laboratory work in physics and chemistry begun for first time in a Southern Negro college.
1894   Elementary grades discontinued.
1896   Series of social studies on Negro life begun; Negro Life Conferences inaugurated; football introduced as an intercollegiate sport.

1905	Endowment amounted to $53,900.
1907	Edward Twitchell Ware elected president upon retirement of President Bumstead.
1922	Myron W. Adams became president.
1924	First efforts at graduate work begun.
1925	Began abolition of high school grades.
1928	No students enrolled below college or junior normal grades.
1929	Affiliated with Morehouse and Spelman to form Atlanta University Affiliation; became graduate institution; John Hope elected president.
1930	Undergraduate courses discontinued.
1931	Began instruction in sculpturing and other fine arts.
1933	Began operating joint summer school with all other Atlanta Negro institutions; total assets of University amounted to more than $10,000,000.
1934	Summer Theatre established.
1936	Death of John Hope; Miss Florence M. Read made acting president.
1937	Rufus Early Clement elected president.
1941	School of Library Service established.
1942	People's College established.
1946	School of Business Administration opened.
1946	Enrollment 294; income $344,000; endowment $4,607,559; library, 85,000 volumes; value of plant, $1,965,000.
1947	Atlanta School of Social Work incorporated into University.
1948	Enrollment 365.

MOREHOUSE COLLEGE (Atlanta)

(Former names: Augusta Institute; Atlanta Baptist Seminary; Atlanta Baptist College)

1867	School established for ex-slaves in Springfield Baptist Church by Richard R. Coulter and William J. White under sponsorship of American Baptist Home Missionary Society; classes began in Augusta with 38 students.

APPENDIX 225

1870 Property secured on Telfair Street at cost of $5,700.
1871 Joseph Thomas Robert elected president.
1879 Moved to Atlanta on property secured at Elliott and West Hunter streets; chartered as Atlanta Baptist Seminary; first building erected at cost of $7,500.
1881 College department opened with one student.
1883 First degree granted.
1885 Samuel Graves elected president.
1889 Graves Hall erected.
1890 Moved to present location; George Sale elected president.
1897 Rechartered as Atlanta Baptist College.
1902 Fourteen students enrolled in college department.
1906 John Hope elected president.
1912 Sale Hall completed.
1913 Name changed to Morehouse College in honor of Henry Lyman Morehouse, Corresponding Secretary of the American Baptist Home Mission Society.
1916 Robert Hall completed.
1921 Operated first summer school.
1924 College department enrollment exceeded academy enrollment for first time.
1928 Began joint operation of summer school with Spelman College.
1929 Became affiliated wtih Atlanta University and Spelman College.
1931 Samuel Howard Archer elected president upon resignation of John Hope.
1935 Control transferred from American Baptist Home Mission Society to Board of Trustees.
1937 Charles D. Hubert elected acting-president upon retirement of President Archer.
1940 Benjamin Elijah Mays elected president.
1946 Enrollment 909; income $395,000; endowment $1,872,-000; value of plant $559,000.
1948 Enrollment 769.

CLARK COLLEGE (Atlanta)
(Former name: Clark University)

- 1869   Primary school opened in Clark Chapel by Rev. J. W. Lee and wife under sponsorship of Freedmen's Aid Society of the Methodist Episcopal Church (North).
- 1870   Building secured at Whitehall and McDaniel streets with financial aid from Mrs. Augusta Clark Cole, daughter of Bishop D. W. Clark. Institution named Clark University in honor of donors.
- 1872   Moved to site on southeast side of Atlanta secured by Bishop Gilbert Haven.
- 1877   Chartered.
- 1879   College department opened with four freshmen.
- 1880   Chrisman Hall completed.
- 1883   Department of Theology created as result of gift from Elijah H. Gammon.
- 1886   Department of Theology separated from Clark to form Gammon Theological Seminary.
- 1902   Thirty-two students in college department.
- 1905   Plant worth nearly $200,000.
- 1925   Matthew S. Davage began one of few long term occupancies of presidency.
- 1940   Name changed to Clark College.
- 1941   Moved to new plant on Chestnut Street opposite Atlanta University. Move made possible by contribution of $1,250,000 from the General Education Board, Rosenwald Fund, and Mrs. Henry Pfeiffer of New York; James P. Brawley elected to presidency.
- 1942   Enrollment 407.
- 1946   Enrollment 777; income, $290,000; library, 15,000 volumes; endowment, $902,000; value of plant, $913,000.
- 1948   Enrollment 886.

SPELMAN COLLEGE (Atlanta)
(Former names: Atlanta Baptist Female Seminary; Spelman Seminary)

- 1881   Founded as Atlanta Baptist Female Seminary by Miss

APPENDIX

Sophia B. Packard and Miss Harriet E. Giles; operated during first two years in basement of Friendship Baptist Church.
1883 Moved to present location. Slater Fund began aid for industrial courses.
1884 John D. Rockefeller, Sr., visited Seminary, paid off debt on property; name changed to Spelman Seminary in honor of family name of Mrs. Rockefeller. *Spelman Messenger* founded; Rockefeller Hall erected.
1886 Packard Hall erected.
1888 Seminary chartered; Board of Trustees organized.
1890 College department opened but teaching only Latin and German.
1891 Miss Packard died after 10 years in presidency; eight hundred students and thirty teachers on campus; property valued at $90,000; Miss Giles succeeded to presidency.
1892 Giles Hall erected.
1897 Full-fledged college department inaugurated, with 2 students.
1905 Plant valued at $350,000; endowment, $10,800.
1909 Miss Giles died. Miss Lucy Upton acting president 1909-1910.
1910 Miss Lucy Hale Tapley became president; emphasis placed on college work.
1925 Tapley Hall erected.
1927 Miss Tapley retired, succeeded by Miss Florence Matilda Read; Sisters' Chapel dedicated.
1928 Elementary School and Nurse Training Department abolished. Summer school operated in cooperation with Morehouse College.
1929 Affiliated with Morehouse College and Atlanta University.
1930 Abolished Spelman High School; opened nursery school.
1940 Enrollment 384.
1947 Enrollment 394; endowment $3,260,000; plant value $969,000; current income $324,000.

MORRIS BROWN COLLEGE (Atlanta)

1881 — Founded by African Methodist Episcopal Church; named for Bishop Morris Brown of the church; property purchased at North Boulevard and Houston Street.

1885 — Chartered; Gaines Hall erected; Mrs. Mary McCree appointed principal; first classes admitted.

1886 — Mrs. Alice D. Cary made principal.

1887 — Rev. E. W. Lee made principal.

1888 — A. S. Richardson appointed principal.

1890 — First class graduated.

1891 — Grant Hall erected.

1892 — Principalship changed to presidency; A. S. Richardson appointed as first president.

1894 — College courses added to curriculum; Theological Department established.

1896 — Rev. James M. Henderson elected president.

1900 — Theological Department reorganized into Turner Theological Seminary.

1901 — Turner Hall erected, uniting Gaines and Grant.

1904-08 — Presidency of Rev. Joseph S. Flipper; new charter granted; tailoring, music, and sewing departments added.

1908-11 — Presidency of Rev. E. W. Lee.

1911 — Lee died unexpectedly; Rev. W. A. Fountain elected president.

1912-16 — Commercial Department established; old dormitory made into Wyley Grammar School.

1913 — Morris Brown University established consisting of Morris Brown College and Turner Theological Seminary in Atlanta, Payne College in Cuthbert, and Central Park Normal and Industrial Institute in Savannah.

1920 — John Henry Lewis elected president.

1928 — William Alfred Fountain, Jr., made president.

1929 — Affiliation with Payne College and Central Park Normal and Industrial Institute discontinued.

1931 — High School and practice school abolished; College became four-year collegiate institution.

1932 — Moved to plant formerly occupied by Atlanta University; Preparatory School abolished; Williams Busi-

	ness College merged with Morris Brown; joined Atlanta University System.
1936	Endowment campaign begun.
1942	Given class "A" accreditation by Southern Association of Colleges and Secondary Schools.
1946	Enrollment 736; library, 7,872 volumes; income, $356,000; endowment, $480,000; value of plant, $403,970.
1948	Enrollment 924.

PAINE COLLEGE (Augusta)
(Former name: Paine Institute)

1882	Committee composed of representatives of Colored Methodist Episcopal Church and Methodist Episcopal Church, South, decided to establish institute; named in honor of Bishop Robert Paine, then Senior Bishop of the white church; Rev. Morgan Callaway elected first president.
1883	Chartered.
1884	Rev. George Williams Walker elected president; instruction begun in rented rooms on Broad Street.
1886	Present site on Fifteenth Street secured at cost of $8,000.
1888	Four-year college course inaugurated with 3 students; $25,000 endowment given by Moses U. Paine.
1899	Haygood Hall erected.
1902	Sixteen students enrolled in college department; began active cooperation with Women's Missionary Council of the Methodist Episcopal Church, South.
1903	Rechartered as Paine College.
1911	John D. Hammond elected president.
1913	Bennett Hall erected.
1915	D. D. Atkins elected president.
1917	Albert Deems Betts elected president.
1921	Theological School discontinued.
1923	Ray S. Tomlin elected president.
1925	Epworth Hall erected, gift of Epworth Leagues of Methodist Episcopal Church, South. Mary Helm Hall erected, gift of Woman's Missionary Council of Methodist Episcopal Church, South.

1929 E. C. Peters elected president.
1938 15,000 volumes in library.
1939 With unification of Methodist Churches, control transferred to Board of Missions and Church Extension of the Methodist Church.
1946 Enrollment 428; income $152,000; library 21,000 volumes; endowment $34,398; value of plant $479,601.
1947 Warren A. Candler Memorial Library completed.
1948 Enrollment 328.

GAMMON THEOLOGICAL SEMINARY (Atlanta)

1883 Department of Theology established at Clark University through efforts of Bishop Henry White Warren and $25,000 contribution from Elijah H. Gammon of Batavia, Illinois; Wilbur P. Thirkield placed in charge.
1886 Department of Theology made separate institution as condition for receiving additional $200,000 endowment from Gammon; Thirkield elected to presidency.
1890 Endowment up to about $400,000, practically all contributed by Gammon.
1894 Stewart Missionary Foundation for Africa established.
1898 Enrollment 80; endowment about $600,000.
1899 Thirkield resigned; presidency rotated among faculty until succession of L. G. Adkinson in 1901.
1905 Nearly 12,000 volumes in library, unusual collection for day.
1906 Adkinson died; succeeded by John W. E. Bowen.
1910 Gammon and Clark again placed under single presidency—that of S. E. Idleman.
1914 School of Missions organized; Philip M. Watters became president of Seminary.
1926-28 Presidency of George Henry Trever.
1928-33 Presidency of Franklin Halsted Clapp.
1933 Willis J. King became president; 21,000 volumes in library.
1937 Enrollment 67; diploma course dropped; bachelor's degree required for admission to Seminary degree course; accredited by American Association of Theological Schools.

1944 King resigned; John W. Haywood elected president; religious education program for women raised to graduate level.
1947 Department of Rural Church and Religion established.
1948 Harry V. Richardson inaugurated as president; enrollment 64.

GEORGIA STATE COLLEGE (Savannah)
(Former name: The Georgia State Industrial College for Colored Youths)

1890 Founded as state institution to provide training as prescribed in Federal land-grant acts of 1862 and 1890. Originally operated under Trustees of University of Georgia, but with local Board of Commissioners in direct control.
1891 Operations began in Baxter Street School at Athens, under direction of Richard R. Wright, principal. October, 1891, classes transferred to present site near Savannah. Wright elected president.
1892 Named "The Georgia State Industrial College for Colored Youths." First college class inaugurated with 4 students.
1893 Began farmers' conferences.
1898 Graduated first student from college department.
1900 Faculty consisted of 14 members as compared to 3 ten years previously.
1921 Institution made headquarters for agricultural extension work among Negroes.
1922 First summer school for teachers held.
1923 Eight students enrolled in college department; Federal survey revealed weaknesses of institution; prodded state to action.
1925 Board of Commissioners replaced by new Board of Trustees.
1926 Benjamin F. Hubert elected president on retirement of President Wright.
1927 State legislature increased appropriation to approximately $50,000 per year. Emphasis placed on college work.

1928 53 students enrolled in college departments.
1932 Integrated into reorganized University System of Georgia under control of Board of Regents. Name changed to Georgia State College.
1938 447 students enrolled in college.
1947 Enrollment 885; income, $343,600; library, 15,500 volumes; value of plant, $880,000; Dr. Hubert resigned presidency; succeeded by James A. Colston.
1949 Enrollment, 1,243.

FORT VALLEY STATE COLLEGE
(Former name: Fort Valley High and Industrial School)

1895 Founded as Fort Valley High and Industrial School by white and Negro citizens of Fort Valley, led by John W. Davison. Five thousand dollar contribution from Anna T. Jeanes for first building marked beginning of Jeanes Fund for education of Negro women.
1903 Henry A. Hunt elected president. Found 145 students and annual budget of about $840. School soon getting support from such well-known benefactors as George F. Peabody, Andrew Carnegie, General Education Board, Julius Rosenwald, and Collis P. Huntington.
1908 Collis P. Huntington gave $25,000 for girls' dormitory.
1913 American Church Institute of the Episcopal Church became sponsor. Held first summer school ever available to Negro teachers in Georgia.
1925 Carnegie library built.
1927 Full-fledged junior college work begun with 13 freshmen.
1936 Began radio broadcasting.
1938 Henry A. Hunt died.
1939 Sponsorship of Episcopal Church ended; institution merged with State Teachers and Agricultural College at Forsyth and became four-year college in University System of Georgia. Horace Mann Bond elected president.

APPENDIX 233

1941　First four-year college class graduated.
1945　Dr. Cornelius V. Troup became president upon resignation of Dr. Bond.
1946　Regents voted to begin graduate work offering master's degrees in education, home economics, and agriculture.
1947　Enrollment, 515; income, $408,445; library, 10,800 volumes; endowment, $38,359; value of plant, $763,509.

GEORGIA BAPTIST COLLEGE (Macon)
(Former name: Central City College)

1899　Founded by Missionary Baptist Convention of Georgia under leadership of Rev. E. K. Love; William E. Holmes elected as first president.
1902　Enrollment 365, but no work of college level being done.
1915　Georgia Baptists reunited under name of General Missionary Baptist Convention of Georgia.
1920　College Department established.
1921　Practically all buildings destroyed by fire.
1924　J. H. Gadson elected to presidency succeeding retiring President Holmes.
1927　Institution $20,000 in debt.
1935　Second split in Baptist Convention threatens existence of college. H. R. Harris elected acting-president.
1937　Mortgage on college property liquidated through philanthropy of James H. Porter of Macon. College came under control of Georgia Baptist Missionary and Educational Convention.
1938　Name changed from Central City College to Georgia Baptist College.
1940　C. J. Gresham elected to presidency.
1945-46　Enrollment in high school 132; college, 53; theological department, 15.
1946　Frederick Douglass Graves elected president.
1949　Peter G. Crawford elected to presidency.

STATE TEACHERS AND AGRICULTURAL COLLEGE
(Forsyth)

(Former names: Monroe County Training School; State Agricultural and Mechanical School)

1902   Founded by William Merida Hubbard. First classes held in Kynett Methodist Episcopal Church; some financial support soon coming from the American Missionary Association.

1916   Became a senior high school.

1917   Slater Fund and General Education Board increased financial support.

1922   Became a state agricultural and mechanical school, but only partially supported and controlled by the state.

1929   Partly destroyed by fire; state took over complete control.

1932   Integrated as a junior college in the reorganized University System of Georgia under Board of Regents; specialties were teacher training and agriculture.

1939   Plant at Forsyth abandoned by Regents and facilities merged with institution at Fort Valley.

ALBANY STATE COLLEGE

(Former names: Albany Bible and Manual Training Institution; State Agricultural, Industrial, and Normal School; Georgia Normal and Agricultural College)

1903   Founded by Joseph W. Holley with financial aid from Anna and Caroline Hazard of New England. First classes held in Union Baptist Church.

1904   Chartered; Board of Trustees organized.

1917   State began appropriations but not complete support. Control transferred to Board of Trustees representing state.

1932   Integrated as a junior college into reorganized University System of Georgia under Board of Regents.

1935   New library built as result of gifts from Caroline Hazard.

1940   Enrollment 253.

APPENDIX 235

1943 Aaron Brown elected president on retirement of President Holley; name changed to Albany State College; became four-year teacher-training degree-granting institution.
1946 Enrollment, 418; income, $275,000; library, 15,000 volumes; value of plant, $600,000.
1948 Enrollment 850.

ATLANTA UNIVERSITY SCHOOL OF SOCIAL WORK
(Atlanta)
(Former name: Atlanta School of Social Work)

1920 Founded by few Negro social workers under parentage of Morehouse College as result of National Conference for Social Workers which met in New Orleans that year. E. Franklin Frazier made director.
1925 Chartered; financial aid for permanent establishment given by Laura Spelman Rockefeller Memorial Fund.
1927 Forrester B. Washington succeeded to directorship of school.
1929 Began cooperation with Atlanta University Affiliation.
1935 Raised admission requirements to four years of college study.
1938 Formally joined Atlanta University Affiliation.
1947 Relinquished corporate charter and became school integrally a part of Atlanta University.

Bibliography

BOOKS

Alvord, J. W., *Letters from the South Relating to the Condition of Freedmen, Addressed to Maj.-General O. O. Howard.* Washington: Howard University Press, 1870.

Bond, Horace Mann, *The Education of the Negro in the American Social Order.* New York: Prentice-Hall, Inc., 1934.

Bowen, Trevor, *Divine White Right.* New York: Harper & Brothers, 1934.

Brawley, Benjamin G., *A Short History of the American Negro.* New York: The Macmillan Company, 1913.

Crogman, William Henry, *Talks for the Times.* Atlanta: Press of the Franklin Printing Company, 1896.

Culp, Daniel W., ed., *The Twentieth Century Negro Literature; or a cyclopedia of thought on the vital topics relating to the American Negro, by one hundred of America's greatest Negroes.* Naperville, Illinois: Nichols & Company, 1902.

Dabney, Charles William, *Universal Education in the South.* 2 vols. Chapel Hill: University of North Carolina Press, 1936.

Douglass, H. Paul, *Christian Reconstruction in the South.* Boston: The Pilgrim Press, 1909.

DuBois, W. E. B., *Black Reconstruction.* New York: Harcourt, Brace & Company, 1935.

DuBois, W. E. B., *The Souls of Black Folk.* Thirteenth edition. Chicago: A. C. McClug & Company, 1922.

Embree, Edwin R., *Brown America, The Story of a New Race.* Seventh Printing. New York: Viking Press, 1936.

BIBLIOGRAPHY

Fleming, William H., *Slavery and the Race Problem in the South, With Special Reference to the State of Georgia.* Boston: Dana Estes & Company, 1906.

Floyd, Silas Xavier, *Life of Charles T. Walker, D.D.* Nashville: National Baptist Publishing Board, 1902.

From Servitude to Service, Being the Old South Lectures on the History and Work of Southern Institutions for the Education of the Negro. Boston: American Unitarian Association, 1905.

Gordon, Asa H., *The Georgia Negro, A History.* Student's edition. Ann Arbor, Mich.: Edwards Brothers Incorporated, 1937.

Haygood, Atticus G., *Our Brother in Black, His Freedom and His Future.* Second edition. Nashville: Southern Methodist Publishing House, 1887.

Holmes, Dwight Oliver Wendell, *The Evolution of the Negro College.* Contributions to Education No. 609. New York: Teachers College, Columbia University, 1934.

Johnson, Charles Spurgeon, *The Negro College Graduate.* Chapel Hill: University of North Carolina Press, 1938.

———*The Negro in American Civilization.* New York: Henry Holt & Company, 1930.

Johnson, James Weldon, *Along This Way, The Autobiography of James Weldon Johnson.* New York: Viking Press, 1938.

Jones, Lance G. E., *Negro Schools in the Southern States.* Oxford, England: Clarendon Press, 1928.

Leavell, Ullin Whitney, *Philanthropy in Negro Education.* Nashville: George Peabody College for Teachers, 1930.

McCuiston, Fred, *Higher Education of Negroes.* Nashville: Southern Association of Colleges and Secondary Schools, 1933.

———*Graduate Instruction for Negroes in the United States.* Nashville: George Peabody College for Teachers, 1939.

McElreath, Walter, *A Treatise on the Constitution of Georgia.* Atlanta: The Harrison Company, 1912.

McKinney, Theophilus Elisha, ed., *Higher Education Among Negroes*. Charlotte: Johnson C. Smith University, 1932.

Paxson, Frederic L., *Recent History of the United States, 1865-1929*. Revised edition. New York: Houghton Mifflin Company, 1929.

Ponton, M. M., *Life and Times of Henry M. Turner*. Atlanta: A. B. Caldwell Publishing Company, n.d.

Reuter, Edward Byron, *The American Race Problem*. Revised edition. New York: Thomas Y. Crowell Company, 1938.

Stowell, Jay S., *Methodist Adventures in Negro Education*. New York: The Methodist Book Concern, 1922.

Swint, Henry Lee, *The Northern Teacher in the South, 1862-1870*. Nashville: Vanderbilt University Press, 1941.

Thomas, William Hannibal, *The American Negro*. New York: The Macmillan Company, 1901.

Thompson, C. Mildred, *Reconstruction in Georgia, Economic, Social, Political, 1865-1872*. New York: Columbia University Press, 1915.

Torrence, Ridgely, *The Story of John Hope*. New York: The Macmillan Company, 1948.

Trawick, A. M., ed., *The New Voice in Race Adjustments*. Addresses and reports presented at the Negro Christian Student Conference, Atlanta, Georgia, May 14-18, 1914. New York: Student Volunteer Movement, 1914.

Washington, E. Davidson, ed., *Selected Speeches of Booker T. Washington*. Garden City, N. Y.: Doubleday, Doran & Company, 1932.

Woodson, Carter G., *Education of the Negro Prior to 1861*. New York: G. P. Putnam's Sons, 1915.

——*The Mis-Education of the Negro*. Washington, D. C.: The Associated Publishers, Incorporated, 1933.

GOVERNMENT PUBLICATIONS

GEORGIA

A Statement from Governor Hugh M. Dorsey as to the Negro in Georgia, 1921.

Journal of the House of Representatives of the State of Georgia, 1890.

Report of the State School Commissioner of Georgia, 1874-1888; 1900-1936. Later issued as *Annual Report from the Department of Education of Georgia to the General Assembly*.

Report of the State Auditor of Georgia, 1931-1938.

UNITED STATES

Alvord, J. W., *Fourth Semi-Annual Report on Schools for Freedmen.* July 1, 1867, Bureau of Refugees, Freedmen and Abandoned Lands. Washington: United States Government Printing Office, 1867.

Eighth Semi-Annual Report on Schools for Freedmen. July 1, 1869, Bureau of Refugees, Freedmen and Abandoned Lands. Washington: United States Government Printing Office, 1869.

Andrews, Benjamin F., *Agricultural and Mechanical Colleges, 1915-16.* A report of the condition of land-grant colleges. Bureau of Education, Department of the Interior. Washington: United States Government Printing Office, 1917.

Blose, David T. and Ambrose Caliver, *Statistics of the Education of Negroes, 1929-30 and 1931-32.* Department of Interior, Office of Education, Bulletin, 1935, No. 13. Washington: United States Government Printing Office, 1936.

Caliver, Ambrose, *A Background Study of Negro College Students.* Office of Education, Bulletin, 1933, No. 8. Washington: United States Government Printing Office, 1933.

Education of Negro Teachers. Office of Education, Bulletin, 1933, No. 10. Washington: United States Government Printing Office, 1933.

Federal Laws, Regulations and Rulings Affecting the Land-Grant Colleges of Agriculture and Mechanic Arts. Department of Interior, Office of Education. Washington: United States Government Printing Office, 1911, 1916.

Jones, Thomas Jesse, *Negro Education, A study of the private and higher schools for colored people in the United States prepared in cooperation with the Phelps-Stokes Fund.* United States Bureau of Education, Bulletins, 1916. 2 vols. Washington: United States Government Printing Office, 1917.

Klein, Arthur J., *Survey of Land-Grant Colleges and Universities.* Office of Education, Bulletin No. 9, 1930. Washington: United States Government Printing Office, 1930.

——*Survey of Negro Colleges and Universities.* United States Bureau of Education, Bulletin No. 7, 1928. Washington: United States Government Printing Office, 1929.

Mayo, A. D., *Southern Women in the Recent Educational Movement in the South.* United States Bureau of Education, Circular of Information, No. 1, 1892. Washington: United States Government Printing Office, 1892.

Negroes in the United States, 1920-32. Department of Commerce, Bureau of the Census. Washington: United States Government Printing Office, 1935.

Statistical Abstract of the United States, 1937. Fifty-ninth number. Department of Commerce. Washington: United States Government Printing Office, 1938.

INSTITUTIONAL RECORDS AND PUBLICATIONS

Atlanta School of Social Work
Bulletin of the Atlanta School of Social Work, 1920-1937.

Atlanta University
Adams, Myron Winslow, *A History of Atlanta University.* Atlanta: Atlanta University Press, 1930.

Atlanta University Bulletin, 1883-1948.

Catalogue of Atlanta University, 1869-1948. Sometimes issued as *Atlanta University Bulletin, Catalogue Number.*

BIBLIOGRAPHY 241

The Crimson and Gray, 1910-1929; 1935-1938. Publication of the Alumni Association of Atlanta University.

The Scroll, 1903-1910; 1913-1917; 1924-1928. Publication of the students of Atlanta University.

Clarke College
Catalogue of Clark University, 1878-1948.

Fort Valley State College
Annual Circular and Catalogue of the Fort Valley High and Industrial School, 1905-1948. Sometimes issued as *Bulletin* or as *The Fort Valley Message.*

Gammon Theological Seminary
Catalogue of Gammon Theological Seminary, 1888-1948.

Georgia Baptist College
Catalogue of Central City College, 1901-1948.

Georgia State Industrial College
Catalogue of the Georgia State Industrial College, 1891-1948. Sometime issued as *Year-Book* and as *Bulletin.*

Morehouse College
Athenaeum, 1898-1924. Publication of students and alumni of Morehouse College and Spelman Seminary.

Brawley, Benjamin, *History of Morehouse College.* Atlanta: Morehouse College, 1917.

Catalogue of Morehouse College, 1878-1948. Issued during earlier years as catalogue of Augusta Institute, Atlanta Baptist Seminary, and Atlanta Baptist College.

Morris Brown College
Catalogue of Morris Brown College, 1899-1900; 1907-1948. Sometimes issued as *Official Bulletin and Catalogue.*
The Wagon Wheel, March, 1939. Publication of the students of Morris Brown College.

Paine College
Annual Catalogue of Paine College, 1887-1899; 1901-1948. Sometimes issued as *Bulletin of Paine College.*

Peters, E. C., *Dr. George Williams Walker, Founder of Paine College.* A leaflet published by Paine College.

Spelman College

Catalogue of Spelman College, 1881-1948. Issued during earlier years as catalogue of Atlanta Baptist Female Seminary, Spelman Baptist Seminary, Spelman Seminary and Normal School. Sometimes entitled *Bulletin,* or *Annual Circular.*

Historicla Sketch and General Catalogue of Spelman Seminary, 1881-1921. Atlanta: Spelman Seminary, n.d.

Spelman Messenger, 1885-1938. Official publication of Spelman College.

University of Georgia

Annual Report from the Regents of the University System of Georgia to the Governor. 1932-1938.

Catalogue of the University of Georgia, 1899-1900.

Report of the Trustees of the University of Georgia, 1899-1900.

REPORTS OF ORGANIZATIONS

American Missionary Association

Annual Reports of the American Missionary Association, 1860-1886. New York: American Missionary Association.

Conference for Education in the South

Bumstead, Horace, "The Practical Value of the Higher Education of the Negro," in *Proceedings of the Third Capon Springs Conference for Education in the South.* 1900.

Hill, Walter B., "Negro Education in the South," in *Proceedings of the Conference for Education in the South.* 1903.

General Education Board

Annual Report of the General Education Board, 1914-1936. New York: General Education Board.

The General Education Board, An account of its activities, 1902-1914. New York: General Education Board, 1915.

Phelps-Stokes Fund

Jones, Thomas Jesse, *Educational Adaptations, Report of Ten Years' Work of the Phelps-Stokes Fund, 1910-1920.* New York: Phelps-Stokes Fund, 1920.

Twenty Year Report of the Phelps-Stokes Fund, 1911-1931. New York: Phelps-Stokes Fund, 1932.

Association of Colleges and Secondary Schools of the Southern States

Proceedings of the Association of Colleges and Secondary Schools of the Southern States, 1930-1934.

Peabody Fund

Proceedings of the Trustees of the Peabody Education Fund, 1867-1874. Boston: Press of John Wilson and Son, 1875. I.

Slater Fund

Bacon, Alice M., "The Negro and the Atlanta Exposition," in *Slater Fund Occasional Papers,* No. 7. Baltimore, 1896.

Curry, J. L. M., "Difficulties, Complications, and Limitations Connected with the Education of the Negro," in *Slater Fund Occasional Papers,* No. 5. Baltimore, 1895.

"Education of the Negroes since 1860," in *Slater Fund Occasional Papers,* No. 3. Baltimore, 1894.

Gannett, Henry, "Statistics of the Negroes in the United States," in *Slater Fund Occasional Papers,* No. 4. Baltimore, 1894.

Haygood, Atticus G., *The Case of the Negro as to Education in the Southern States.* Report to the Board of Trustees of the John F. Slater Fund. Atlanta: Jas. P. Harrison & Company, 1885.

Proceedings and Reports of the John F. Slater Fund, 1882-1936. New York: John F. Slater Fund.

"Reference List of Southern Colored Schools," in *Slater Fund Occasional Papers,* No. 20. Three separate issues have been published in 1921, 1925, and 1929.

"Report on Negro Universities and Colleges," in *Slater Fund Occasional Papers,* No. 21. Baltimore, 1922.

Williams, W. T. B., "Duplication of Schools for Negro Youth," in *Slater Fund Occasional Papers,* No. 15, Baltimore, 1914.

MANUSCRIPTS
Schools
Atlanta University
> Minutes of the Faculty of Atlanta University, 1872-1930.
> Minutes of the Trustees of Atlanta University, 1895-1911.
> President's Report to the Trustees of Atlanta University, May 26, 1914.

Fort Valley Normal and Industrial School
> Faculty Records of Fort Valley Normal and Industrial School, 1916-1938.
> Minutes of the Trustees of Fort Valley High and Industrial School, 1895-1938.

Gammon Theological Seminary
> Auditor's Reports and Financial Statements of Gammon Theological Seminary, 1911-1939.
> Minutes of the Trustees of Gammon Theological Seminary, 1888-1939.

Georgia State Industrial College
> Minutes of the Meetings of the Commission Governing Georgia State Industrial College for Colored Students, 1916-1926. (In possession of A. Pratt Adams, Savannah, Georgia.)
> Minutes of the Faculty of Georgia State Industrial College, 1891-1915.
> Students' record of Georgia State Industrial College.

Morehouse College
> Faculty Records of Atlanta Baptist College, 1899-1913.

Morris Brown College
> Auditor's Reports of Morris Brown College, 1935-1938.

Paine College
> Minutes of the Trustees of Paine Institute, 1882-1936.

Spelman College
> Students' Record of Spelman Seminary, 1897-1912.

Organizations and Individuals

Annual Report, Division of General Extension of the University System of Georgia, 1937-38.

Ayer, Frederick, Collection of Letters, 1865-1867. The bulk are from E. M. Cravath, agent of the American Missionary Association, to Ayer. In the possession of Atlanta University Library.

Blauch, L. E., "The Georgia State Industrial College." A survey in mimeographed form issued June 15, 1923, by the U. S. Department of Interior, Bureau of Education, Washington, D. C.

Bumstead, Horace, Collection of Letters, 1902-1919. The bulk are from Horace Bumstead to Edward Twitchell Ware. In possession of Atlanta University Library.

Christler, Ethel Maude, "Participation of Negroes in the Government of Georgia, 1867-1870." Master's thesis in Atlanta University Library, 1932.

Cocking, Walter D., Director, "Report of the Study on Higher Education of Negroes in Georgia." Athens: University of Georgia, 1938. Issued in mimeographed form.

Earl, Charlotte Alma, "The Racial Attitudes of One Hundred Negro College Students." Master's thesis in Atlanta University Library, 1938.

Freedmen's Bureau Weekly and Monthly Reports for 1870. These are loose sheets in the possession of Atlanta University Library.

Reddick, Jamie Lawson, "The Negro and the Populist Movement in Georgia." Master's thesis in Atlanta University Library, 1937.

Rodriguez, Edward Rudolph, "A Study of the Discriminations in Race and Color Current in the City of Atlanta." Master's thesis in Atlanta University Library, 1934.

Steely, Fred Lynn, "Social Work as a Pedagogical Device for Sociologists." Manuscript prepared in 1935 by Professor Steely of Paine College.

Thomas, Harriet Franceska, "Legislation as it Affected Public Education for Negroes in Georgia." Master's thesis in Atlanta University Library, 1935.

Walker, Charles Hilliard, "The Attitude of Georgia Toward the Education of Negroes, 1865-1935." Master's thesis in Atlanta University Library, 1935.

Ware, Edward Twitchell, "Sketch of the Life of Edmund Asa Ware." A typewritten manuscript in Atlanta University Library.

Webster, Edgar H., "The Georgia Negro's Fight on Ignorance." In possession of Edgar H. Webster, Fairhope, Alabama.

Webster, Edgar H., Notes on early Negro education prepared for the author by Professor Emeritus Edgar H. Webster of Atlanta University. 1939.

NEWSPAPERS

Atlanta Independent, 1905.

Atlanta Constitution, 1883.

Boston Journal, 1888.

Savannah Advertiser, 1872.

Savannah Morning News, 1891.

Savannah Tribune, 1890-1891, 1907, 1911, 1918, 1921, 1926.

PAMPHLETS

Clark, Elmer T., *A Methodist Romance*. Published by Paine College, 1933.

Clark, Elmer T., *The Unique Adventure*. Published by Paine College, 1933.

Down Where The Need Is Greatest. New York: The American Church Institute for Negroes, c. 1937.

DuBois, W. E. B., ed., *The College-Bred Negro*. Atlanta University Publications No. 5. Second abridged edition. Atlanta University Press, 1902.

DuBois, W. E. B., ed., *The College-Bred Negro American.* Atlanta University Publications No. 15. Atlanta University Press, 1910.

Emery, E. B., *Letters from the South on the Social, Intellectual, and Moral Condition of the Colored People.* Boston: Beacon Press, 1880.

Ethridge, Mrs. W. S., *An Aristocracy of Achievement.* Concerning the Hubert family of Hancock County, Georgia. 1929.

Floyd, Silas X., *A Sketch of Rev. C. T. Walker, D.D.* Augusta: Sentinal Publishing Company, 1892.

Love, E. K., *Annual Address to the Missionary Baptist Convention of Georgia*, in Atlanta, May 24, 1899. Nashville: National Baptist Publishing Board, 1899.

Orr, Gustavus J., *The Education of the Negro, Its Rise, Progress, and Present Status.* Atlanta: Jas. P. Harrison & Company, 1880.

Wright, Richard R., *A Brief Historical Sketch of Negro Education in Georgia.* Savannah: Robinson Printing House, 1894.

PERIODICALS

The American Freedmen, I, 11 (February 1867). Organ of the American Freedmen's Union Commission.

The American Missionary, 1865-1897. New York: Organ of the American Missionary Association.

Clement, Rufus E., "The Church School as a Factor in Negro Life," *Journal of Negro History*, XII, 1 (January 1927).

Funke, Loretta, "The Negro in Education," in *Journal of Negro History*, V, 1 (January 1920).

Garrison, Curtis W., ed., "Slater Fund Beginnings: Letters from General Agent Atticus G. Haygood to Rutherford B. Hayes," in *The Journal of Southern History*, V, 2 (May 1939).

The Journal of Negro Education, II, 3 (July 1933). A Survey of Negro Higher Education, *The Yearbook*, No. II.

The Journal of Negro Education. Washington, D. C.: Howard University, 1932-1948.

Peters, E. C., "Paine College Serves its Community," in *World Outlook*, XXVIII, 9 (September 1938).

Quarterly Review of Higher Education Among Negroes. Charlotte, North Carolina: Johnson C. Smith University, 1937-1948.

Sims, David H., "Religious Education in Negro Colleges and Universities," in *Journal of Negro History*, V, 2 (April 1920).

Steely, Fred Lynn, "A Partial Explanation of the Individualism of the American Negro," in Social Forces, XII, 3 (March 1934).

Wesleyan Christian Advocate, January 14, 1882 (Supplement).

Woodson, C. G., "Negro Life and History in the Schools," in *Journal of Negro History*, IV, 3 (July 1919).

Index

Abbott, Allen O., 45
Adams, A. Pratt, 191, 192
Adams, Myron W., 149, 154, 163, 166, 195, 196, 197, 223, 224
Adkinson, L. G., 230
African Civilization Society, 14
Albany Bible and Manual Training School. See Albany State College
Albany State College, founding, 185-187; absorption by state, 187, 201; transition to four-year college, 202; academic rating, 203; extension work, 216-218; summer school, 218; chronological table, 234-235
Alvord, J. W., 16
American Baptist Home Mission Society, 25, 51, 103, 165, 224, 225
American Bible Society, 87
American Church Institute, 184, 232
American Missionary Association, origin and first schools, 6, 8, 12, 13; sponsors Atlanta University, 21-22, 61, 103, 233
Anthony, Susan B., 113
Anti-Tuberculosis Association, 178
Archer, Samuel Howard, 219, 225
Armstrong, Samuel Chapman, 69, 70
Association of Colleges for Negro Youth, 163-164
Atkins, D. D., 174, 229
Atkinson, W. Y., 113
Atlanta Associated Charities, 178
Atlanta Baptist Female Seminary. See Spelman College.
Atlanta Baptist Seminary. See Morehouse College.
Atlanta Community Chest, 179
Atlanta Constitution, 47, 106, 177
Atlanta Journal, 112, 113
Atlanta School of Social Work, founding, 178-179; merger, 198, 200, 224; curricula, 210; graduate study, 212-213; chronological table, 235

Atlanta University, 41, 43, 49, 52, 55, 59, 88, 89, 91; founding, 21-22; curricula, 27-31, 78-86, 171-172, 181, 210-218; student aid funds, 32, 123; financial support, 34-36, 61, 100-108, 175, 198, 207; library, 38, 87-88, 197-198; attitude of whites, 43-46, 59-61, 62, 112, 157, 160; buildings and equipment, 47, 97; industrial education, 70-78, 194; extension work, 85-86, 216-218; enrollment, 92-96; Negro control, 108; early students, 116-121; student life, 121-147, 172-173; faculty, 147-154, 174; academic rating, 162-170; affiliation, 193-200; graduate study, 211-213; chronological table, 223-224
Atlanta University Affiliation, establishment, 193-197, 224, 225, 227; development, 197-200; library, 215; joint summer school, 218
Atlanta University Center. See Atlanta University Affiliation.
Atlanta University Publications, 85-86
Augusta Institute. See Morehouse College.
Avery College, 5
Ayer, Frederick, 8-9, 10, 21

Ballard Normal School, 18
Baxter Street School, 63
Beach Institute, 18
Betts, Albert Deems, 229
Biddle University, 183
Bill, Jennie, 87
Bond, Horace Mann, 219, 232, 233
Bowen, John W. E., 151, 230
Bradwell, Charles, 3
Brawley, Benjamin, 80, 150, 163, 171, 172
Brawley, James P., 219, 226
Brittain, M. L., 177
Brooks, Phillips, 61
Brown, Aaron, 219
Brown, Joseph E., 16, 20, 42, 47

[249]

Brown, Joseph M., 112
Brown University, 25
Bryant, M. Edward, 118
Buck, A. E., 40
Bullock, Rufus B., 20, 35, 40
Bumstead, Horace, 41, 61, 85, 97, 101, 104, 114, 134, 146, 154, 165, 166, 168, 170, 173, 194, 195, 223
Buttrick, Wallace, 65, 183

Cable, George W., 61
Calloway, Morgan, 54, 55, 229
Campbell, William J., 3
Candler, Warren A., 54, 106
Capers, William, 53
Capon Springs Conference, 113
Carnegie, Andrew, 97, 232
Carnegie Corporation, 213-214
Carnegie Foundation, 162, 175, 210
Carter, E. R., 122
Carter, R. A., 55, 120
Cary, Mrs. Alice D., 228
Central City College. See Georgia Baptist College.
Central Park Normal and Industrial Institute, 228
Champney, Miss, 51
Chase, Thomas N., 40-41, 223
Clapp, Franklin Halsted, 230
Clark College, 38, 47, 49, 57, 59, 174; founding, 22-24; curricula, 28-31, 78-86, 171-172, 181, 182, 210-218; student aid funds, 32; faculty, 41; department of theology, 58; industrial education, 71-78, 194; enrollment, 92-96; buildings and equipment, 98, 175, 215; financial support, 102-108, 175, 207; student life, 121-147; early teachers, 147-154; academic rating, 163-170; merger, 196; cooperation with Atlanta University, 199; chronological table, 226
Clark, D. W., 23, 226
Clark University. See Clark College.
Clement, Rufus Early, 219, 224
Coffin, Charles C., 45
Cole, Mrs. Augusta Clark, 226

Colquitt, A. H., 47
Colston, James A., 219, 232
Commission on International Cooperation, 177-178
Conference for Education in the South, 113-114, 162
Conley, Ben, 20
Cooke, Anne, 215
Cook, Josiah W., 106
Cotton States Exposition, 73, 91, 109
Coulter, Richard C., 24, 224
Cox, John, 3
Crogman, William, 150, 151-152
Cravath, Erastus M., 21
Crawford, Peter G., 221, 233
Curry, J. L. M., 70, 100, 107, 113, 161, 194

Dartmouth College, 41, 90
Davage, Matthew S., 219, 226
Davidson, J. W., 182-183, 232
Davis, Richard Harding, 175
Degrees, 31, 80, 88-89, 212
Dixon, J. L., 177
Dorsey, Hugh M., 178
Drew, Charles, 195
DuBois, W. E. B., 9, 77, 84, 86, 90, 95, 112, 149, 150, 152-153, 160, 161, 162, 163, 164, 166, 171, 186, 213

Edmunds, George F., 94
Elder-Carswell Act, 180
Eliot, Charles W., 77, 105
Emory College, 38, 47, 54, 121

Fisk University, 21, 104, 165, 167, 168, 173
Flipper, Joseph S., 228
Ford, Henry, 158
Fort Valley Normal and Industrial School. See Fort Valley State College.
Fort Valley State College, founding 182-185; merger with State

INDEX

Teachers and Agricultural College, 202; academic rating, 203; graduate study approved, 212; extension work, 216-218; summer school, 218; chronological table, 232-233
Fountain, W. A., 171, 219, 228
Fountain, W. A., Jr., 228
Francis, Cyrus W., 41, 223
Frazier, E. Franklin, 179, 235
Frazier, Garrison, 3
Freemen's Aid Society, 12, 23, 57, 103, 226
Freedmen's Bureau, 61, 119; origin and early activities, 7-8, 9, 12; reports of, 14, 16, 17, 18; financial aid to schools, 22, 35
Friendship Baptist Church, 51, 227
Froumontaine, Julian, 4

Gadson, J. H., 221, 233
Gaines, W. A., 56
Gammon, Elijah H., 57-58, 86, 226, 230
Gammon Theological Seminary, 84-85, 169, 174, 199; founding of, 49, 57-59; library, 87; buildings and equipment, 97, 175; financial support, 100-106, 207; attitude of whites, 113; student life, 121-147; faculty, 147-154, 174; curricula, 172, 212, 216; cooperation with Atlanta University, 200; extension work, 218; chronological table, 230-231
Garrett Biblical Institute, 87
Gate City Free Kindergarten Association, 178
General Education Board, 90, 162, 164, 166, 183, 192, 195, 196, 197, 198, 207-208, 226, 232, 234
Georgia Baptist College, founding, 110-111; student life, 121-147; early teachers, 147-154; financial support, 174-175, 207, 221; name changed, 207; chronological table, 233
Georgia Normal College. See Albany State College.
Georgia State College, founding, 59-65; industrial education, 72-78; curricula, 79-84, 181; extension work, 85, 216-218; library, 87, 190, 215; enrollment, 92-96, 192, 208; buildings and equipment, 99, 175, 190; financial support, 100-101, 104, 191-192; Negro control, 109; early students, 121; student life, 121-147, 173; faculty, 147-154, 174; academic rating, 163-170, 203; reform, 189-192, 205; summer school, 218; chronological table, 231-232
Georgia State Industrial College. See Georgia State College.
Georgia, University of, 47, 62, 95, 101, 159, 201
Georgia, University System of, 187, 188, 202-203, 206, 217, 234
Gilbert, John Wesley, 150, 152
Giles, Harriet B., 50-52, 114, 194, 227
Gillespie, Joseph, 118
Glenn, G. R., 113
Gordon, John B., 16, 62
Grady, Henry, 68, 152
Granderson, Jane Anna, 53
Graves, Frederick Douglass, 233
Graves, R. R., 38
Graves, Samuel, 97-98, 225
Greene, Charles, 3, 6
Gresham, C. J., 233
Grover, C. M., 51

Hamlin, Augustus C., 45
Hammond, John D., 229
Hampton Institute, 69, 103
Harreld, Kemper, 173, 213
Harris, H. R., 233
Harris, Joel Chandler, 113
Harris, Julian, 178
Harris, William T., 77
Harrison, Alexander, 3
Harrison, Benjamin, 133
Harvard University, 90, 167, 169, 173
Haven, Gilbert, 24, 226
Hayes, Rutherford B., 77, 102
Haygood, Atticus, 38, 42, 47, 54, 70, 71, 76, 99, 102, 113, 114, 161, 194

Haywood, John W., 219, 231
Hazard, Anna, 187, 234
Hazard, Caroline, 187, 234
Hazard, Rowlin, 185
Henderson, James M., 228
Herndon, Alonzo F., 173
Herndon, Mrs. Alonzo F., 133
Higginson, Henry L., 105
Hill, Benjamin H., 16
Hill, Walter B., Jr., 180, 190
Hilo Labor School, 69
Holley, Joseph W., 185-188, 219, 234, 235
Holmes, William E., 42, 108, 110, 149, 150, 233
Hope, John, 55, 150, 170-171, 172, 175, 185, 195, 196, 197, 214, 219, 224, 225
Hopkins, John L., 113
Howard University, 88
Howe, Julia Ward, 105, 113
Howell, Clark, 157
Howells, William Dean, 175
Hubbard, William Merida, 188, 219, 234
Hubert, Benjamin F., 192, 216, 219, 231, 232
Hubert, Charles D., 219, 225
Hubert, John, 150
Hughes, Charles Evans, 175
Hunt, Henry A., 183-185, 202, 219, 232
Huntington, Collis P., 232
Hutchins, J. G., 88

Idleman, S. E., 230
Industrial education, 66-78

Jeanes, Anna T., 182, 232
Johnson, Henry Lincoln, 132
Johnson, Herschel V., 16
Johnson, James Weldon, 126, 127, 130, 145
Jones, C. C., 5
Jonesboro, 17
Journal of Negro Education, 206
Junior College Movement, 181-188

Kidder, D. P., 87

King, Henry Andrews, 171
King, Willis, 219, 230, 231
Ku Klux Klan, 16, 25, 39, 119, 135, 177, 178

Land, Fort E., 177
Lee, E. W., 228
Lee, J. W., 23, 226
Leonard Street Orphanage, 178
Lewis, John Henry, 228
Lewis, J. R., 14, 40
Lincoln University, 88
Love, E. K., 109-111, 233
Lucey, Daniel, 182
Luther, Mrs. Mary, 123
Lyons, J. W., 89

McCree, Mrs. Mary, 228
McKinley, William, 113
Macon Messenger, 16
Magill, S. W., 6
Mays, Benjamin Elijah, 219, 229
Markham, Edwin, 175
Massachusetts, 79
Massey, Rebecca, 149
Meldrim, P. W., 63
Mercer University, 47, 101
Monroe County Training School. See State Teachers and Agricultural College.
Morehouse College, 47, 55, 59, 89, 179; founding, 23, 24-26; curricula, 31, 78-86, 181, 214-215; student aid funds, 32; library, 38, 175; faculty, 42; industrial education, 71-78; extension work, 85; enrollment, 92-96; buildings and equipment, 97-98, 175; financial support, 100-103, 198, 207; Negro control, 108-110; student life, 121-147, 173-174; early teachers, 147-154; academic rating, 162-170; name changed, 170; affiliation, 193-200; summer school, 218; chronological table, 224-225.
Morehouse, Henry Lyman, 170, 225
Morrill Act, 35, 62, 63, 72, 76, 99, 189, 223
Morris Brown College, 59, 89, 171; founding, 49, 55-57; curircula,

INDEX

82-84, 171, 182, 209-218; library, 87; buildings and equipment, 98, 175; Negro control, 108; student life, 121-147; early teachers, 147-154; academic rating, 163-170, 229; cooperation with Atlanta University, 199; chronological table, 228-229

National Association of Teachers in Colored Schools, 162
National Conference of Social Workers, 178
National Temperance Society, 87
National Theological Seminary, 25
Negro Life Conferences, 85-86, 223
Nelson, Walter H., 28
Northen, W. J., 63, 113

Old Bryan Slave Mart, 6
Orr, G. V., 47

Packard, Sophia B., 50-52, 194, 227;
Paine College, 59, 89, 159, 171, 174; founding, 49, 53-55; industrial education, 70-78; curricula, 79-84, 181; library, 87, 216, 217; enrollment, 92-96; buildings and equipment, 98-99, 175; financial support, 100, 103, 105, 207; attitude of whites, 113; student life, 121-147, 173; early teachers, 147-154; academic rating, 163-170; name changed, 170; extension work, 217-218; summer school, 218; chronological table, 229-230
Paine Institute. See Paine College.
Paine, Robert, 55, 229
Parker, J. W., 25
Parsons, G. W., 63
Patterson, R. W., 62
Patterson, William, 144
Payne College, 228
Payne, Daniel A., 82
Payne, Moses U., 106, 229
Peabody Fund, 32, 102, 161
Peabody, George F., 183, 232
Pease, Giles, 38
Penny, Edgar J., 149
Peters, E. C., 219, 220, 230
Peters, Richard, 26

Pfeiffer, Mrs. Henry, 226
Phelps-Stokes Foundation, v-vi, vii, 167, 168, 170, 181, 205
Phelps-Stokes, Mrs. Caroline, 167
Pickard, John, 152
Porter, James H., 233
Prophet, Elizabeth, 214

Quarles, "Father" Frank, 26, 51, 98

Read, Florence Matilda, 196, 219, 224, 227
Richardson, A. S., 228
Richardson, Harry V., 219, 231
Richardson, Mary, 88
Richardson, W. T., 6
Riley, James Whitcomb, 175
Robert, Joseph Thomas, 25, 27, 31, 42, 97, 129, 148, 225
Rockefeller, John D., 52, 96, 105, 162, 175, 227
Rosenwald Fund, 226
Rosenwald, Julius, 163, 192, 232

Sale, George, 74, 98, 114, 170, 194, 225
Savannah Advertiser, 140
Saxton, Rufus, 5
Scarborough, William, 4
Sherman, William T., 3, 7, 63
Shorter College, 47
Siegfried, W. D., 25
Slater Fund, 75, 76, 100, 102, 107-108, 227, 234
Slater, John F., 102
Smith, George S., 118
Smith, Hoke, 157
Smith, Joseph E., 108
Smith-Lever Act, 163
South Carolina Medical College, 25
Spelman College, 59; founding, 49-53; industrial education, 72-78; curricula, 80-86, 171-172, 182, 213-215; missionary training, 84-85; library, 87-88; enrollment, 92-96; buildings and equipment, 96-99, 175; financial support, 100-106, 175, 198; Negro control, 108-109; attitude of

whites, 113; student life, 121-147; faculty, 147-154, 174; academic ratings, 165-170; affiliation, 193-200; extension work, 216-218; chronological table, 226-227
Standing, George, 15
Stanton, Edwin M., 3
State Agricultural and Mechanical School. See State Teachers and Agricultural College.
State Teachers and Agricultural College, founding, 188; absorption by state, 188, 201; merger with Fort Valley State College, 202; chronological table, 234
Stephens, Alexander, 16
Stewart Missionary Foundation for Africa, 84, 87, 230
Stewart, William F., 85
Stone, Mrs. Valeria G., 97
Storr's School, 22, 119, 223
Student life, 121-147, 219-220

Tapley, Lucy Hale, 171, 227
Taylor, George C., 55
Teachers, crusade of, 7, 9-10; native white Georgian, 14-15; treatment of, 15-17, 39-40; need of, 17-18; early missionary spirit of, 38-46; early college teachers, 147-154
Thirkield, W. A., 58, 113, 230
Tomlin, Ray S., 229
Toronto University, 169
Towns, George A., 89, 143, 150, 173
Trever, George Henry, 230
Troup, Cornelius V., 219, 233
Turner, Charles H., 152
Turner, John, 142
Turner Theological Seminary, 228
Tuskegee Institute, 69, 78, 103, 134, 183, 192
Twiggs County, 111

United Negro College Fund, 207
Upton, Lucy, 227

Urban League, 178

Vardell, Arthur, 3
Varnell, Annie, 143

Walker, C. T., 122
Walker, George Williams, 55, 78, 89, 98, 104, 150, 153, 229
Wallack, John, 118
Wardlaw, C. H., 150
Ware, Edmund Asa, 10, 16, 21-22, 38, 39, 40, 41, 45, 48, 52, 59, 71, 91, 100-101, 117, 142, 165, 200, 211, 223
Ware, Edward Twitchell, 166, 168, 170, 173, 195, 224
Ware High School, 63
Warren, Henry White, 57, 58, 230
Washington, Booker T., 69, 70, 73, 76, 78, 83, 85, 109, 163, 186, 192
Washington, Forrester B., 179, 235
Watters, Philip M., 230
Watson, Thomas E., 111
Webster, Edgar H., 86
Weltner, Philip, 195
Wesleyan Christian Advocate, 47
Wesleyan College, 47
West Medford Baptist Church, 50
Wheeler, Joseph, 113
White, Claudia T., 53
White, William Jefferson, 8, 16, 25, 53, 108, 224
Wilberforce University, 4, 5
Williams Business College, 228-229
Wofford College, 55
Women's Baptist Home Mission Society, 50
Woodruff, Hale, 214
Wright, Richard R., 63, 76, 96, 109, 117, 135, 161, 173, 190, 231
Wright, Richard R., Jr., 64

Yale University, 8, 21, 25, 41, 121
Young, John, 150

www.ingramcontent.com/pod-product-compliance
Lightning Source LLC
Chambersburg PA
CBHW030133240426
43672CB00005B/117